From Empire to Anthropocene

From Empire to Anthropocene

The Novel in Posthistorical Times

BETTY JOSEPH

Johns Hopkins University Press
Baltimore

© 2023 Johns Hopkins University Press
All rights reserved. Published 2023
Printed in the United States of America on acid-free paper
2 4 6 8 9 7 5 3 1

Johns Hopkins University Press
2715 North Charles Street
Baltimore, Maryland 21218
www.press.jhu.edu

Cataloging-in-Publication Data is available from the Library of Congress.
A catalog record for this book is available from the British Library.

ISBN: 978-1-4214-4697-4 (hardcover)
ISBN: 978-1-4214-4698-1 (paperback)
ISBN: 978-1-4214-4699-8 (e-book)

Special discounts are available for bulk purchases of this book. For more information, please contact Special Sales at specialsales@jh.edu.

ACKNOWLEDGMENTS

I would like to thank a number of people without whose attention and help this book would not have been possible. The initial idea for this project came from a paper written for "Feminism and Time," a panel that Robyn Wiegman organized for the MLA's Women's Studies Division two decades ago. Kelly Oliver's invitation to spend a semester at Stony Brook University provided the opportunity to rehearse various arguments in a seminar on gender and globalization.

In addition, I am grateful for the support of colleagues and their institutions for opportunities to lecture or conduct seminars on various topics related to this book. I gave individual lectures at the Humanities Institute at Stony Brook University; the Kroc Institute for International Peace Studies at University of Notre Dame; the Department of English at University of Houston; the Center for 21st Century Studies at University of Wisconsin, Milwaukee; the Global Fellows Program and the Department of English at University of California, Los Angeles; the Glasscock Center for the Humanities at Texas A&M University; the Departments of History and English at University of California, Riverside; and the Department of English, University of Illinois–Chicago. For stimulating conversations during these visits, I thank E. Ann Kaplan, Lamia Karim, Hosam Aboul-Ela, Daniel Sherman, Françoise Lionnet, James M. Rosenheim, Randolph Head, Ali Behdad and Sunil Agnani.

Parts of two chapters have appeared in other forms: "Gendering Time in Globalization: The Belatedness of the Other Woman and Jamaica Kincaid's *Lucy*," *Tulsa Studies in Women's Literature* 21, no. 1 (Spring 2002): 67–83; and "Neoliberalism and Allegory," *Cultural Critique* 82 (Fall 2012): 68–94. I am grateful to Susan Swenson, the Lombardi family, and Pierogi Gallery for permission to reproduce Mark Lombardi's *Oliver North, Lake Resources of Panama, and the Iran-Contra Operation, c. 1984–86* (4th version).

I assigned many of the novels discussed in this book in my graduate and undergraduate classrooms over the years. I thank the students in "Global Fictions," and "What Is the Contemporary?" for their willingness to read and think about the texts and contexts of globality.

In the early stages of writing, Susan Koshy's generous feedback during a workshop sponsored by the Feminist Reading Group at Rice and Susan Lurie's attentive reading of a first draft provided valuable direction and encouragement. Many thanks to my colleagues Marcia Carter, Susan Lurie, Helena Michie, and Scott Derrick for the many years of camaraderie. Alexander Regier deserves special thanks for hours of argumentation, shop talk and Guy Clark, and for nudging me from time to time to get this book done. I am grateful to my department chairs, Cary Wolfe, Rosemary Hennessy, and Kirsten Ostherr, and to Kathleen Canning, dean of Humanities, for their collegiality and guidance at various stages. Anne Smith and Linda Evans have helped me balance my departmental research-teaching-service obligations with their admin skills. Lora Wildenthal's mentorship was instrumental in planning release time and reordering professional priorities to complete the writing.

In addition to those mentioned above, many friends and interlocutors at Rice and other institutions have helped me imagine what a book about critical globality should look like. For their conversations and support at various stages, I thank Suvir Kaul, Eric Hayot, Felicity Nussbaum, Ratheesh Radhakrishnan, Tani Barlow, Carl Caldwell, Diana Strassman, Nicole Waligora-Davis, Samhita Sunya and Elora Shehabuddin. As this book goes to press, I salute the memory of the late Theresa Munisteri, our department's copyeditor extraordinaire, who passed away in 2022. Over three decades, Terry read our manuscripts with unparalleled attention and care. I missed our conversations when this manuscript was done. I am grateful to the two readers for Johns Hopkins University Press whose rigorous and helpful review of the manuscript gave me a chance to decide what mattered most and to revise accordingly. At the press, Catherine Goldstead and Juliana McCarthy were patient and professional at every stage of the process. Carrie Watterson's expert copyediting has made this a much better product.

Last but not least, I want to thank my family in the United States and India, especially Poth, Geema, Jeff, Louie, Rajen, Amma, Kunju, Elsa, Rose, the Erlers, and the Laubachs. I am fortunate to have friends who have enriched my life in Houston more than they know—Jaspal, Tulsi, Indranil, Nusrat, Yaksha, Jim, Sophie, Dean, Krupa, Sunita, Oskar, Aman, Ashwini, and Yunuen. This book is dedicated with love to my mother, Cicily Joseph, who is glad to see it finished and now believes I have better things to do.

From Empire to Anthropocene

INTRODUCTION

What Is the Contemporary?

> People today are not prepared to coexist consciously with a billion other subjects.
> —Peter Sloterdijk, *Der Spiegel*, June 22, 2017

If the word "global" generates unease about a world that is too large for comprehension, it is not without cause. Stabilizing the globe as an object of thought is to intuit a large spherical surface that is abstract, like the World Bank logo crisscrossed only by lines of latitude and longitude. However, any further consideration of globality reveals that the seamless surface possesses natural edges that in turn form boundaries for islands of humans all over it. In a world that is commonly represented today as boundless and undifferentiated, as a result of the ever-growing reach of new teletechnologies, such representations are always interrupted when the temporal discontinuities of the earthly edges come into contact with the globe's abstract contours. When edges become political or cultural boundaries, do they constitute the limits of our ability to conceptualize a collective larger than our own spatially defined social networks? This book proposes that we think of the collective not only as an ideological problem about the lengths to which our interests and identifications can stretch spatially but as a problem of temporality as well.

When Francis Fukuyama, the best-selling guru of neoconservatism in the 1990s, proclaimed that history had come to an end, he did so with the optimism that the contemporary world had reached a new phase in which the breakup of the Soviet Union and the fall of the Berlin Wall could only mean that old atavistic conflicts would cease, that capitalism had won out against communism as the only viable option for all nations, and that the world had entered a perpetual state of peaceful coexistence in which democracy, hand in glove with free markets, would spread like a wave all over the world.[1] This world community imagined in arrested time, as homeostasis, did not, however, come to be. Now, almost three decades later, Fukuyama has had to postpone the end of history.[2] At the time of this book's writing, the imaginative hold of political parties that based their electoral successes on bad anachronisms—the promise of making a nation great "again"—suggests that political collectivities can still form in the heartland of first world capitalism with shared tropes of decline, of falling behind, of abandonment, and of being unequal in a shared present with others. This temporal disjuncture is also discursively supported by widespread talk of retreat from a once-shared world to a reshaped future isolated behind walls constituted by economic nationalism, trade barriers, and immigration controls. If anything at all has come to an end, it is the promise of neoliberal globalization with dreams of prosperity for all. What has taken its place is the paradoxical coincidence of a world that is, on the one hand, overwhelmingly reshaped everywhere by transnational capital connected by teletechnologies, and on the other hand, decidedly less optimistic about economic prosperity, political freedoms, and cultural hybridity.

The progressive march of neoliberalism has been replaced by an imaginative dead end in which archaic dreams of times past generate collectives based on religious, racial, and cultural purity. Also emergent are forms of labor identities (such as the "white working class") based not on the tertiary sector of the new virtual and service economies but on a secondary industrial base that has long since ceased to dominate in the very areas where such identities are mobilized. If the desire for the political is tied to apprehensions of time, then what happens when those temporal relations begin to fray? How are our imagined relationships to other social beings affected by the ways in which we think about our deliverance from a difficult past, our feelings of being uprooted in the present, or our anxieties about an uncertain future? How might political life depend on feelings of being in the same time with others like you or being separated from others who have left you behind and moved on?

This book argues that we must place these contradictory intersections of time and globalization at the center of any cultural analysis of the "contemporary." I place this term in quotation marks not only to draw attention to the word itself as a conceptual point of departure, for modes of inquiry that are needed to engage the pressing social, economic, political, cultural, and ecological issues that characterize our times, but also to address a related but narrower disciplinary question: "What is contemporary literature?" This question, inscribed on the threshold of this project, was prompted in part by practical concerns like the training of graduate students in a still-central, perhaps even venerable field of literary studies; however, the practicality of this endeavor has done nothing to lessen the difficulty of representing the conditions of our historical present in a textual corpus that is often indexed simply as "twentieth- and twenty-first-century literature."[3] If there is anything at all that might be designated as the literature of "our time" in the United States, it seems to exist either as an ever-extending period that began after the Second World War—"post-1945 literature"—or as an array of special topics that fan out into various regional literatures, minority and ethnic literatures, stylistic modes, and thematic constellations.

All this is not to say that the lack of consensus in characterizing the past eighty years is a problem we should solve once and for all. Indeed, as more time passes it is possible that scholars will make such determinations to satisfy curricular constituencies. My aim is to gauge the extent to which the difficulty of slicing up or defining the contemporary is also a contemporary problem—one of our own time's making and attributable in no small part to two political-economic trends that have been underway since the 1960s: First, the interruption of a continuously transmitted national literary-historical tradition in the United States (and this is true also of Britain) by the growing body of immigrant and diasporic writing that focuses on the lives and experiences of people from the non-European world. Second, the imaginative dissolution of the geographical boundary of the nation-state by the powerful teletechnologies of communication that have brought with them an awareness of a world out there impinging on the lives of citizens here and now. Substituting "global literatures in English" for previous categories like "postcolonial literature," "world literature," or "Anglophone literature," suggests that an active recoding of contemporary literature into a borderless literature in English is under way, and this literature finds its source materials primarily in transnationality, migrations, and new diasporas—all of which are effects of the economic restructuring that we call globalization. In this setting "global fiction" might include immigrant and ethnic writers from North America and the United Kingdom (like Jamaica Kincaid, Teju Cole, and Hari Kunzru), but it also moves into the national "mainstreams" when North American writers like Don DeLillo and Barbara Kingsolver use global or transnational themes as content or employ time-space expansions that create millennial or planetary-scale narratives. Postcolonial fiction, or the work of writers from decolonized space, like Aravind Adiga and Mohsin Hamid, occupy only part of this new, wider set.

If we move away from the literary texts themselves for an understanding of their contemporaneity to the context in which we assert the right to delineate a segment of "our time" (medieval Latin *contemporarius*, from *con-* "together with" + *tempus, tempor-* "time"), then the question of contemporary literature is inextricable from the more philosophical question that Giorgio Agamben posed in an essay of the same title a decade ago: "What is the contemporary?"

In answering that question, he arrives at the key insight that the contemporary is inevitably an ahistorical idea. Contemporariness means to have "a singular relationship with one's own time, which adheres to it and, at the same time, keeps a distance from it." More precisely, as he puts it, "it is that relationship with time that adheres to it, through a disjunction and an anachronism." Adopting the stance in proximity with and distance from a time that is also shared with others ("Of whom and of what are we contemporaries?") is therefore not tied to any specific historical era. However, the content of the response and the stakes of this distancing depend on the historical moment in which the question is posed, and thus, contemporaneity must imply much more than the mere simultaneity or plain coexistence suggested by in the ordinary usage of the term. As Agamben characterizes this form of distancing, if we are totally immersed in our present, we will be blinded by its light and unable to see anything that emerges in its shadow. The truly contemporary poet (or writer) then, is "he [*sic*] "who firmly holds his gaze on his own time so as to perceive not its light, but rather its darkness."[4] Thinking of the present in this differentiated way is to think of the contemporary spectrally, neither as shadow nor as light but as a living present that holds within it the multitemporality of historical time, of pasts that have endured as well as the futures that are possible or likely. Although Agamben himself does not adopt a historical or geopolitical perspective (except to say how September 11, 2001, has forever changed the "first glimpse" of New York City's skyline for its future visitors), I think his insight, about disjunction and anachronism as expressions of a necessary alienation from *and* belonging to one's time, is especially relevant when there is widespread perception that the world is undergoing systemic change—a change that may not be singularly defined but is perceived in terms of one or more overriding crises: systemic changes from economic restructuring, global warming, automation, subversion of democratic institutions, people displaced from conflict zones, and demographic change within nation-states.

When the representation of historical change is perceived not as a single beam of light that catches all people equally (like the empty homogeneous time of national history in which "we the people" continue to march), then the vanishing of the present into the past is intuited in different temporal speeds and rhythms. For instance, geopolitical changes wrought by wars, revolutions, and economic downturns are often represented as the ground suddenly vanishing from under one's feet, but technological change that is too sped up to be grasped by human sensory apparatuses is represented as space collapsing into a synchronous time that erases history. In contrast, environmental change unfolding at nonhuman or geologic scales is represented as a kind of slow violence that is hardly visible, sometimes even over a generation. Of these different modalities of historical and cultural change, the most spectacular are of course the ones where dates and events have themselves become metonyms for a time into which we have all arrived. One remembers how events that were initially represented as singular and dramatic in their unfolding, like the fall of the Berlin Wall or the attack on the Twin Towers, later became significant thresholds for signaling the end of the Cold War or the ushering in the "post-9/11 world" of unending wars on terror.

This book considers relations of temporal belonging and disjunctiveness as ways of understanding political desires and, in so doing, reorients contemporary literature, especially the rich body of transnational Anglophone fiction, as a literature *of* our time. The book uses the literary text to analyze apprehensions of temporality in the contexts of historical, affective, technological, economic, and environmental change. These contexts are instantiated by a series of concepts associated with them that are now undisputedly ubiquitous in the analysis of contemporary culture. The five that I discuss in the book—specters, attachments, networks, markets, and assemblages—instantiate, in turn, each of the contexts listed above. We will see that concepts, too, are embedded with their own temporal structures and temporal framing that determine their metaphorical processing of the phenomena they seek to understand. Because concepts come with metaphorical entailments, as concept metaphors they allow us to access the various disciplinary domains that have hatched them as well as the historical changes in signification that have necessitated their use today. I imagine this book as primed to answer a question like this: "What has changed to make these concepts necessary in our analysis?" A satisfactory answer requires, I argue, taking a distanced view of our own time and looking at the theoretical tools we use to create our understanding of the contemporary world.

The novels I read in each chapter work less as sources of empirical information about the world and more as sites for the staged performances of these concepts. Just as a mise-en-scene is the act of placing on stage and of drawing a viewer into the world of a film, a play, or a novel, my method of reading draws upon what Adi Ophir has called "conceptual performances."[5] Each concept "plays" the text like an actor plays a character, and the mise-en-scene is achieved as we execute a reading of the novel, call upon its author, borrow metaphors, and follow the rhetorical and narrative tools of linguistic expression that are all mobilized to bring the novel's world into presence. Adhering to the principle that conceptual terms should not work in the manner of a theory "applied" in a flat-footed way to a text, I link each of these concepts to the complex, often unpredictable, play of meaning constituted by the text's literariness, especially by those rhetorical figures that provide complex permutations in our apprehension of time, such as metalepsis, analepsis, parataxis, personification, and prolepsis.

At the center of these literary readings are two premises, one narratological and the other political. Novels allows us to distinguish between *fabula* (or story), "the temporal-causal sequence of narrated events," and *sjuzhet* (or plot), the "way in which these raw materials are formally manipulated."[6] Without adjudicating between the two in terms of priority or hierarchy, I mobilize this distinction, first discussed by the Russian formalist Viktor Shklovsky, as a useful lever for demonstrating how the novel defamiliarizes the systems of coherence imposed on reality by the codes and conventions of other, sometimes earlier, forms.[7] For instance, the sequenced events of a novel, as they occur in a past-present-future continuum, are "told" in such a way as to constrain and reveal the narrative conventions of the time of their "telling" (or writing). Furthermore, the critic's own reading, which may or may not coincide with the contemporary time depicted in the novel, wrests a living present from the abstract temporality of the past-present-future continuum of the story. What might appear as a logically sequenced argument is itself, both in its plotting as well as in its belated retelling (as a critical rereading), a breaking apart and rejoining of bits and pieces of narrative. In the literary texts chosen for analysis, I aim to draw attention to narrative anachronies involved in the metaleptic transpositions of effect before cause, the analeptic flashbacks to the past, the simultaneous juxtapositions of parataxis, the time lapses of description, the proleptic anticipations of the future, and the personification of concepts into historical and futuristic allegories.

In what follows in this introduction, I address the intersection of time and globalization as a form of chronopolitics. I then show how an analysis of the contemporary requires attention to the incommensurability between two schemes of temporality, two ways we talk about time itself—as abstract and concrete—and how their incommensurability poses constraints as well as possibilities for thinking about political collectivity. Next, I make a case for the methodological specificity of literature, literary readings, and concept metaphors in an analysis of the contemporary. Finally, I outline the book and lists the novels and critical material that are the focus of each chapter, its conceptual performance, and the rhetorical-narratological elements that are attached to the concrete-abstract relationality of the temporal schemes.

The Chronopolitics of Globality

Since its use in a well-circulated 1983 article in which Theodore Levitt announced that the multinational corporation was nearing its end and the "globalization of markets [was] at hand," the term "globalization" has become a discursive celebrity.[8] But such currency for a word also brings its own perils, such as the blunting of its conceptual edge. "Globalization" facilitates an uninterrupted conversation about a restructured world and works as a placeholder that because of its relative emptiness allows it to assume different contents like "networks," "flows," "migration," "markets," "downsizing," "offshoring," "virtuality" and so on. To turn "globalization" back into a concept with a cutting edge thus requires interrupting the flow of conversation with a "What is x?" question.[9] To ask such a question is to refuse to take a term's usage as sufficient. It is to establish new discursive terrains within which the word can be mobilized, perhaps even connected to a whole network of other concepts and phenomenal fields. This, I hope, is what happens when this study stages a series of conceptual performances using the literary text as the opening into a phenomenal field within which it is to be grasped. As "globalization" takes shape as a concept in this book, the literary readings are meant to draw attention to different aspects of our uneven and seemingly within-reach contemporaneity, especially the ways in which time as opposed to space structures our understanding of the world and determines what can be accessed or remains concealed.

To conceive of globalization in its broadest cultural (as opposed to economic) sense is to think of it as an intensified consciousness of the world as a whole. But the distinctiveness of this connection is not merely in the linking of local and distant localities, for such connections have obviously been underway in archaic as well as modern historical contexts whenever trade, urbanization, or colonialism were involved. What is distinctive today, as Edward Soja puts it, is not globalization as such but "its intensification in popular (and intellectual) consciousness and in the scope and scale of globalized social, economic, political and cultural relations.".[10] Along these lines, the historian Stephen Brooke points out with regard to Britain, the newness of a widely accepted "new times" was forged primarily by the technological supports that accompanied economic restructuring: "There is a sense in the 1980s that lives are lived or life is experienced across a wide spatial register, from the local to the national to the global. This is not to say that people were not transnational or cosmopolitan before.... '[W]hat is new is the technological component that makes the transmission and circulation of these transnational experiences more immediate.'"[11]

The cultural aspects of this technological change, described by geographers like David Harvey as "time-space compression" and by sociologists like Manuel Castells and Hartmut Rosa as the experience of a "timeless present" and "social acceleration," despite their allusions to temporality, have not had any significant impact on the continuing emphasis in globalization studies on spatial rather than temporal phenomena. Even Harvey's catchphrase, "time-space compression," which he defines as the shrinking of "the time horizons of both private and public decision-making," is understood by him as a prelude to spatial expansion. As Harvey puts it, "Satellite communication and declining transport costs have made it increasingly possible to *spread those decisions immediately over an ever wider and variegated space.*"[12] For Harvey, even in the recent period of flexible accumulation, accelerations in turnover time are only short-term palliatives that cannot be indefinitely continued. At some point or the other, Western capitalist economies will resort to what he calls a "spatial fix"—a displacement that uses the "production of new spaces," or geographical expansion, to absorb excess capital and labor by way of new trade, direct or infrastructural investments, and new possibilities for exploiting labor power.[13] Similarly, a notion like "social acceleration" that seeks to understand the shrinking present of everyday life may lose its analytical edge if such an analysis incorporates a temporal perspective only to represent society as a constellation of temporal ghettos whose multitemporality is the sign of a "progressive disintegration of society."[14]

Without the ability to narrate sequence, time ostensibly falls away, and we cannot intuit or grasp these technologies and their accelerated cultural work except in the spatialized figure of something along the lines of a "network"—a concept metaphor related to mapping and scapes that promote flattened ontologies rather than the sort of heterotemporalities that signal cultural change.[15] Another reason for the dominance of spatial figures lies, as I suggested in the beginning of this introduction, within the mental grasping facilitated by the figure of the globe itself as a bounded seamless flat surface across which capitalism has spread and rendered the space itself abstract. No longer tied to actual locations or places, space, it seems, becomes abstract and loses its significance for orientation. Economic processes and cultural changes are no longer located, and locations become nonplaces without history, identity, or relation. This analytical resistance to temporality is counterintuitive because there is enough empirical evidence to suggest that all the crises catalyzed by economic globalization in the past three decades, whether financial crashes, environmental catastrophes, the disappearance of manufacturing jobs, increased income disparities, or even the displacement of people from the South to the North, are all understood as signs that the world is going badly. Imagining the fate of the world we live in through the lens of optimism or pessimism always involves temporally laden fantasies about anticipated futures.[16]

In a recent *New York Times* article on the decline of coal mining in the United States, the town of Grundy, Virginia, is described as one of the "victims" of the technological and other dislocations that have wreaked havoc on small-town America. In the article, Lawrence Summers is quoted as an expert on such phenomena. It is hard to miss the irony of Summers sounding the alarm, given the notorious memo he penned while serving as president of the World Bank in 1991, in which he proposed the economically rational solution of offloading rich nations' toxins on poor African countries on the premise that people living in places with lower life expectancy are less likely to feel the effects of the slower violence of environmental poisoning.[17] The chronopolitics of this solution is so blatantly cynical that it hardly needs foregrounding here. Suffice it to say that even if this claim about life span is statistically true, Summers's sleight of hand is to calculate the environmental impact only for a single life's duration when in reality the lives of many generations of people are at stake. It is as though the incremental effects on succeeding generations, so well chronicled in the environmental debates in wealthy countries, ceases to be violence in Africa because it is a place without a future. In the *Times* article, Summers also repeats an argument that has now become commonplace: the United States has reached a point where globalization does it more harm than good. As Summers puts it, "There is probably no issue more important for the political economy of the next 15 years, not just in the United States but around the world, than what happens in the areas that feel rightly that they are falling behind and increasingly left apart."[18]

The tropes of falling behind, feeling abandoned, and looking on from the sidelines are now part and parcel of a political discourse that constitutes the backlash against globalization. These tropes are most apparent in the self-representations of those who were once the working classes in the farming and manufacturing sectors and show how social alienation begins in an affective register, of not being in the "same time" with others (the feeling of being uprooted in place). Furthermore, these tropes register how feelings of alienation can become the basis of alarming chronopolitical mobilizations whose political antagonists are not those who stand in the way of dismantling the economic conditions of inequality but those "others" who are now stealing "our" futures from us—the poor on government assistance, the new immigrants, the undocumented, the refugees, and so on and so forth. This chronopolitics tells us that when liberal institutions constituted by principles of inclusion and equality are seen to be the tool of political parties who deliver a future only for the nation's external "others" or its internal others like LGBTQ people, Blacks, Hispanics, Muslims, and Jews, the newly disenfranchised are no longer interested in maintaining a democratic system that does not benefit them but has indeed betrayed them by prioritizing the interests of other victims. What is now often coded as "revolution" in popular media is not only an anti-capitalist politics from the left but also an anti-establishment politics from the right that advocates electing leaders who will "shake things up" or "blow up" the "status quo" of "elites" without actually engaging the problematic of global capitalism.

We are now far afield from that post-Soviet moment when prophets of neoliberalism like Fukuyama proclaimed that history had run its course and the world would move toward a common horizon, converging on a similar political and economic model—the great alliance between liberal democracy and free markets that would bring all nations into the Promised Land. But what has happened since then is not the much-awaited world of common marketization, a world that has achieved homeostasis; instead, we have now entered a phase in which economic deregulation precipitates financial crashes that have the potential for generational impact and cause unprecedented levels of income inequality in rich and poor countries alike. For philosophers like Bruno Latour writing on the state of affairs today, we are now facing a "wicked universality" where globalization and the effects of climate change are "one and the same threat" and all of us find ourselves, rich and poor alike, inhabitants of North and South, facing a "universal lack of shareable space and inhabitable land."[19] Latour sees some historical irony in his assertion that the former Euro-American colonizers of the world now recognize their predicament to be similar to that of the people they once colonized: "But where does this panic come from? From the same deep feeling of injustice felt by those who found themselves deprived of their land at the same time of the conquests, then during colonization, and finally during the era of 'development': a power from elsewhere comes to deprive you of your land and you have no purchase on that power. If this is globalization, then we understand retrospectively why resisting it has always been the only solution, why the colonized have always been right to defend themselves."[20] For Latour, in the Anthropocene, we have all become subjects of globalization's empire. While my own propositions do not disagree with Latour's assertion that people in the nations that benefitted most from globalization may be seeing their worlds shrinking, his insistence on thinking about today's climate crisis primarily as a problem about space and land (invoked in his essay by metaphors of orientation, landscapes, and maps) does not address the equally pertinent temporal displacements demonstrated in the tropes he uses to describe how people perceive the problem: tropes such as "remaining in place," "left behind by their own countries," "attachments," "backward-looking," "nostalgia," "preserve," "maintain," "arrow of time," "old inhabitants," "future inhabitants," "future wars," and the dreams of a common globe toward which all countries "seemed to be headed."[21] It is curious that Latour's propositions seem unconstrained by some of his earlier formulations of actor-network theory (ANT) that instructed social theorists to resist the temptation "to jump to the global." The Latour of ANT analysis advises us thus: if anyone speaks of a "system," a "global feature," a "structure," a "society," an "empire," or the "world economy," our first reflex should be to ask, "In which building? In which bureau? Through which corridor is it accessible?"[22]

In a recent book, aptly titled *Down to Earth*, the writing of which seems to have been prompted by President Donald J. Trump's election and the withdrawal from the Paris Accord, Latour seems willing to dispense with buildings, bureaus, and corridors. The work invokes a number of terms from his forbidden list, although the word "globalization" substitutes for global economy or capitalism in every case. Without overstating the case, I am suggesting that one of the ways we manage to get away from talking about globalization as economic restructuring is by referring to it as an undefined process of changes in space and place, as uprooting and migration that is happening to everyone, everywhere. But Latour is not the only space theorist doing that kind of cultural analysis today. Globalization is still understood primarily in its spatial dimensions as the transnational "spread" of capitalism, and it will take more than the notion that one is losing "land" to bring us to confront the common fate that awaits the world, as the accelerated resource exploitation of capital proves to be the primary catalyst for catastrophic climate change. Will the descendants of those whose lives were transformed by previous empires have to forget or reimagine the legacies of that history to become partners of the nations in this shared world of impending species demise? Will the dreams of the poor in the formerly colonized nations, who desire the lifestyles of Europeans and Americans and who want to "catch up" and be in a coeval time with the rest of the world, have to be put aside for a common cause of survival?

I argue that we cannot reimagine these futures unless we find ways to reconcile the incommensurabilities between concrete and abstract time. These two schemes of temporality may be understood in terms of what Fredric Jameson has called the "living present" (the basis of individual subjective experience) and the "past-present-future continuum" (the abstract "common" time out of which the former is captured).[23] The reconciliation, I must add here, is not simply the act of the concrete canceling out the abstract but, rather, an imaginative act that uses our simultaneous living in both these temporal schemes as a dialectical opening to imagine common presents and common futures that displace the designs of capital to colonize the living presents of human and nonhuman lives. My next section unpacks these schemes of temporality and shows their constitutive role in imagining political community and its looser forms or collectivities.

Non-contemporaneity and the Living Present: Abstract and Concrete Time

How does one unlearn the tendency to think of the contemporary world as "flat"?[24] How do we analyze the complex play of temporality that has always served as the basis for imagining collectivity and its chronopolitics? There is little doubt that a double process is unfolding today. On the one hand, economic globalization continues to be a homogenizing force that strives to synchronize or even annihilate diverse temporalities associated with cultures, locations, histories, and human practices and experiences, whatever we might signify as the "local."[25] On the other hand, we are seeing temporal/spatial disjunctures as different groups and segments of society demonstrate a differential capacity to keep up with the technological acceleration (automation and virtual work transforming the workplace) and to survive the cynical "futurity of speculative finance" in economies designed for the few or to withstand the effects of prolonged exposure to environmental harm (slow violence).[26] Thus, even as we concede that more of the world's population today is aware of globality, by which I mean understand that our daily lives are affected by activities and circuits that operate at big scales and far away from us, this experience does not result in everyone entering an imagined community of world citizens existing in synchronous time. It is true that size and scale have never stood in the way of constituting powerful forms of modern imagined collectivities like the nation. Benedict Anderson's argument that mass communities are imagined by way of a shared empty homogeneous time, simultaneous existence, is now an axiom in cultural studies; however, we cannot imagine a global community in similar terms.

Why is it so hard to imagine "global community"? The sheer mass of billions that Peter Sloterdijk conjures up as an unconscious paranoia-inducing presence is the stumbling block for the subject who cannot grasp this multiplicity in older formulations of otherness and who cannot leave behind the experience of temporalities established by more easily recognizable cultural communities (shared histories based on identities or locations).[27] Unlike the speculative fantasies of sci-fi, there is no malevolent alien force that comes from another galaxy and persuades the citizens of our world to unite against it. The closest candidate for such imaginings of alterity—climate change—requires a planetary rather than global consciousness or, in other words, a consciousness that can withstand the powerful lobbies of global capital that strive to defeat its formation by pitting geographical locations, resources, and labor pools against each other in order to exploit their comparative advantages. Global connections are occluded when economic restructuring affects whole swaths of people who have not believed themselves to be part of a transactional globe. Such is the case for those who have not been dislocated in recent memory or who have stayed in one place for a long time, like Indigenous peoples and people in rural communities. Such connections also remain invisible when global capital cancels out and devalues other temporal schemes through the technological acceleration of its own temporality. Thus "local" decisions are often disarticulated from their transnational calculations by time lags and not readily apprehended as connections that emanate from the Latourian building, bureau, or corridor. Consider, for instance, that the sneaky Lawrence Summers memo about toxic waste disposal "tells" us about a global connection because it was leaked to the press by a critic of the World Bank's environmental record.

It is important we keep in mind that any formulations of the global, like Manuel Castells's "timeless present," will always be haunted by traces of the non-global and the untimely. For those who encounter the global as a radical change in their everyday lives, the experience is not represented as a sort of cosmopolitan cultural openness (such as the perspectives of some of our elite fictional narrators) but as a sort of uprooting-in-place.[28] For people whose livelihoods have been affected by technology transfers, automation, cheaper migrant labor, resource mining, and business outsourcing, the experience of globalization is not recorded as the smooth transfer of technology or the unruffled movement of borderless flows but rather, as Anna Tsing's powerfully evocative metaphor suggests, as "friction," or as a "drama of uncertainty." Tsing's powerful ethnographies of deforestation in Indonesia show that when the shibboleths of globalization declare that the future is clear and well known, cultural criticism can turn away from these false assurances of a "self-making future" and reopen "a sense of mystery" that might yet sustain and enrich the possibilities for imagining "the about-to-be-present."[29] This means that no meaningful imaginings of collectivity can emerge out of a contemporary that lies before us like a flat world of simultaneous synchronicity. It is only by passing through the various heterotemporalities that already exist in the global (and cause friction) that any politically viable imaginings of shared synchronic experience can emerge to confront a world run by capital.

This is why the question of the past—of historical consciousness as a source of mystery that produces the about-to-be-present and a future imagined beyond the trajectory of the individual's life—is central to this book. The flat worlds of mobility and flows (see chapter 3) promote the disappearance of a sense of history. In the world of networked coexistence, our entire contemporary social has, little by little, lost its capacity to retain its own past. When the word "archive" is used for digital media, for instance, we sense that it is operating as a metaphor for a much more precarious mode of preservation. Furthermore, a contemporary world linked by teletechnologies enables the imagining of lives lived in a perpetual present and caught in a perpetual process of change that obliterates the very traditions (whether personally desirable or not) that earlier social formations have striven in one way or another to preserve. As Gayatri Spivak warns us, what passes for history can be references to "one's own hallucinatory heritage for the sake of the politics of identitarian competition."[30]

Andreas Huyssen has posed the provocative question of whether "contemporary memory cultures in general can be read as reaction formations to economic globalization." Is it that media-saturated culture creates such overload that "the memory system itself is in constant danger of imploding, thus triggering the fear of forgetting?"[31] I do not share Huyssen's view that globalization has produced a singular cultural obsession with memory in the same manner that modernism was engaged by a "present future" and postmodernism by space.

My inclination is to let the novels discussed here speak for themselves and in so doing, bring into view forms of experience and sensibility of time that we as readers try to explain historically, phenomenologically, and textually. This book therefore presents the contemporary as an interplay between an abstract idea of time and the concretization of it in a lived present: a "past-present-future" that is defamiliarized by breaking the chronological order in the way that a familiar story can be made unfamiliar by reformulating it into a plot with jarring twists, omissions, digressions, and the postponement of important information. This use of the literary as a way to surprise the historical is staged in Agamben's aforementioned essay where "an age" is represented as a beast ("my century, my beast") that has a "shattered backbone of time." Agamben's use of this disjointed figure from Osip Mandelstam's poem "My Century" establishes the point that poets, insofar as they are the contemporary, are the "fractures" that impede time from composing itself as well as that which "must suture this break or this wound." If we think of "our time" in an abstract way as a scene where empty, homogeneous, calendrical time is unfolding in a linear fashion, like the interlocking vertebrae of the backbone, then the literary text breaks this abstract time by introducing a "dys-chrony" by virtue of its noncoincidence with the empirical. This noncoincidence asserts itself in two ways: first, between the text and context when a novel does not fully coincide with its historical referents or a context that is defined by the empirical accounts of the journalist, the sociologist, and so on. There is a second kind of noncoincidence, of which we become aware when a fictional text shapes a particular story by rejoining bits and pieces in a different way than it would have unfolded if told in chronological sequence. In the first case, like Agamben's poet, the novelist's work is empirical evidence, but not in the manner of a social document that establishes empirical truth; rather, the text is incontrovertible evidence of a different kind: evidence that it was possible, at a particular historical moment, *to think this way*.

The novel's procession of historical referents must keep this figurative work in focus. Here, the lesson comes to us from deconstruction: literature takes the empirical and sees in it the logic of the metaphor.[32] Unlike the historical, journalistic, or sociological document, literary expression takes the literal and disfigures it, defaces it, by turning the empirical into the rhetorical, tropological, and narratological. In other words, literature is unverifiable. It works, unlike the cases of the historian, by way of a singular case, a single example. In his important essay on the interpretation of history, "Shelly Disfigured," Paul de Man's most provocative assertion is that the main act of literature is not the confirmation of literality, or the putting of faces on things, or the creating of the truth of history, but rather, it is, to use Orrin Wang's useful gleaning from the same essay, the act by which "language disfigures history by revealing the insubstantiality of the historical monuments we reconstruct."[33]

This is why I do not assert that the content of the selected novels, although written in the past three decades coinciding with economic globalization, are empirical windows onto the contemporary world. Indeed, they are poor conveyors of an exhaustive list of events, places, identities, and cultural themes that might satisfactorily address what is important about the empirical conditions of globalization. If the empirical world is what I wanted to access, I could turn to very important work done by economists, sociologists, anthropologists, and political scientists. Furthermore, to say that these works of fiction are representative of "their time" in terms of empirical references would be to monumentalize them, to fix them as embodiments of a time, and to make them into statues that will fall into ruin as their "literal" meanings are lost to us down the road. I am more interested in the very traits that are often seen to be the weaknesses of the expansive so-called global novels in English: their tendency to border-cross in ways that preclude the possibility of any linguistic complexity or cultural nuance.[34] I contend that the inauthenticity and homogenizing tendencies, if they can be characterized thus, are precisely what allows a deemphasizing of the particularities of space and place and a foregrounding of different ways of thinking about time.

The lack of neat fit between the literary and the empirical world brings me to the second kind of noncoincidence I mentioned above—the noncoincidence a reader of the novel notices between a past-present-future of abstract time in the story and the ways in which the narrative breaks and rejoins bits and pieces in its telling or plot. As readers of novels, we interrupt the continuous flow of a fictional story in the same way that a narrator interrupts the abstraction of an empty time by asserting a present for the "I" who is speaking. Foregrounding these fractures allows us to exercise the imagination and think of contemporaneity in the way we intuit the text: we know that nothing ever happens in a text to anything that precedes, follows, or exists in it but as a random event whose power is due to the randomness of its occurrence. This randomness, or the imaginative play that is preserved in literary reading, is lost when literature is read only as a social document to be mined for its information about what is going on in the world. As a scholar who is attentive to the intellectual compromises of living in an era when information technology and Big Data are misread as interdisciplinarity, Spivak reminds us why literary analysis must remain paramount in our times. Electronic acceleration and big data have no time for the patience required of close reading: "Some of us like to think that although we can think of different ways of thinking of space and time, and thus organize our thinking of space and time in different stories, in fact the human being thinks—does, as in performs—space as extension and time as sequence and this does not change."[35] The limits of the human sensory apparatus imply that no amount of information rendered as empirical description can rival machinic data. What is essentially human is also what is singular about literature—it gives us different ways of thinking about time and reorganizing it through stories; however, in the end, time has to be thought as sequence, and space has to be thought as expansion.

Fredric Jameson's renaming of the elements of *fabula* and *sjuzhet* as "schemes of temporality" allows us to think of abstract time or the "formal continuum of past-present-future" as a scheme that is subjected to cancelling at every moment by a "living present" or the instinct that each individual subjectivity in the novel is given to live as best as it can. The "present of time" thus challenges the "official requirement of the form to integrate that moment in a formal continuum."[36] Although these two schemes are ahistorical in their functions in all modes of narrations, the way they relate to each other can be historicized because attention to continuity "changes and evolves with the complexity and also the dimensions of the historical situation as such," and although we live in both temporalities simultaneously, each one takes its significance or preponderance from the immediate situation in the novel. Thus, in a modernist text like *Mrs. Dalloway* that represents sensory overload in subjective experience, the stream-of-consciousness technique is an example of "other features of time [that] offer to displace the older organizational schemes of temporality and to propose new and more plausible substitutes."[37] This does not mean that the tripartite continuity of past-present-future is a "mere" abstraction and the present is the only "really" concrete experience. Such a relationship would stand, Jameson points out, "only if the present were a mere instant of the other kind of time, a moment or point on the continuum, a mere break in the flow: in which case the line is as real as the point."[38] What we need to imagine instead is the possibility that there might be "many kinds of presents," and that the living present asserted by the time of narration in a novel might include a great deal of complexity, that it would be unjust to reduce it to the discontinuity of "the Deleuzian schizophrenic, the confinement in the present of the amnesiac or the Alzheimer's patient, the fixation on the eternal of the mystic."[39]

All this is to say that if we think of the living present as a single, unchanging, or absolute interlocking backbone of events following one after another, we would exclude all negation or critical distance of the kind that I have argued for in this introduction and elsewhere in the book. Each chapter attends to the ways selected novels respond to the dawning, and sometimes inescapable, awareness of the sheer mass of the new globality and the billions of people with whom we have to coexist whether we like it or not. There is no experience of a "present" that is not tied to the subject, because it is the subject whose life cuts into abstract time and renders it into manageable concrete units and sequences. Globalization thus provides an imaginative stumbling block because it is impossible for any individual (even in the guise of a cosmopolitan character or omniscient narrator in the novel) to encompass this heterogeneity in older ethical notions of alterity or through recognizable cultural communities with neat geographical boundaries. Instead, contemporary writers, more so today than ever before, write fiction with this awareness of those billions whose lives are comingled with ours.

I want to end this section on abstract and concrete time by addressing the relationship between temporality, ethics, and the political. Why are different ways of thinking of time—or accessing, through the literary, ways to organize our thinking of time in different stories—integral to the idea of coexistence and collectivity? I will address this question by way of Jacques Derrida's discussion in *Specters of Marx*, which, one may remember, is also a pointed philosophical critique of Fukuyama's vision of a contemporary world coming into being by way of a fundamental break with the past. Derrida questioned the temporality of homeostasis, Fukuyama's end of history, by introducing what it could not account for—the figure of the specter, or the ghostly figuration of a fundamental disjuncture, or disjointedness, between an empirical now (that is supposedly perfect) and a future to come (the unrealized ideal), the difference between democracy now and the more perfect union one hopes for. As that which is and is not, the specter represents temporalities that cannot be grasped adequately in terms of the present time. Specters therefore represent a past that has not passed (the ghosts of Karl Marx or Hamlet's father) as well as a future that breaks with the present (the specter of communism haunting Europe in *The Communist Manifesto*). The past is other and yet it calls to us, but like Hamlet's father, the past is also mute, and we have to be haunted by it, accept responsibility, to give it voice.

Similarly, ethical relationships are not fixed in an empirical present. More often than not, we imagine relationships with those "who are no longer or for those others who are not yet there, presently living, whether they are already dead or not yet born." Is it possible for us to respond to one of the pressing issues of our time, the problem of climate change, without a kind of a temporally extended ethics? As Derrida says, "No justice seems possible or thinkable without the principle of some *responsibility*, beyond all living present, within that which disjoins the living present . . . be they victims of wars, political or other kinds of violence, nationalist, racist, colonialist, sexist, or other kinds of exterminations." There can be no ethics and no politics without the ghost. As a concept metaphor the specter possesses rich literary and historiographical potential for it lets us imagine a temporality that takes us beyond a passively experienced "chain of presents." What Derrida adds to Agamben's idea of noncoincidence is the transformation of this distancing, or otherness, into the possibility of others who are not with us in our time: "Without this *non-contemporaneity with itself of the living present*, without that which secretly unhinges it, without this responsibility and this respect for justice concerning those who are not there, of those who are no longer or who are not yet present and living, what sense would there be to ask the question 'where?' 'where tomorrow?' 'whither?' "[40]

Reading as Conceptual Performance

Literary analysis can become a cultural analysis of the present if it keeps in mind the lessons learned from these modes of temporal distancing and if it questions the very concepts that we bring to our analysis of the contemporary—if we demonstrate how they are abstractions that express social relations we believe to be historically present. As a case in point, when Marx argues in *Poverty of Philosophy* that money is not the problem because it is only the phenomenal form of an abstract social mediation, he is saying that money only expresses a form of social relations already present. We cannot wish away those social relations by abolishing money. In the same vein, I argue that key concept metaphors that have gained considerable traction in literary and cultural studies of the contemporary must be deconstructed to show not only the diverse domains of knowledge that have parceled out the analysis of the present, but also how their arrival in analysis today is a sign of historical change—change for which we need new terms, or in many cases, old terms remade into new concept metaphors. Just as the living present is a projection of the experience of individual memory onto an ideological construction, like a narrative genre, to show how a present, any present, is not a slicing up of a "chain of presents" but a complex reshuffling of the past-present-future continuum in which neither the past nor the future are fully subsumed by present time, we must think of our "theories" not as a chain of new ideas, or new theories for new times (a break with the old), but as analytical practices that involve a temporal differentiation. Concepts work by displacing a term from the context of its use, what we might call its "natural" environment, in which its discursivity and metaphorical resonances usually go unnoticed. When we use a term as a concept metaphor, we move it into another context in which its discursivity is thematized and explicated. As Ophir has pointed out, the conceptual statement is "simultaneously linked to two distinct sets of statements, the distance between which is not fixed and depends on the kind of discourse in which conceptualization takes place."[41]

This recontextualizing ability is the reason that the five concepts I have made central to each of the chapters in the book—specters, attachments, networks, markets, and assemblages—are grounded in literary performances that reveal those concepts to be not only topographical but also temporal. What Étienne Balibar says about concepts shows us how the conceptual comes with an inherent spatial bias: "[The] formation of concepts—does not work as an instrument to distinguish, *isolate* the faculties or elements of intellectual activity that could generate conflicts from one another, be they ideologies, subjectivations or sensibilities, but, on the contrary, to bring them together and transport them into a single *topos*, in order to problematize the uncertain effects of their encounter."[42] To think of concepts as the act of herding meaning into a topos is to think of them as sites of internal differences. My analysis seeks to make the literary text into the topos where the concepts themselves are encountered. When these theoretical abstractions are pressed into service of understanding contemporary problems through literary readings, they too are enriched as they grapple with the global as a necessary stumbling block. Making these concepts work for globality means using the awareness of an expanded world to think about how its sheer mass is connected to us historically, affectively, technologically, economically, and environmentally.

"Specters" (chapter 1) is the existing term for a ghostly figure as a concept metaphor to problematize the durability of the historical past in the present, how we are haunted by our past. Specters can become narrative tropes that transport the past-present-future of colonialism into the lived presents of poor migrants in their new homes and reveal in their wake the standardizations of global capital that undermine community through a creative destruction of its own past of colonialism and imperialism. In "attachments" (chapter 2), we see a term that is suggestive of a subject's personal and intimate emotional connections to others, whether people, places or things. But this term can be reworked as a concept that helps us access the power of affective investments. Thinking of attachments in the way Lauren Berlant does, as "affective structures," allows us to think of how the past-present-future continuum works in discussions of citizenship and the formation of a present in the imagined community of the nation that undergoes demographic transformation by immigration. "Networks" (chapter 3) is a term that is now used to describe a variety of communication grids, ranging from epistolary and print technologies to transportation and electronic media; however, when we encounter the stumbling block of the sheer mass of connections enabled by globalization, this problem is imperfectly solved by imagining network as a synchronous simultaneity that overcomes space but not the heterogeneity of living presents. "Markets" (chapter 4) are age-old sites of economic exchange; in their new conceptual rebirth under neoliberalism, they have become ideological constructs repurposed to imagine an abstract global space of exchange where everyone is on the same coevally constructed playing field—a future heaven of temporal equivalence. When markets appear as action verbs like "marketization" and in the personifications of the entrepreneur as *Homo economicus*, markets elicit a metaphysical power that transforms the abstraction itself into a principle governing the most individualized kind of temporality we experience, our finite life spans and our imaginings of the "good life." Finally, with "assemblages" (chapter 5), a term that commonly indicates a collection of things, its use as a concept has reshaped ideas about agency and collectivity, allowing us to imagine a new relationship of the human and nonhuman. Yet this concept, which has far-reaching political and ethical implications for thinking about the future and the impending catastrophe facing us as planetary beings, also has a tendency to create a flattened world. I ask whether assemblages can factor in the kinds of historical residues and inequities of the living presents experienced by those who cannot yet imagine their lives in such proleptic terms.

It is part of this book's argument that these five concepts, in their literary unfolding, privilege one aspect of the past-present-future continuum because of the particular temporal emphasis the *sjuzhet* and the genre place on the story. Therefore, the first two chapters discuss narrative anachronies that are oriented toward the past, like metalepsis, analepsis, palimpsest, and parataxis, while the third generates a synchronous, timeless present. Chapter 4 draws out the abstract future beyond the temporal calculations of financial markets, while chapter 5 reveals the nonhuman time scales of climate change using the proleptic time lapses of narrative description. Taken together, these conceptual performances reveal the implicit temporal structures that underlie the use of these terms in debates about globalization today, while the literary texts give us ways to access how living presents use features of time that displace older organizational schemes of temporality and propose new and more plausible substitutes.

I realize that there will be no agreement about how one names new narrative forms, especially given the diverse set of novels and writers, so I will simply list some of the designations already in use, rather than make a case for why they should be categorized this way: the migrant narrative, the city novel, the internet novel, the neoliberal allegory, and cli-fi, or climate fiction.

Chapter Outline

The first two chapters constitute one unit in answer to the question, "What do the temporalizations of migrancy tell us about the lingering effect of histories that have been rendered as 'legacies' of the past, as remainders rather than as active forces in the world today?" Acknowledging colonial presence may have as much to do with how nations require the political expediency of belonging somewhere as it does with how spectral and affective connections are necessary for community and citizenship. The book then proceeds to the scene of economic restructuring and ecological damage in the developing and developed globe through a series of literary readings that track the temporalizations of networks, markets, and assemblages. Each chapter explores stories that ask what forms of collectivity a subject can embrace when the experience of temporality, especially the "now," is increasingly mediated by the virtual and is no longer interpretable by neat oppositions such as colonial/postcolonial, local/global, capitalist/socialist, and tradition/modernity.

Chapter 1, "Specters: Durabilities of the Past in the Present," introduces the specter as a concept metaphor for temporalities that cannot be grasped adequately in terms of present time. My reading of Jamaica Kincaid's *Lucy* (2000) attends specifically to scenes of the present that include a past that has not passed and a future that breaks with the present by holding on to the past and its inheritance. Lucy's predicament, I argue, is inherent to the time of the migrant, who must live with this double bind in a new community. How might discussions of cultural assimilation embrace this unsettledness as a positive force in the globalized world?

Whereas chapter 1 shows how global time remains haunted by traces of the colonial and the untimely that are carried over from older social formations, chapter 2, "Attachments: Affective Palimpsests and the Habits of Citizenship," explores the politics of time implicit in questions of citizenship and national belonging. Drawing on recent work on the affective components of citizenship by Lauren Berlant, Judith Butler, and others, I ask how we might read the affective structures of personal attachments in terms of a "historical sensorium." How does the constitution of the "we" (in "we the people") happen in the wake of the demographic transformation of the United States today? In Teju Cole's *Open City* (2012), we imagine collectivity from the perspective of a more highly educated migrant who brings with him the contradictions of the global elite class to which he belongs.[43] I argue that a reading of history and the subject's psyche as palimpsestuous temporality is necessary for working through the political effects of affective structures and attachments in the formation of "new" racisms and the distribution of inequities today.

The becoming abstract of land and the earth, which was hinted at by the lack of geographical markers in *Lucy* and by the spectrality of urban spaces of *Open City*, is at the front and center of chapter 3, "Networks: Sheer Space as Synchronous Experience." This chapter explores the now ubiquitous concept metaphor of the network through a fictional representation of technologically driven global capitalism. Networks show global expansion by flattening time and space, by representing the world as a synchronic simultaneity effected by the connectivity of these teletechnologies. Hari Kunzru's *Transmission* (2005), a novel about a cyberattack of global proportions, plays with the idea of communication across this flattened globe and in so doing allows us to examine the intersectionality of globalization, time, and technology through the tempos and rhythms of the narrative. By taking up the representational attraction that technological networks have provided for thinking of globalization itself as a kind of cyberspace, where capital is virtual and dematerialized and has become pure transmission, I ask whether such a fascination might foreclose the imagining of collectivities that depend on temporalities that are harder to see in the network time that Manuel Castells calls the "timeless present."

Chapter 4, "Markets: Capital and the Resource of Time" has two foci: one, the tension between the lived present of subjective experience and the time of capital; and two, allegory as a symptomatic representation of the present, an "outdated" literary form that is reappearing or "flashing" (to use Walter Benjamin's term) in a time of danger to show us the colonization of human life by economic reason. I show how writers like Aravind Adiga, Mohsin Hamid, and Don DeLillo repurpose allegory and its popular rhetorical device of personification into a narrative mode that challenges economic reason's stealth project of making all human conduct into economic conduct. In the novelistic tradition of characters like the Dickensian Mr. Bounderby, who personified utilitarianism by never failing to remind us of his bootstraps, the neoliberal heroes of Adiga's *White Tiger* (2008), Hamid's *How to Get Filthy Rich in Rising Asia* (2013), and DeLillo's *Cosmopolis* (2003) show us how the "market," a term that has lost its empirical grounding as a place where human beings exchange goods, is now a concept metaphor for free-floating capital in various spaces of expansion, extraction, and production. Reading the three novels comparatively as allegories of the market—in different spaces of expansion, different modes of production, and different forms of extraction of surplus value, and also from feudal-tributary agriculture and primitive accumulation, to manufacturing, commercial, and venture capital—offers us different heterotemporalities for considering capital's colonization of the lived present through the universal equivalency of exchange.

While neoliberal allegories show how the finite life of an individual, a life span, can become a way of thinking that which is not identical with the present and can provide an imaginative distancing from an economic rationality that tells us how we should live our lives, the final chapter compares the seeming timelessness of accelerated economic globalization that is centered on the human with the nonhuman scales of time that have subsumed all manner of ethical and political considerations today, in short, climate change imagined within the problematic of the global. Chapter 5, "Assemblages: Ethico-aesthetic Compositions for the Future," explores a radical form of human-nonhuman collectivity imagined as a response to environmental crisis. Drawing on theorists like Jane Bennett, I explore the assemblage as an imaginative "coexistence of mutual dependency with friction and violence between parts" that shares a structural similarity to twentieth-century globalization's transformation of the earth into a space of events, as well as the part-whole relationships of "network," "meshwork," and "empire." I argue that assemblage brings with it a much more radical shift in the way in which we see temporality: not only how this part-whole relationship is imagined outside human scales of time but also how political agency, which is normally understood as calculated and directed collective action toward an anticipated end, is reconceptualized as an embrace of uncertainty. This chapter focuses on Barbara Kingsolver's *Flight Behavior* (2012), a novel that fashions various narrative reconfigurations of humans, nonhumans, and material objects into composites and constellations that offer alternatives to the assemblages theorized by Bennett and others like Latour and Manuel DeLanda.

The book begins and ends with discussions of novels that foreground perspectives often rendered invisible in the enforced abstract universality of economic globalization and climate change. Novels like *Lucy* and *Flight Behavior* invite us to think about our historical present through the imagined perspectives of poor women and racial minorities in the gendered work of caring and sharing. It is literature that reminds theory about the lessons we have learned from four decades of feminist, deconstructionist, Marxist, and postcolonialist work in the humanities. In the global and transnational Anglophone fiction of today, we encounter writers who aim to detach themselves from older modes of national allegorizing, cultural authentication, and identitarian contests. Even as the fictions of our time demand a different kind of attention to the entangled and interconnected lives they show, the contemporary novel's expansionist trend coexists with a growing resistance to the kind of globality that invokes the sheer mass of populations. There is a sort of weariness with a world that is too much with us, resulting in the desire to close off considerations of other histories and demographics and opt for the analytical comforts of the local, the descriptive, the empirical, the affective, and the formalist. I hope this book will encourage the jaded reader who desires such a retreat to undertake a renewed engagement with the novel's unrelenting worldliness and its ability to bring to its readers worlds whose abstract scales and temporalities are tamed by stories of living presents that refuse to concede to world-time.

CHAPTER ONE

Specters
Durabilities of the Past in the Present

The specter is a form of living-on of a present being through time. In *Echographies of Television*, Jacques Derrida says that "live" television (or film) casts an uncanny spectral shadow over the instant, the present of an event. This uncanniness is a spatial and temporal *différance* constituted by the mediatic capture of the image.[1] As viewers, we are reminded that the sound-image is happening in the moment, here, in this space, although the person may have been somewhere else in the world. We may also believe that the image is the virtual afterlife, a spectral form, of a person who is speaking as if alive although long since dead. A recorded voice, a body image, or a gesture in the virtual medium—they are all instantiations of spectrality. Described this way, it is not difficult for us to see that the sort of spatiotemporal differentiation created by the displaced sound-image is not limited to virtual media. This aspect of spectrality is fundamental to the way in which one constitutes identity, selfhood, or for that matter, the very notion of presence.

The formal survival of spectrality is a never-ending process that follows from the reality that as beings *in* time we are finite. We persist and live on as the *form* of our present beings *through* time. To persist means to carry on after something has ended, and thus, paradoxically, the specter represents both death and living-on at the same time. Without this formal survival, nothing can be present because, to identify the person we encounter or the thing we see, we have to assume that they remain the same throughout all their possible repetitions. This is a paradox we encounter in Shakespeare's "Sonnet 18," in which the poet addresses his beloved by comparing her to a summer's day. Having done so, he realizes that summer's lease is short as seasons change; he wants an "eternal summer [that] shall not fade." The final couplet brings the resolution to this problem: "So long as men can breathe, or eyes can see, / So long lives this, and this gives life to thee." "This" is the poem, by the writing of which the poet will preserve the beloved after her death, keep her living-on and growing "in eternal lines to Time." But the beloved's eternal life is assured only if we assume that all subsequent conjuring of her by readers and their readings are of one and the same person. This principle works in autobiography too, where the uncanny spectral shadow over the instant, or the present of the self who writes her life (autobiography), is a spatial and temporal *différance* constituted by the capture and unification of that self in a series of repetitions of the pronoun "I" through time.

When we come to the question of history, spectrality is complicated by the necessity of thinking in terms other than that of personal genealogy—history as the consensual cultural memory of a collectivity. For instance, in the intellectual debates about the post–Cold War "future" of Europe in the 1990s, spectrality was a way of invoking Europe's heritage as less than "pure"—its memory haunted by the inscriptions within it of colonialism and anti-Semitism. Spectrality at this scale is simply an acknowledgment that collective memory can seem intuitive and intimate, as not needing disciplinary knowledge of history, but such identifications (without distancing) can also make history "private" or something to be owned. On the one hand, the transformations of cultural, financial, state, and media apparatuses by virtual teletechnologies might suggest that distinctions between cultures are harder and harder to define. On the other hand, such a flattening of the cultural is only possible because we privilege the power of spatial connectivity, the power of these teletechnologies to homogenize interactions. Teletechnologies encourage a flattening of time when "universal privilege [is] accorded to 'today' and to everything that advances under its temporal stride."[2]

Yet, all indications are that even though the postmodern age of teletechnologies may have in fact prioritized the "now" and made the past less valuable, these technologies also create a fear of forgetting. Mayra Rivera, for instance, sees an intense "hunger of memory" in the contemporary US cultural scene: "vows never to forget, museums and memorial sites, and public apologies for the wrongs of the past" are all part of this preoccupation with the past, which she understands to be a "symptom of anxiety affecting a culture that cannot hold on to the present long enough."[3] For Andreas Huyssen, the culture of globalization is "socially produced amnesia." Could it be, he asks, that "the surfeit of memory in this media-saturated culture creates such overload that the memory system itself is in constant danger of imploding, thus triggering the fear of forgetting?"[4] If the dialectics of this forgetting implies an even more intense focus on memory, we can expect to see growing calls for a kind of revisionism that Gayatri Spivak calls "privatizing history," when cultural claims to retrieve the past refer to "one's own hallucinatory heritage for the sake of politics of identitarian competition."[5] The ever more fragmented memory politics of today raises the question of whether forms of collective consensual memory are even still possible, and, if not, whether and in what form this divided world can share in appeals to the past. Although it is hardly possible to make everyone part of one story, it seems to me we can learn something about our own (common) complicity by acknowledging the role of spectrality by thinking of the past as Other, calling to us, asking us to read it and speak to it responsibly.

"*Thou art a scholar; speak to it, Horatio.*" This is the last line of Derrida's *Specters of Marx*, and it is quoted from William Shakespeare's *Hamlet, Prince of Denmark*.[6] In the play, an officer says these words to Horatio, Hamlet's friend, as they watch the ghost of the king, Hamlet's father, enter the castle ramparts. The ghost is familiar and its form is known to all, even intimately to Hamlet, Horatio, and the court officers. Yet, it is as a "scholar" that Horatio is asked to speak to the ghost. Derrida's message at the end of a book that reads Marx by talking to his ghost is that "it's not just enough to emote" or to intuit the past.[7] The ghost is a figure, but it is a silent one. Scholars implicate themselves, because, in the end, it is they who take responsibility for the past by studying it in order to speak to it. "Hauntology," as Spivak puts it, "is a name for reading."[8]

Jamaica Kincaid's *Lucy* (1990) is a novel that lends itself to a reading of spectrality in these terms. As an "autobiographical novel" narrated by the eponymous heroine, it captures the principle of an "I" who persists and lives on as the *form* of a once-present being *through* time. As a story of a young woman's migrancy to the United States from a Caribbean island, we get an additional spatiotemporal dislocation, a *différance* that distances the narrator not only from the time of the events that are narrated but also the home or place that is being remembered. The prestructure of *Lucy* allow us to consider the use of memory in subject formation as a model for thinking about the ethical and political openings provided by spectrality—as a responsibility borne to the past as well as the future. After all, the specter appears, not to draw us into the past but because it has a message or directive for the future. To give in to the workings of spectrality is to recognize affirmative potential in the virtual destabilization of the very grounds of our belonging—spectrality is a challenge for any politics based only on native soil or delimited and localized affiliations.

The unusual structure of Kincaid's novel adds another layer to the question about an ethical relationship to the past. Although it is "Lucy's story" that we read, narrated in the first person, it is only at the end of the novel that Lucy actually begins to "write" her autobiography. It is as though the novel itself is the narrator readying herself for that task: preparing to move beyond an emoted and intuited past of her childhood and youth in the Caribbean, resisting the pull of identity in a story about herself, and striving to reevaluate her own relationship to and complicity with the past. When we read *Lucy* this way, the past appears not merely as events to be accessed or recovered but as a past that is being revised in the present for the future. In the novel, the literary figure that facilitates such a relationship to the past is the figure of metalepsis—a trope that enacts a series of substitutions as well as achronic reversals of cause and effect in temporal sequence. In metalepsis we sense only a faint far-fetched allusion to a previous text and it is easy to miss the allusion unless one has studied the text or event to which the figure alludes or one can recognize the old word or meaning that is now reappearing in a new context. Thus, the novel's metaleptic narrative retroversion focuses our attention on these allusions being "revisions" in the present rather than recovered memories of the past. In other words, *Lucy* is not the kind of novel in which memory retrieval is being used to constitute a "Caribbean identity" for a poor immigrant woman. To the contrary, as the novel brings into view a spectral past, it also reveals the conditions in the present that create the susceptibility for the past to appear and be transformed by the context of its appearance. We may have lost the large swathes of historical memory that created the national histories and the parastate collectivities of the three worlds, but the spectral appearance of other times in a contemporary—the lived present of a subject who is narrating her story—may provide other ways of relating to the past that do not depend on sanctioned authority or constructions of the past as our own genealogy. Metalepsis is the figure that replicates the experience of haunting not as a nostalgic return to the past but as a look toward the past as a way to the future.

At first glance, Jamaica Kincaid's novel might seem an unusual choice for a book on the global contemporary. Although published in 1990 at the cusp of globalization's emergence as an object of study with a scholarly niche and experts, the time of narration in the novel is 1969.[9] The primary setting is an unnamed city somewhere in the United States, but Lucy's narrated past draws in a Caribbean island that is still under British colonial rule. The novel ingeniously uses a productive anachronism—an achronicity by which the literary text captures the faint outlines of what is an emergent structure of feeling and proleptically figures what is not yet social "fact." By staging Lucy's time in the United States as a present inherited from the British Empire, the novel performs a historical transition through the spectralized memory of its narrator. It reminds a contemporary reader in the 1990s of a different status of a "present" in which the United States has emerged as the world's sovereign superpower and brought about a waning of Europe's global role. At another level, legacies of the past in Lucy's subject-formation also show the durabilities of the colonial past in the present. Historically, as a social formation, the second British Empire depended for the effectiveness of its centuries-long rule on what Ann Stoler calls a "partial visibility"—haunting structures that were both distant yet also "strangely familiar" in their "'uncanny' intimacies."[10] In the novel Kincaid, too, mobilizes such a vertiginous past-in-the-present to bring to the foreground what cannot fully appear as a known background or historical context to its young narrator. In this veiled background, the reader is asked to imagine the diffuse operations of modernity, colonialism, and capitalism as overlapping formations whose effects are overdetermined and discontinuous at the same time. By leaving the traces of the past in an unassimilated form in the present, Kincaid enacts neither rupture nor seamless continuity between this backgrounded past and a foregrounded present; rather, she places them side by side, as the undeniable appearance of the past-in-the-present. In other words, spectrality is the force that holds Kincaid's narration in place.

If we understand spectrality as a form of appearance of the abstracted workings of history, empire, or the capitalist world system, it is to be expected that a normal post-Enlightenment response (on the part of the reader) might be to strive to demystify this knowledge—to make the abstract into concrete phenomena, the systemic into the quotidian, and history into individual memory. However, setting ourselves such a task simply skirts the question of abstraction itself because we would not understand *how* subjects imagine their relationship to what we refer to as the "systemic": structures that are ungraspably complex and only partially material. We would lose an opportunity to examine the process of interpretation embodied by a novel, a process where language, as a system of ordering and signification, provides its own tools and levers for accessing phenomena, even if it escapes a subject's full cognition and comprehension. In *Lucy* we see how it is the aesthetic and linguistic dimension, rather than the empirical, that is the privileged field of spectrality. Conversely, to privilege spectrality means letting go of the concrete details through which literature often offers itself as a form of social documentation of the "real" rather than of the fabricated. Instead of reading *Lucy* contextually, as a realistic albeit fictional document that references a particular historical and cultural situation, I focus on its literariness—its rhetorical, narrative, and aesthetic elements.[11] Indeed, my sense is that Kincaid's novel resists the idea that the literary text is all about showing us a social reality about which concrete details about geography, location, culture, and history are to be reproduced faithfully. If readers were to act on such a desire for social documentation, they would read *Lucy* as a fictional autobiography about the experience of a young woman moving from a poor Caribbean country to a rich North American one. However, as readers of *Lucy* soon notice, the novel is startlingly opaque in this regard. It is as though Kincaid deliberately withholds the very particulars that would make this a novel about an immigrant's "race-class-gender predicament" in her new home.[12] Lucy gives us one historical date, 1969, but no names of locations, not even everyday details about her work as an au pair. We can only approximate the narrator's country of origin and the country to which she has emigrated through vague details. As readers, we sense an interconnected world in the novel only in an abstract way without the familiar tent pegs that pin down a subject's identity or the cultural, national, and historical attributes that provide the neat ontopological (ontological value linked to territory or *topos*) comparisons on which much multicultural and transnational fiction depends.[13]

This opacity is partly necessary because *Lucy* is a narrative that is meant to make us feel as though we are squinting at a smoky background, a background to which we gain access only through what I call a "metaleptic reading." Instead of working our way from presupposed abstractions like history and economy (the intangible totalities that can never appear fully to our consciousness) to their concrete manifestations in Lucy's lived reality, the novel demands that we reverse our direction of reading. What we have to work with are the fragmented, far-fetched memories of a young and assertive but unreliable self-engrossed informant. As we watch the play between the past and present, between Lucy's origin and destination, her old home and her new, narrative unconsciousness and consciousness, and as Lucy's memories emerge spectrally from an archive that cannot be fully present to the subject who remembers, as a finite repository, these memory traces nudge the novel's readers to a reconstruction of the spatial and temporal sedimentations of a history that nowhere appears as an autonomous background narration: as an isolatable historical "context" with places, dates, events, and personalities. Rather, it is through the untidiness of subjective memory, narrated as autobiography, that readers retroactively encounter the spectral return of colonialism in a present that seems discontinuous from it—discontinuous because it is a present that now includes Lucy as well as her affluent employers as beneficiaries of capitalism in the global North. The novel seems to ask, Who inherits Lucy as a spectral transmission? It is only when we read the narrative retroactively from the time of the present to the past, from memory-effect to absent cause, from the intimate impressions of autobiography to the spectral but determining structures of history, and from concretion to abstraction that the novel reveals how Lucy becomes an agent in shaping her own story.

In the sections to follow, I begin with a discussion of the novel's representation of the past and present as a play between levels of the text that results in a doubled vision, like an inverted telescope—as Lucy sees what is there before her as something that has been encountered before in the past. I then move to a discussion of metalepsis as the exemplary spectral figure of doubling that builds a transactional bridge between the backgrounded but invisible past and the present in which the subject dwells. Metalepsis thus carries the concrete details of autobiography into a more abstracted level, that is, from personal memory to a systematization of the past as "history." In the following section, my reading of metalepsis in *Lucy* joins Karl Marx's famous use of the trope as an exemplary figure for unpacking the historical movement of capital. This is where I move metalepsis from the level of the personal story to the systemic story. We know that political economy has always had an affinity for specters; famous examples include Adam Smith's invisible hand, Marx's specter of communism, and Max Weber's spirit of capitalism. Ghostly presencing has also intensified in contemporary discussions of the economic world-system because of the mystification posed by the accelerated movements and abstract structures of the finance economy. Descriptions of contemporary globalization abound in spectral metaphors.[14] Popular notions like "intangible value" and "shadow banking," for instance, represent mystification as a sort of invisibility. Through a reading of Marx's discussion of the commodity, I show how the spectrality of metalepsis is a representation not only of the instability of globalization's timeless present but also of the movement of capital itself—a point that Anna Kornbluh has made persuasively through her own reading of Marx's use of metaleptic argumentation.[15] A final section looks closely at the dialectical movement of spectrality in *Lucy* as a subjective response to violence in the present, on the one hand, and a defense against history's determinations as decided fate, on the other. I end by fleshing out some of the ethical lessons that imaginative framing of Lucy's experience by way of metalepsis teaches us, the novel's readers, as we try to make sense of a fragmented world in which, for each one of us, and groups of us, globalization is "an island of languaging in a field of traces."[16] By this Spivak means that globalization, rather than being a field of translation where we can exchange appropriate signs for preexisting concepts, is more akin to what Antonio Gramsci called a relationship to an "inventory of traces." In the time of globality, the lived present of the subject is a product of the historical processes to date, which has deposited in her "an infinity of traces" but "without leaving an inventory."[17]

The Inverted Telescope of History

As we enter the novel, its opening lines describe a border crossing, from the Lucy's previous home to the unnamed city where she is to work and live:

> It was my first day. I had come the night before, a gray-black and cold night before—as it was expected to be in the middle of January, though I didn't know that at the time—and I could not see anything clearly on the way in from the airport, even though there were lights everywhere. As we drove along, someone would single out to me a famous building, an important street, a park, a bridge that when built was thought to be a spectacle. In a daydream I used to have, all these places were points of happiness to me; all these places were lifeboats to my small drowning soul, for I would imagine myself entering and leaving them, and just that—entering and leaving over and over again—would see me through a bad feeling I did not have a name for.[18]

Despite the assertion of a starting point—the "first day" of Lucy's new life— that we expect to unfold in the story, what we get is a vertiginous moment. Looking out the car window, Lucy finds that she is at the end of an inverted telescope. The landmarks that are singled out for her, although she sees them passing by, are experienced as though from afar. They appear without any concreteness—they are not named for the reader and have no identifying details. Instead, "a famous building, an important street, a park, a bridge" appear in Lucy's telling as shadowy forms, as shells of themselves not in the clear light of day but as places she had dreamed of in another place and time. These places, Lucy says, now "looked ordinary, dirty, worn down" in "real life" because they were no longer a "fixture of fantasy" (4). The substitution of Lucy's experiential reality of the city with the recurring motif of a spectrally doubled vision accomplishes two narrative effects: the doubling constitutes history itself as an effect of spectrality (access to what one is not living right now), and it renders the concretion and immediacy we might associate with the present into a deferred moment (the here and now already encountered in the past as image or fantasy). This dizzying circularity, like that of vertiginous virtual global technologies I discussed earlier, is also at work in the novel's narrative sequencing. We notice, for instance, that the entire opening paragraph (quoted above) is, in fact, a digression from its opening sentence: "It was my first day" is immediately followed by the narrator's description of her arrival the previous night. The reader has to wait several paragraphs till Lucy is done describing "the night before," and the narration moves forward, starting again with these words: "That morning, the morning of my first day, the morning that followed my first night" (5).

For this narrative vertigo to take hold, the story itself (as a sequence of events) must give way to a reversal of cause and effect. Whereas Lucy begins the narrative with her abrupt arrival, an entry into a new space and time, the retroactive force of a prior moment—"all these places were points of happiness to me"—is actively shaping what should have been a moment of newness into a shabby ordinariness. In this push and pull between past and present, the world of Lucy's childhood and that of her adulthood always remain unbridgeable because of their spatial and temporal distance from each other, not least of all because Lucy herself wants to make a fresh start. But the language of the novel strives toward commensurability at another level. It strives to make a passage, a bridge, between what appears as Lucy's thought and an absent cause, an "origin" for this thought, sometimes through translation and at other times through the transferential work of tropes or rhetorical figures. For the most part, tropes are figures of substitution that identify one thing with another that has a familiar meaning, but sometimes the association is remote and lacks the direct comparison that is available in the case of metaphor. The effect of this omission is that the reader has to make an effort to provide the bridge between the thing and its referent, as opposed to straight metonymy where this association may already be in conventional use. Thus, links created by a far-fetched association are like the relationship of the subject to a spectral totality that is barely perceptible but alluded to in a text where language operates in the manner of a trace rather than of a direct referent. Here is Lucy as she looks around herself on the first day in her new home:

> The room in which I lay was a small room just off the kitchen—the maid's room. I was used to a small room, but this was a different sort of small room. The ceiling was very high and the walls went all the way up to the ceiling, enclosing the room like a box—a box in which cargo traveling a long way should be

shipped. But I was not cargo. I was only an unhappy young woman living in a maid's room, and I was not even the maid. I was the young girl who watches over the children and goes to school at night. (*Lucy*, 7)

We notice the disavowal in Lucy's description, but what is not acknowledged in the statement itself emerges at the level of the narrative's allusiveness. When Lucy asserts that she is not "cargo," the series of quick transfers she has already described from the airport, to the car, to the elevator, and then into the box-like room reminds the readers that she is, but not quite. And when she asserts that she is not a "maid," the placement of the au pair's room off the kitchen tells the reader that she is like a maid, but not quite. The narrative thus works metaleptically by forming a kind of intermediate step between the term transferred and the thing to which it is transferred, having no meaning in itself but merely providing a transition. The terms "cargo" and "maid" operate in this way—both are rejected at the level of sense but stay around long enough to make an associative leap, long enough to let us think of affective labor in the domestic sphere as a form of paid labor and as cargo imported from somewhere. The au pair in particular (as sponsored student-worker) performs a kind of domestic work that blurs the distinction between employee and guest, intellectual and menial, domestic and foreign. What might seem an initial confusion of terms is actually a displacement or substitution without real alternatives. Just as certain forms of production and labor, like the factory floor and the working class, are displaced by globalization today, these substitutions indicate an intensification of the categorical confusion that is ongoing but was always part of gendered work in the domestic sphere. The au pair's work is not just the gendered labor of surrogate mothering but a form of "affective labor"—a job that carries a special status by virtue of taking care of another's needs.[19]

What the novel lets us sense through Lucy's confusion is a structural aspect of gendered work that is not fully apparent in its performed aspects. In the social sciences, however, this sort of labor is well on its way to becoming a recognized social fact. Take, for instance, that classic analysis of gender and international relations *Bananas, Beaches and Bases*, which appeared the same year *Lucy* was published. In it, Cynthia Enloe titles a chapter on nannies "Just like One of the Family," drawing attention to the transformation and substitution of hired domestic work as "inside" work and the increasingly affective component of it.[20] That analysis can act as context for what is happening here, but Kincaid's text provides some other important displacements. As "cargo," Lucy alludes to the transnational element in this mode of outsourcing of work that is done by the "family," but as "maid" the text links her to another figure of domestic labor that has now been displaced from most middle-class homes in the United States. The maid-cargo–au pair substitutions therefore present Lucy as reprising an older role, now somewhat invisible because of the rhetoric of transactional equality that characterizes such affective labor in households today. Such displacements are useful to track because they allow an analysis of what goes on behind the rhetoric of newness, unprecedentedness, and discontinuity that often pervades accounts of the "new" world order. In what was regarded as a pathbreaking work in 1999 on gendered globalization, the social theorist Saskia Sassen describes the shifting nature of gendered work in the global cities of London and New York. In her account we notice the language and scare quotes that mark spectrality and reappearance, but these elements, it seems to me, are also foreclosed by her emphasis on the novelty of the "new cultural forms":

> The expansion of the high-income workforce in conjunction with the emergence of new cultural forms has led to a process of high-income gentrification that rests, in the last analysis, on the availability of a vast supply of low-wage workers. This has *reintroduced—to an extent not seen in a very long time*—the whole notion of the "serving classes" in contemporary high-income households. The immigrant woman serving the white middle-class professional woman has *replaced the traditional image of the black servant serving the white master.*[21]

In Sassen's account, real-life Lucys are the new face of a labor that supplements the domestic work of white (and increasingly nonwhite) professional women in the United States who often subsidize their careers and lifestyles through the direct importation of women's labor from poor countries. This is no doubt one of the continuing paradoxes of the international division of affective labor that Enloe also records in her book. But Kincaid's novel shows the apprehension of this discontinuous feminist agency in the manner in which an assertive, independent, young female narrator sees her own subject position through a series of displacements. Social theorists today now freely admit that globalization makes possible things that, though perhaps always there, "remained hidden during the stage of the welfare-democratic taming of capitalism." In the intensification and increased visibility of what is already present here and now, there, too, is the acknowledgment of a spectral or mutual haunting of the "old" and the "new" in ways that allow capitalist accumulation to continue—not only through expansion into noncapitalist or peripheral spaces but also through a reconstitution of the relationship between spaces of cores and peripheries around new forms of unequal exchange. Spectrality is thus shorthand for what was meant to disappear but has reappeared in another form.[22]

The novel goes further in its historical sedimentation and allows us to see the connection of its new arrival, Lucy, to an older history of racialized labor in the United States, which Sassen alludes to in the passage I quoted earlier, through a series of associated images seen through her eyes. While on a train journey to the family's summer house on the "Great Lake," Lucy notices in the dining car that the "people sitting down to eat dinner all looked like Mariah's [her employer's] relatives," while the "people waiting on them all looked like mine." The missing link arrives a few sentences later when Mariah tells Lucy to look out the window at the "freshly plowed fields" that she loved so much. Lucy looks out and sees "mile after mile of turned-up earth" and retorts with a cruel tone to her voice, "Well, thank God I didn't have to do that." Lucy ends this anecdote with these words: "I don't know if she understood what I meant, for in that one statement I meant many different things" (*Lucy*, 32–33). As readers we cannot know exactly what Lucy means here, but we can surmise through the text's allusiveness that Mariah's aestheticized freshly plowed fields are a reference to US slavery, to which Lucy, as a migrant from the Caribbean, has only an oblique relation. Nevertheless, the text encourages the reader to make a connection between the old diaspora of enslaved Africans in the Americas and the new one represented by Lucy, of twentieth-century migrant labor moving from poorer to richer countries. Through this distinctive allusive quality, the reader is guided to see a relationship, albeit perceived and made visible in a partial way by Lucy, as a form of knowledge not in terms of expert explanations about political economy that serve as the better-known formulas of globalization but as the apprehension of the systemic through a spectral logic. In the next section I focus on some of more complex ways in which the trope of metalepsis directs our attention to the spectral elements of Kincaid's novel.

Metalepsis as Spectral Figure

One of the most complex allusive references in the novel is offered by way of an explanation for the narrator's name. When Lucy asks her mother about it, she says, "I named you after Satan himself. Lucy for Lucifer" (*Lucy*, 152). This throwaway remark by her mother transforms Lucy's relationship to a name that she had come to dislike as "slight, without substance, not at all like the person I thought I would like to be even then" (149). As a child who memorized portions of John Milton's *Paradise Lost*, the stories of the fallen were familiar to her, but she had not known that her situation "could even distantly be related to them. Lucy, a girl's name for Lucifer" (153). Lucy decides that she would have much preferred to be called Lucifer "outright" but whenever she saw her name, she admits that she always "reached out to give it a strong embrace."

The distant relation constituted by allusion involves a metaleptic substitution. The Miltonic character Lucy encounters only after receiving her own name is now the cause of her own projection, an agential projection into the future of the person she "would like to be." Lucy as Lucifer distances her from the "slight" and "insubstantial" present in which her name exists; Lucy as Lucifer is a subject-effect of a past that is revised and made into a catalyst for the future. Ironically, this is the very movement that Harold Bloom identifies in the allusive work of Milton's epic poem: "Milton re-writes Spenser so as to *increase the distance* between his poetic father and himself."[23] For Bloom, metalepsis is an allusive scheme that refers the reader back to a previous figurative scheme, in which the earlier object is incorporated "so as to overcome it." As Bloom puts it in spectral terms, "The present vanishes and the dead return, by a reversal, to be triumphed over by the living."[24] If the metaleptic substitution Milton achieves over Spenser is the child becoming the father of man, then Lucy gives us one better than the substitution and distancing from the patronymic: "That my mother would have found me devil-like did not surprise me, for I often thought of her as god-like, and are not the children of gods devils?" What I want to emphasize here is how Lucy's agency is metaleptic: it acknowledges the anxiety of (the mother's) influence even as she seeks to distance herself from her. But that distancing from her mother's time, her Caribbean home, her daughter's role has her now reprising her mother's role—as a poor woman desiring upward mobility, Lucy's path lies through the social rather than biological mothering of someone else's children.

As a spectral figure, metalepsis is richer than metaphor and metonymy; its active use of words in a different sense differs from the latter two in an important way. John Hollander explains it thus: in most descriptions of rhetorical figures, "a kind of implicitly spatial language connects the representation with what it replaces—part for whole or vice versa," but metalepsis is the only one (besides dramatic irony) that seems "to involve a temporal sequence."[25] Thus, it can operate as a trope that takes "the consequent for the precedent," effect for cause, or sometimes the other way. The consequence may be of a "narrative pre- and post- —or, more generally, of a kind of allusive—connection" that is far-fetched.[26] Discussing Quintilian's treatment of metaleptic transitions, Hollander points out how such tropes act collectively as a bridge by forming "an intermediate step between the term transferred and the thing to which it is transferred, having no meaning in itself, but merely providing a transition."[27] This is one of the key ways in which metaleptic narration works in *Lucy* (even when the text is not strictly substituting a literary allusion). For one, the novel reveals metaleptic transitions or bridges in its play between narratorial unconsciousness and consciousness, in causal invisibility and appearance, and most compellingly, in the spectral appearance of an absent and receded background that is still active in the foreground. The temporal reversal of spectrality is evident whenever Lucy distances herself from the powerful historical influence of colonialism—a past that constantly appears in her present, which she has to incorporate and overcome while also distancing herself from a future she desires (social mobility) in a new economic world order that she cannot yet name.

Spivak has argued that what often appears as a change in cultural practice might be symptomatic, or a recoding, of a change in the historical determination of capital.[28] If she is right, then we should be prepared to read texts of so-called transnational culture metaleptically not only as texts about "cultural change" but also as coded narratives that actively substitute the cultural for what are, in effect, changes brought about by the economic restructuring of the world. In the previous section, I showed how the novel calls forth abstractions of economic restructuring that are beyond Lucy's collective cognitive, linguistic, and epistemological reach when she substitutes terms that describe her present situation with others that are far fetched—either remotely associated with contemporary economic globalization such as those signifying the mobility of commodities and labor or referring to a prior moment of globalization like slavery that also turned human beings into capital and transported them halfway around the world. The historical overlay created by these substitutions allows us to read Lucy's transnational movement not only as a mode that is distanced from the past as introjection but also as the projection of a new form of international labor migrancy that is emergent. In the next section I explore how metalepsis works against forms of reification that fetishize locality, place, or social groups. The novel does this primarily when it asks us to read concrete things not just as objects (a flower or a poem) but also as representations of the political-economic processes that are becoming ever more "universalizing in their depth, intensity, reach, and power over daily life."[29] Here metalepsis works to counter Max Horkheimer and Theodor W. Adorno's notion that "all reification is a forgetting."[30] To the contrary, I will show that reading Kincaid's repeated allusive use of a flower (such as the daffodil) reveals how the definite social relations between Lucy and her employer have assumed the fantastic form of a relation between things. The metalepsis potential of this thing ("reification"—from the Latin *res* [thing]), renders it more than a token of exchange in a circulation that has forgotten its roots in human activity.

The Metaleptic Rhythm of Capital

In an astute reading of *Capital*, Anna Kornbluh shows us how the "drive" of capital, its "self-infinitizing, subjectifying, repetitive motion," is captured in Marx's prevalent use of metaleptic substitutions.[31] The proliferation of serially replaced images that eventually brings us back to the starting point, only to take off again, allows Marx to represent how capital grows, becomes, takes on new forms of appearance. This proliferative structure is replicated in *Lucy* by one of the most sustained and striking uses of a literary allusion—to the Romantic poet William Wordsworth and his famous poem on daffodils, "I Wandered Lonely as a Cloud." This classic poem creates an inventory of historical, economic, and cultural traces through which Lucy remakes herself as a historical agent by the supersession of a postcolonial subjectivity and, in so doing, allows us to see a symptomatic cultural act—an aesthetic objectification of daffodils—operating as a form of appearance of the economic. The use of Marx's phrase "forms of appearance" is deliberate here.[32] I want to make the point that capital, too, is spectral, as is the concept metaphor of value, for both can appear only in another form—embodied in goods and commodities, represented by numbers, tables, currencies, and so on. Marx isolates the commodity in chapter 1 of *Capital* only to discover that there is nothing elemental about it. The natural form of a thing relinquishes its own use value when it serves as the body inhabited by the "value-form" of the coat or when, like money, it serves as the general "equivalent form" to express the value of a number of commodities.[33] Thus, a simple concrete object may have secret qualities like exchange value or weight that "hide" in it and can only be expressed through another measure or another commodity. When this relationship of value is expressed, concrete objects become embodiments of intangibles, or abstractions, like human labor and value, and it is metalepsis that recruits these abstractions into a relationship of temporality. As Anna Kornbluh's reading of the tropological aspects in Marx's prose reveals, the movement of capital is itself metaleptic, a succession of forms of appearance embodied in familiar, everyday objects that hold within themselves a global history of capital. Furthermore, Marx's prose shows that *Capital* (the work, not the concept) effects a "metaleptic rhythm" in its textual movement through "its succession of paradoxes, what it calls 'double results' and dual forms of appearance, and through its perpetual motion of lifting the veil, starting anew the analysis from a different point of view."³⁴ It is thus not surprising that when Kornbluh discusses the analytical reading that will transform these concrete things into the abstract, it is the language of haunting that is pressed into service: "When value is conjured as spiritual abstraction that authorizes exchange, the spirit transforms material bodies; personification discloses this spiritualization of the commodity body."³⁵

In *Lucy* when an object like the daffodil comes to life, it operates like a commodity that bears within it, as a form of appearance, all the prior moments that have gone into the creation of its embodied value (the labor of human beings, the social relations of production, and the exchange of commodities). In *Lucy* we see a rhythmic metaleptic movement in the way a flower, the daffodil, is successively substituted, one figure by another, expressing its value within varying forms of appearances that start the analysis again from a different point of view. Narratively, metalepsis transposes cause and effect; figuratively, when metalepsis alludes to another figure or text from the past, it also generates origin and distancing from that origin through repetition. Both aspects (reversal and movement) coalesce to constitute the temporality of history in *Lucy* as a form of haunting that leads from a present appearance to a forgotten but remembered prior existence in the past.

Metalepsis also has a spatial aspect when it is working as all tropes and allusions do—linking with other texts, substituting for other words, and disfiguring other images in the play of meaning across the body of the text. This spatial order of meaning is organized in *Lucy* by the totality of the novel itself. For instance, while describing the morning of her first day, Lucy tells us that it was a sunny morning: "not the sort of bright sun-yellow" that she was used to but a "pale-yellow sun." This sentence might pass the reader without notice; however, the next appearance of color in the novel is a description of Lucy's skin: "I knew my skin was the color brown of a nut rubbed repeatedly with a soft cloth" (*Lucy*, 5). We only notice the act of substitution when the word "yellow" appears again. When it does, we notice that the word has left behind its earlier reference to the sun and taken up a retroactive contrast between the light-colored hair of her host family and Lucy's dark skin: "The husband and wife looked alike and their four children looked just like them. In photographs of themselves, which they placed all over the house, their six yellow-haired heads of various sizes were bunched together as if they were a bouquet of flowers tied by an unseen string" (12). The heads of the yellow flowers are now a "bouquet" of blond heads bunched together for family portraits. At this point, the figurative use of yellow is beyond doubt, but it is the repetition of the word that retroactively adds another layer of meaning to its very first appearance in Lucy's description of the temperate weather. A few pages later the metaleptic allusion is already in play but perhaps still far fetched for most readers when Lucy describes Mariah and Lewis thus: "Their two yellow heads swam towards each other and in unison, bobbed up and down" (15). The reference is clinched when Mariah asks Lucy, "Have you ever seen daffodils pushing their way up out of the ground?" (17). At this point Lucy remembers the "old poem" that she had been made to memorize as a schoolgirl; a poem that she had forgotten until Mariah mentioned the word "daffodils."

In the poem by Wordsworth, the poet describes coming upon a "crowd" of golden daffodils, "tossing their heads in sprightly dance"—a catachresis that Lucy undoubtedly modifies to describe the family portraits.[36] But where Wordsworth, like Mariah, finds great pleasure in the sight of daffodils, for Lucy the flowers only unearth a structure of feeling that she associates with the cultural hegemony of imperial Britain. The mere mention of the flower summons a memory of linguistic coercion, when as a ten-year-old schoolgirl she was made to memorize Wordsworth's poem and recite it to an auditorium full of parents, teachers, and fellow pupils. For the young Lucy, the poet's language was purely instrumental. Literature's use in colonial education is for cultural indoctrination, and the colonized manipulate it to acquire cultural capital rather than epistemic access: "After I was done, everybody stood up and applauded with an enthusiasm . . . and later they told me how nicely I had pronounced every word, how I had placed just the right amount of special emphasis in places where that was needed, and how proud the poet, now long dead, would have been to hear his words ringing out of my mouth." For Lucy, the poem is also the spectral voice of the canonized dead poet, and she, who declares elsewhere in the novel that she would "rather be dead than become just an echo of someone," makes a vow to erase from her mind every word of that poem; however, the flowers don't just go away but reappear as malevolent beings. The night after she recited the poem, Lucy dreamed that she was being "chased down a narrow cobbled street by bunches and bunches of those same daffodils that [she] had vowed to forget," and when she finally fell down from exhaustion, "they all piled on top of [her], until [she] was buried deep underneath them and was never seen again" (*Lucy*, 18). The return of the daffodils in Lucy's dream, despite the vow to erase it from her mind, is a compelling analogy of how metalepsis works like dream content, as the ungraspable transaction between consciousness and unconsciousness, the background and foreground that structures Lucy's own telling of her story. This is why reading metaleptically, it seems to me, is literature's way of training us to read history and the economic as coded content: something that was supposed to have gone away but has reappeared in another form.

By its next iteration in the novel, the daffodil reveals the complexity that lies hidden in its appearance as a simple object. One day Mariah takes Lucy to the garden after blindfolding her. She walks Lucy to a spot in the clearing and says, "Now look at this" (*Lucy*, 28). Lucy looks. Here is the novel's description of the scene:

> It was a big area with lots of thick-trunked, tall trees along winding paths. Along the paths and underneath the trees were many, many yellow flowers the size and shape of play teacups, or fairy skirts. They looked like something to eat and something to wear at the same time; they looked beautiful; they looked simple, as if made to erase a complicated and unnecessary idea. I did not know what these flowers were, and so it was a mystery to me why I wanted to kill them. Just like that. I wanted to kill them. . . .
>
> Mariah said, These are daffodils. I'm sorry about the poem, but I am hoping you'll find them lovely all the same. (29)

We can assume that Mariah's blindfolding of Lucy is to help her experience the flower's singularity as an unmediated "first" impression. Unaware of what she is looking at, because she and her fellow students had never actually seen a daffodil on their tropical island, Lucy at first sees a "simple" thing, but she also suspects that the simplicity belies something hidden, that it may be a form of appearance standing in place of a "complicated and unnecessary idea." The daffodils are now like an allusive trace that moves a familiar object into ghostliness and spectrality, where the only trail to its prior meaning and its complicated abstracted meaning lies in the affect that remains.[37] Lucy confesses, "I did not know what these flowers were, and so it was a mystery to me why I wanted to kill them" (29). When the reader tries to follow Lucy's affective response back to its absent source, the daffodil takes on the temporal looping that metalepsis enables by directing us back from an effect or form of appearance to the absent cause or essential truth that lies within the daffodil.

If we read this scene alongside that unforgettable moment in *Capital* when Marx, instead of delving headfirst into the systemic complexities of capitalism, decides to begin with an analysis of how simple objects like coats and linen acquire their value-in-exchange, the analytical richness of metalepsis becomes clearer.[38] Here we might think of *Lucy* and the text of political economy as analogous: both read "back" from a form of appearance to its invisible or illegible systemic meaning (colonialism, capitalism) by a rhetorical tracking through language (as signifying system), using substituted terms, allusions, generated oppositions, and tropes. In chapter 1 of *Capital*, when Marx arrives at the section on the fetishism of the commodity and its secret, he substitutes another simple object, a table, warning us in advance that what looks at "first sight" to be "an extremely obvious, trivial thing" will, with analysis, turn out be a very "strange thing."[39] This ordinary thing may have all kinds of use values, but as soon as it takes on the form of a commodity, it changes into a thing that "transcends sensuousness" (the realm of use) and reveals itself to be a form of appearance of its opposite, exchange value.[40] In the passage above, the flower, unknown at first sight (till Mariah names it for Lucy), moves from sensuous descriptive detail to possible use value (tiny teacups, fairy skirts for children's play) to something strange, evoking an emotion for which Lucy, as yet, has no cause. For Lucy, the word "daffodil," when added to this sensuous detail ("Mariah said, 'These are daffodils'") initiates the allusive work of a trace rather than simply referring to the flowers in front of her. The trace, kept at bay by Mariah's insistence on the phenomenology of the phenomenon ("Now look at this," she says, after removing the blindfold she had placed on Lucy), however, escapes that act of containment. Despite Mariah's attempt to remove all prior traces and meaning so that what Lucy sees is a fully present "first sight," Lucy already senses, even before she recognizes the flower, that its uncanniness has something to do with the flower's prior appearance in her life. Metalepsis asserts continuity where Mariah imagines a rupture or a new beginning, a beginning in which the daffodil will lose all the historical dirt clinging to it and become the object of a shared aesthetic experience. But Lucy tells us, "I did not know what these flowers were, and so it was a mystery to me why I wanted to kill them." And when Mariah finally identifies the flowers, saying, "These are daffodils," Lucy responds with silence: "There was such joy in her voice as she said this, such a music, how could I explain to her the feeling I had about daffodils—that it wasn't exactly daffodils, but that they would do as well as anything else?" (*Lucy*, 29).

At this moment of communicative failure between Mariah and Lucy, two forms of cultural commodification confront each other: in one, a social class uses a beautiful object to demonstrate taste and aesthetic appreciation, and in the other, the same object serves literary representation—in a poem whose role is that of instrumental linguistic training for social mobility (to acquire correct speech and pronunciation rather than critical or aesthetic appreciation). A structural clarity emerges in the novel as these two women are placed in a set of relations to the same thing, where the value relation of both women's products of labor (as aesthetic object and as recited poem) appears in the daffodil in a manner that has no relationship to the physicality of the flower itself. Lucy's daffodil gains its mystical character not simply from its use value (as a decorative or aesthetic object) but also from a set of social relations in a colonial education system, where the object has become a product of intellectual, linguistic, and physiological labor, of brain, nerves, muscles, sense organs, and vocal chords. As Marx puts it, "It is nothing but the definite social relations between men themselves which assumes here, for them, the fantastic form of a relation between things."[41]

When metalepsis makes the spectral fleshly, the daffodil comes to life and operates uncannily like the coat in Marx's *Capital* that bears within its form of appearance all the prior moments that have gone into the creation of its embodied value. However, it is part of my argument that Kincaid is not merely after analogy or allusion but, rather, after the added element of recoding that makes metalepsis more than an echo of an older figure or text. The daffodil appears in the present as an object of cultural and aesthetic value for Lucy's employer, but Lucy's introjections and projections reveal this aesthetic and cultural object to be a recoding of previous meanings and valuations, hearkening back to the historical formations of colonialism and postcolonialism in the Caribbean, as well as a proleptical figuration of the economic restructuring under way in the United States. I will say more about this in the last section.

In *Lucy,* Kincaid leads us through the thickets of language, shuttling between the particular (or the singular instance) and the abstraction that it metonymizes. In so doing, the text allows Lucy, an unself-conscious victim, and Mariah, a beneficiary of the same global system, to realize their relationship to each other within a social formation not only as employer-employee but also as gendered subjects whose individual lives are scripted by global capital. Both have to work their way through the spatial and temporal disjunction that has as its immediate consequence the inability to grasp the way the system functions as a whole.[42] Here, a simple flower acts in the way the commodity fetish does—as an elemental form in a world of appearances. Lift the lid on this form, and what is revealed is the work of capital.

In Mariah's directed moment under the trees when Lucy's blindfold comes off, she (Lucy) "sees" the flowers for the first time, but she also understands that beneath this moment of attempted equality (sisterhood established by consensus over an aesthetic object) is the unequal cultural work of self-making. Through the relations that this attempted act of equal exchange establishes between the two different productions of "daffodils," and through their mediation, the structural hierarchy between the two women is made visible. Yet to say this outright is to refuse the solidarity that can exist in the shared experience, for as Lucy notes, "I felt sorry that I had cast her beloved daffodils in a scene she had never considered, a scene of conquered and conquests; a scene of brutes masquerading as angels and angels portrayed as brutes. . . . It wasn't her fault. It wasn't my fault. But nothing could change the fact that where she saw beautiful flowers I saw sorrow and bitterness" (*Lucy*, 30).

As a process that reveals the site of Lucy's unconsciousness, metalepsis resembles what Louis Althusser calls "determinate absence," or a governing structure that allows us to read a text as a play between what it says and what it cannot say, as a text of unconsciousness, that is, not as a text that depicts capitalist structures as expressed content but as one that through its "dispositions" ("traces and effects") provides a bridge to the "structures" that govern the connections that are depicted.[43] Historical experience is mediated because subjects are decentered by the determinate conditions under which they live and work. Subjects find themselves in circumstances and conditions that are not of their making and that they do not enter of their own volition. As such they cannot, in any full and uncontradictory sense, be, as Stuart Hall puts it, "the collective authors of their actions."[44] Yet the task of putting together this history is inextricably part of the autobiographical. Martin Jay has pointed out that if all reification is a forgetting, then dereification is a process of remembering "what had been torn asunder (dis-membered), an anamnestic recovery of the wholeness of laborer and fashioned object, process and product, theory and practice, and essence and appearance."[45] As a result, such a recovery would denaturalize unjust social relations that seemed to be an eternal "second nature," for what needs to be recovered is "the fundamentally productive, constitutive role of a collective subject, which has made history unconsciously in the past but will make it consciously in the future and recognize itself in its creation."[46] Metaleptic recovery can thus be a fundamental resource for proceeding from the autobiographical to the collective subject; what was made unconsciously in the past can be made consciously in the future, and what is understood as a singular experience of autobiography in the present can become an occasion for the recognition of the historical role of a collective subject. It is to an exploration of this role of the metaleptic that I turn in the final section of this chapter.

"How Does a Person Get to Be That Way?": The Viciousness of the Present

When Antonio Gramsci wrote the scattered pieces that were later published as *Prison Notebooks*, he thought of the autobiographical as a preparation for the intellectual labor he himself undertook: "The starting-point of critical elaboration is the consciousness of what one really is, and is 'knowing thyself' as a product of the historical process to date which has deposited in you an infinity of traces, without leaving an inventory."⁴⁷ Here Gramsci thinks of the memory "trace" as the unprocessed record—the raw material with which we all work—even as he understands "the inventory" to be a code that might have provided the trace's missing connection to history. It is this invisible or vanished mediator that has to be reconstituted by the subject who remembers. Once this connection is established through a "critical elaboration," Gramsci says, the consciousness of oneself as a product of history prepares the subject to "take an active part in the creation of the history of the world."⁴⁸

In a similar vein, in his introduction to *Orientalism*, Edward Said alludes to these lines from Gramsci to illustrate how the "personal dimension" factored into the research for his path-breaking work. Said's awareness of being an "Oriental" as a child growing up in two British colonies was overwritten by a Western education, but the earlier traces remained: "In many ways my study of Orientalism has been an attempt to inventory the traces upon me, the Oriental subject, of the culture whose domination has been so powerful a factor in the life of all Orientals."⁴⁹ For Said we note that "Orientalism" is not just the book but, rather, a coherence-creating concept that brings together as a discursive formation (a signifying system) the traces left by a powerful history of domination. By revealing how the "personal" when made sense of as the "historical" becomes a powerful impulse to rewrite that history, not just for himself but for everyone positioned similarly by that history—"all Orientals"—Said testifies to the way in which abstractions are powerful modes of understanding the world and how they shape us collectively. Regarding Gramsci and Said's quest for self-knowledge, we might say that autobiography is a first stage—the moment of self-awareness when the traces are recorded and the effects of history are felt. What we get in Kincaid's *Lucy* is a fictional second stage that reveals how these traces are transformed into a "critical elaboration," or "a critical form" of truth and the story of one individual remade into a story that is shared and socialized as a collective history. It is important to note that in the two famous examples of successful systematizations mentioned, we cannot see the actual dialectical process by which, as subjects of history, Gramsci and Said arrive at this juncture. Indeed, I would argue that unlike their characterization of the autobiographical as unprocessed traces that have to be refitted (inventoried) as historical record, Kincaid offers a much more radical idea of this remembering.

What *Lucy* offers is the possibility of thinking that retroactive meaning is closer to how the signifying structures of language function as a whole and that all historical understanding is also retroactive. What was originally a meaningless event retroactively acquires meaningful impact. It is only later that the traces of this meaningless event are included in a symbolic network. In this sense, to borrow a formulation from Slavoj Žižek, history is like psychoanalysis—not concerned with the past "as such," as pure evidence, but in the way that past events are included in the present, synchronous field of meaning.[50] Indeed, we might go a step further and ask, If the trace of an old encounter (like Lucy's memorization of the Wordsworth poem) begins to exert itself in the present, is it because the "present symbolic universe of the subject" is structured in a way that is receptive to it?[51] Metalepsis, by focusing our attention on the revision in the present, rather than on the recovery of the past, brings into view the conditions in the present that create the susceptibility—for the past to reappear and be transformed by the context of its appearance. One of the best examples of how conditions of susceptibility underlie the appearance of metaleptic logic lies in nationalist discourse.

Nationalism is an imagined community that arises in response to an external oppression like colonialism. It is constituted through mass resistance to this form of rule and, therefore, does not exist in the precolonial era. The struggle for national liberation is a struggle for something that comes into being only through being experienced as "lost" or "endangered."[52] Nationalist ideology attempts to elude this contingency and circularity by inventing and projecting backward a fictive moment of origin—a golden age before colonialism when the "nation" was already there. This reversal of antecedent and consequence makes the nation into that to which we will "return" as a result of the struggle for liberation.[53]

This mode of projection that deflects "origin" is apparent in the novel when Lucy's desire for a break with the past is represented as an anxiety about her mother's influence: "I had come to feel that my mother's love for me was designed solely to make me into an echo of her; and I didn't know why, but I felt that I would rather be dead than become just an echo of someone"(*Lucy*, 36). When Lucy acknowledges later on, "My past was my mother," her feeble attempts to draw a line between them are deemed in vain: "I was not like my mother—I was my mother" (90). Lucy learns the lesson via metalepsis: she cannot not be an echo of her mother, and to not acknowledge that influence is to indulge in a fantasy of origins—a time when she was (and a time when she will be) free of her mother. If Lucy does not learn this lesson, she will also not learn about complicity, by which I mean our participation in the very structures from which we believe we have freed ourselves. What the presence of metalepsis makes it possible to ask (and what the example of nationalism makes clear) is this: How is the past being transcoded in a way that represses the viciousness of the present?

It is telling that Lucy's attempt to distance herself and differentiate herself from her rich, white employer is by seeking absent causes for Mariah's behavior. When Mariah tells Lucy that she feels glad to be alive when she sees daffodils, it is hard to miss the sarcasm in Lucy's silent response: "So Mariah is made to feel alive by some flowers bending in the breeze. *How does a person get to be that way?*" (*Lucy*, 17; my emphasis). Lucy's question is undoubtedly rhetorical because no proper (psychobiographical) answer is ever offered to Lucy's various renditions of the same question. There is the time when Mariah is disappointed when a snowstorm ruins a spring day and Lucy muses, "How do you get to be a person who is made miserable because the weather changed its mind, because the weather doesn't live up to your expectations? How do you get to be that way?" (20). And then there is this: "Mariah was beyond doubt or confidence. I thought, Things must have always gone her way and not just for her but for everybody she has ever known from eternity. . . . Again I thought, How does a person get to be that way?" (26). It is only in this last instance that Lucy suspects that what could just as easily be attributed to Mariah's personality could simply be the confidence that comes from privilege, a privilege that she shares with all those around her. The recurring question suggests that, for Lucy, while Mariah's privilege is most apparent, open, and manifest and takes place on the surface and in the view of everyone, what is hidden, repressed, and out of sight are its real foundations. By keeping the various iterations of the same question in play without really answering it, the novel asks its readers to read the "source" or "site" of privilege's unconsciousness.[54]

Thus, the answer to Lucy's bewildered question about her employer's reaction to daffodils, "How does a person get to be that way?" is not the reified response "Everyone responds differently to daffodils" but, rather, the insistence on an underlying connection between the two women's responses. The reader recognizes that although Mariah and Lucy have "different" daffodils to exchange, the daffodils are not really commensurate. Mariah's aestheticized flower appears seemingly shorn of coercion, imbued with pleasure and self-presence, and her assumption is that anyone seeing a daffodil would react to its unquestionably universal beauty. With Lucy's silent question, one is asked to imagine the unconsciousness that structures Mariah's and Lucy's disparate reactions. For Lucy the track from flower to English poetry includes colonialism, access to elite education, the cultural capital of English, international division of gendered labor, class formation in diaspora, and social mobility in the United States. In Mariah's case the text moves us from flower to aesthetic taste and, then, abruptly to postindustrial ecological crisis. The flower is a form of appearance for all these abstracted social relations. The recurrence of the flower as "trace" in these and other allusions in the text is one of the ways by which literary language *performs* rather than rationalizes the links between the two women, between the postcolonial Caribbean and the postindustrial United States, between cultural indoctrination and immigrant assimilation. Here, one might say, the text stages Kant versus Marx.[55]

But even as the novel seeks the origin of the daffodil's meaning for Lucy in a colonial past, it also projects how a perception of the past arises out of a present synchronous field of meaning. Does the daffodil appear in the aesthetic form of value, as an object of beauty, concealing the viciousness of the present? Here we might think of the daffodil as a metonym for Nature: globalization continues to engage the rural (for which the daffodil is also a metonym) through disembodied practices like biotechnology, genetics, chemical fertilizers, and urban development, while financial capital, homeworking, and international subcontracting displace the familiar sites of production like the factory floor.[56] In such a scenario the idea of organized labor (Lucy as the collective representation of domestic workers) is hidden by these changed conditions. She cannot appear as such. What was concrete once is more abstract than ever. Thus, if we are to ask why Mariah is so intensely moved by the sight of daffodils, we also have to ask what present conditions make that aesthetic response possible.

In the novel, when Lucy accompanied the family on its summer vacation, they drove through miles and miles of countryside. At the sight of a small town, Mariah became excited, and Lucy reports her reaction thus: "She would exclaim with happiness or sadness, depending, as things passed before her. In the half a year or so since she had last been there, some things had changed, some things had newly arrived, and some things had vanished completely" (*Lucy*, 34). Mariah, the novel tells us, works actively in the cause of nature preservation. She and her friends regularly attend events organized in honor of some "endangered" and "vanishing" marshland; they are upset at the "destruction of the surrounding countryside." Many houses were built on what used to be farmland (49, 71). Once, Mariah shows Lucy a place that used to be an open meadow, where as a child she went looking for robin's eggs and wildflowers. Lucy conveys Mariah's disappointment about the "vanishing idyll" with the skepticism we would expect from someone who is not from a privileged class. It is a point of irony that the question that unnerves Mariah, and exposes the paradox of this suburban housewife's ecological resistance to capitalism, is posed by her own daughter, and not Lucy: "Well, what used to be here before this house we are living in was built?" Lucy's judgment is harsher: "Mariah decided to write and illustrate a book on these vanishing things and give any money made to an organization devoted to saving them. Like her, all the members of this organization were well off but they made no connection between their comforts and the decline of the world that lay before them" (72).

If Mariah's ecological activism is constituted as resistance to an economic system that spectralizes the rural, then Lucy's tart remark raises the possibility that imagining preindustrial nature as a vanishing idyll is also a defense, a myth that conceals the viciousness of the present.[57] What is foreclosed here is the forbidden mediator, the invisible, slow violence of environmental degradation that creates the conditions for an idealized nature. The point is that Lucy sees that it is a projection back into the past of something idyllic that supposedly existed and to which Mariah and her friends hope to return through environmental preservation. This vicious cycle is implied in Lucy's telling remark about Mariah's feelings about nature: "I couldn't bring myself to point out to her that if all things she [Mariah] wanted to save in the world were saved, she might find herself in reduced circumstances. I couldn't bring myself to ask her to examine Lewis's daily conversations with his stockbroker, to see if they bore any relation to the things she saw passing away forever before her eyes" (*Lucy*, 72–73). Through her brilliant economy of expression, a hallmark of Kincaid's prose, the daffodil becomes a metonym for the spectralization of the rural as it comes into proximity, paratactically, with another metonym of the financialization of the globe—corporate stocks. The novel's slow steps to this process of unveiling are marked by several deferrals of the question posed many times over and over in the novel, "How does [Mariah] get to be that way?" The question, which must be asked of Lucy herself, too, indexes how ideology is what is most open, apparent, and manifest on the surface and yet not easy to grasp, for as Stuart Hall asks, "How can the realm in which we think, talk, reason, explain and experience ourselves—the activities of consciousness—be unconscious?"[58] In *Lucy*, it is this surface that is ruffled when Kincaid—instead of finding the origins of the subjective and the affective in a wide-armed gesture toward a spatial background that we might call US capitalism (in Mariah's case), or a temporal background, that is by turns slavery, colonialism, and neocolonialism (in Lucy's case)—turns to metalepsis, which collapses this background and foreground distinction into a temporal and spatial confusion.

Through the metaleptic figuration, the subject both occludes and resists. The unconsciousness of the consciousness resists and conceals violence and, in so doing, also creates a fantasy of an uncontaminated origin (Lucy's island before the violence of colonialism, Lucy's language before English and Wordsworth, Lucy's distinctiveness before her mother) or a fantasy of the environment before ecological destruction (Nature). We have seen that even if the metalepsis aims to create an external starting point, exposing the retroactive constitution of its meaning is the only way to resist the complicity of becoming part of a system of self-reproduction and self-generation. We cannot gentrify violence or efface its traumatic effect by transforming it into a meaningful totality. After all, it is colonialism and colonial education, the vanished mediators, that allow Mariah and Lucy to participate in a commensurate exchange of ideas, culture, and history through a common (English) language.

In her reading of *Lucy*, Spivak has argued that the "removal of the place of origin" of the migrant allows figures (like Lucy) to be read as "culturally destabilized" subjects that effectively substitute for class subjects that have disappeared. As she puts it, "The stability of the factory floor disappeared overseas with post-Fordism, international subcontracting, and the progressive feminization of labor. The predominance of financial capital and the 'spectralization of the rural' in globalization today . . . occlude the question of organized labor."[59] Because the relationship between Lucy and Mariah is represented through psychological and cultural antagonism, rather than class antagonism, the novel invites us to read what is concealed even in the assertions of Lucy's story. Here is a clue:

> In books I had read—from time to time, when the plot called for it—someone would suffer from homesickness. A person would leave a not very nice situation and go somewhere else, somewhere a lot better, and then long to go back where it was not very nice. How impatient I would become with such a person, for I would feel that I was in a not very nice situation myself, and how I wanted to go somewhere else. But now I, too, felt that I wanted to be back where I came from. (*Lucy*, 6)

Moments like these, when Lucy acknowledges in hindsight that she has become the very person that she had disavowed, gives the story its cyclical and vertiginous quality that I described at the very beginning of this chapter. Indeed, the narrative movement of Lucy's story does not create a whole, "real" person. There is little progress in the story as such. The novel makes this point by repeating its opening scene in the final chapter: "It was January again; the world was thin and pale and cold again; I was making a new beginning again" (*Lucy*, 133). Ironically, it is the last chapter, simply titled "Lucy," that shares the title of the book as a whole. Is the insistence on "again" a texturizing rather than progress—metalepsis?[60]

The Lacanian insight that the subject is actually a subject-effect, and not the effective presence of "flesh-and-blood" agents that make instrumental use of language (as a tool) suggests that we learn more by approaching Lucy's autobiography not as a means of access to Lucy's "real" self but as the task of putting together a spectral "I." In that sense, it is only appropriate that the last chapter of the novel is the summation of this exercise rather than a definitive or conclusive picture of Lucy herself. In the final chapter, when she tells us, "The person I had become, I did not know very well" (*Lucy*, 133), the novel puts Lucy's own story under scrutiny for the very elements of defensive fantasy that might conceal something about the present. Spivak reads this narrative ambivalence as the guilt of social mobility—as a poor woman from the postcolonial underclass enters the diaspora created by "Eurocentric economic migration."[61] In the new metropolis, the United States, as a new migrant who eagerly severs her physical connection with postcolonial space, Lucy must face these questions: Is she part of the solution or the problem? Is she now a privileged subject in the belly of imperial power rather than a victim of colonialism?[62]

Just as the constitution of the "I" in autobiography is the result of a retroactive transcoding, a metaleptic logic exposes Lucy's own thinking about colonialism as a blocked way of resisting the present by imagining an absolute past when she was not an echo of someone (her mother, European culture). The point Kincaid's novel makes by its insistence on temporal confusion is that Lucy is an echo and there are conditions in the present circumstances that have caused the echo to appear. There is also the important lesson that Lucy cannot resist multicultural hybridity in the United States by falling back on colonial acculturation. The narrative makes this throwback impossible by its use of the past and present not as a clearly delineated background and foreground but, rather, as a side-by-side arrangement in paratactic sentence constructions and as the deferred, blurred, spectral chain of metalepsis.[63] The metaleptic chain reminds us that activist solutions for improving the lives and opportunities of migrant maids and nannies in the here and now are not unimportant, but if they consider the arrival of the workers as a rupture, only wage raises and support systems are at issue. For counterbalancing the systematic transfer of caring work from poor countries to rich, where real mothers there are now surrogate mothers here, more is at stake—such as humane immigration laws and family reunification.

In the closing lines of the novel, as Lucy picks up an empty notebook and begins to write her autobiography—not the defensive story we are reading but the planned one, in which she is an agent of her own story—the act signals progress. As she writes her full name on the top of the page, "Lucy Josephine Potter," the name is already an echo—of Wordsworth's Lucy, Milton's Lucifer, and an English enslaver called Potter—but in writing it and the sentence that follows, Lucy's signature is not a demand for authorial autonomy but rather the desire for the love of another—the mother whose labor is now reproduced in her daughter's surrogate mothering: "I could write down only this: 'I wish I could love someone so much that I could die from it.' And then as I looked at this sentence a great wave of shame came over me and I wept and wept so much that the tears fell on the page and caused all the words to become one great blur" (164). With this ending we move from the question of who is doing the forgetting and what is being forgotten to the more general question of how remembering may produce planned change in actual social practices and institutions. The imaginative act of being haunted draws us affectively, sometimes against our own wishes and always somewhat unpredictably, into the structure of feeling of a reality we come to experience not as cold, concrete facts but as a transformative recognition of otherness through the mode of spectrality. In the next chapter, I move the question of spectrality into the subject formation associated with political citizenship, a stage that a figure like Lucy will inevitably negotiate in a near future as she enters the collective temporality of the nation-state.

CHAPTER TWO

Attachments

Affective Palimpsests and the Habits of Citizenship

Attachments may be optimistic in the way they draw one to objects of desire, but the enduring nature of such objects—whether they be people, places, or things, dead or alive—can also be a drag on the present and stand in the way of attempts to form new solidarities and new attachments. This chapter is about the implications of that push and pull in Teju Cole's *Open City* (2012), a sprawling novel that, despite its grounding in New York City where the narrator resides, mobilizes the retroversion of autobiographical memory and the narrator's past to bring the world into the city. As the novel expands spatially, we realize not only that its title is a reference to a US city but also that openness is what this novel is about. The openness of the polis lies at the heart of the term "cosmopolitanism," which is related to the Greek *politês* (citizen), or the inhabitant of the city who is welcoming of the foreigner and the world. "Civic" and "civil" are also related to *civitas*, the abstract body of citizens (*cives*) bound together by law and responsibility. Because of this link between the urban subject and citizenship, it is not surprising that the global metropolis has become a privileged site for the analysis of processes of economic globalization. If, as the sociologist Saskia Sassen argues, the growth of global cities is a sign that the national economy has decomposed into a variety of subnational elements, then a literary focus on the megapolis as the site of inclusion and exclusion suggests that the city novel, too, is at odds with the nation.[1]

Open City attempts to hyphenate two spheres, the metropolitan space of migrancy and the postcolonial former home, through the figure of a privileged cosmopolite who mourns his personal past.[2] The expanded space of the global, generated by memories and events tied to Germany, Nigeria, and Belgium, enters the novel as the life story of Cole's narrator, Julius. This expanded space, enabled by the narrator's hybrid identity, his biracial German and Nigerian heritage, exists in tension with his lived present. Julius seems uninterested in these spaces as locales that require their own sedimented histories and descriptive detail (only New York City gets this treatment). Rather, these places appear as sites of attachments that have endured from his past and are temporalized as recollections of scenes of loss, suffering, and fantasy. The novel's rich ruminations on the relationship between the narrator and his time makes this a text about contemporariness. The enduring attachments of familial ties, instantiated by the stories of the narrator's grandmother, mother, and father, lock the gaze of the autobiographical "I" on the entire twentieth century. Like Osip Mandelstam's poet, Julius welds with his own life, his lived present, the "shattered backbone of time" that spans two centuries and is fractured in ways that prevent the continuum of an abstract past-present-future from composing itself.[3] In so doing, the synchronous temporality of the spatially expanded global city, the city-as-the-world, is impeded by historical pasts that still operate within it, not unlike the way in which the chronological past of the narrator's childhood continues to operate in a novel that has a much shorter narrative span than the individual and systemic temporalities it wants to narrate. Julius's extended family contributes six decades of a mediated historical past while the city itself, subjected to constant excavations and rebuilding, expels from time to time the human remains of centuries-old prior inhabitants who predate the arrival of the nation-state. All these temporalities crowd into the much shorter time span of the narration itself—the twelve months that Julius works as a resident psychiatrist in a city hospital.

In this chapter I argue that the affective distancing and nearness generated by attachments defines the novel's contemporariness and provides a valuable opening for thinking about citizenship in the era of globalization. As the demographic transformation of the United States directs our gaze toward a future political collectivity of hyphenated identities, now swelling with increasing non-European immigration, I ask whether we can afford to promote an ideal of citizenship that asks new arrivals to start from scratch with new attachments, rather than a form of citizenship that is imagined as "being with" the migrant's entanglements and enduring loyalties. In what follows, my reading of *Open City* explores the form of openness that the polis provides as a model for the nation. I read the migrant's time in the nation's history in the way that Sigmund Freud and others, like Judith Butler, who follow his work theorize the power of attachments as a residue within the subject. The analogies between the persistence of the historical past in the subjective present and the child in the psychic life of the adult allow us to see a palimpsestic subject, vulnerable to its own attachments, as a model for openness and citizenship; in the place of a closed-off, impermeable, autonomous subject that remains the basis of conventional discourses on national sovereignty. The narrator's attachments in *Open City* intensify a migrant temporality that is akin to the linguistic transfer of creolization—"diffracted times coming together"—when there is not only a temporary fracture of old alliances but also the creation of new and perhaps looser collectivities whose boundaries do not lie neatly on top of the former.[4] Thinking of history and the subject as temporal palimpsests, like a document that is copied over and rewritten many times but whose older inscriptions, albeit faint, continue to appear on the surface, asks that we think of attachments to the past as scenes of mourning that can be attached not only to the living but also the dead, not only to scenes and objects associated with pleasure but also to those associated with suffering, loss, and trauma. As such, the challenge *Open City* poses for us is this: How does a narrator whose history lies somewhere else find a place in another history? If the imagining of a community requires being in the same time with the others, then how does one share a nation's history that is not one's own? My reading of *Open City* probes the relationship between the time of the subject and the time of the nation, between the psychic and historical palimpsests that constitute an imagined community of citizens.

The Nation, Attachments, and the Migrant's Time

At the time of writing this book, it is clear that, whereas the social movements against global capital's drive to create new markets in land, resources, and labor have been ongoing, and discontinuous and limited in their success, the cultural backlash against globalization has found common cause in electoral politics. Fortified borders have sprung up everywhere, and still more are on their way. The renewed urge to build walls and close national borders comes at a juncture when all over the world national economies are more internationally interdependent and interconnected than ever before. Political rhetoric that channels a paradoxical desire to open up the economy but close off the border, in rich and poor countries alike, is linked, as scholars like Saskia Sassen and Wendy Brown have argued, to a fundamental tension that has overtaken nation-states in the globalized world. The nation-state's sovereignty, premised on a long-standing but fictional idea of supremacy, perpetuity, completeness, and territoriality, has been severely compromised by transnational flows of capital, people, goods, ideas, violence, and political and religious loyalties. These flows, as Brown describes them, "both tear at the borders they cross and crystallize as powers within them, thus compromising sovereignty from its edges and from its interior."[5] Thus, walls that appear at first sight to be the manifestation of unassailable state sovereignty are more likely "hyperbolic tokens" expressing vulnerability and anxiety at the core of what they hope to express.[6]

When sovereignty operates as a concept-metaphor for a form of unified power premised on autonomy and exclusivity, we understand it to be a common way of talking about the power of the nation-state and the formation of a collective "we the people." This discourse of sovereignty has a long reach in the history of Western subject formation: the short version of this imagining of the human as the autonomous and sovereign subject of possessive individualism is the story of the social contract and individual rights; however, the story of the consolidation of the "individual" as political subject also runs parallel to that of the "nation" as an imagined community of citizens, and these two stories find an exemplary site of intersection in the modern novel.[7] If, as Brown contends, economic globalization has thrown the nation-state's sovereignty into crisis and created a fantasy of containment that seeks succor through the political discourse of closing borders and building walls, can we not imagine an intellectual endeavor wherein old and rigid ideas of political citizenship may also be brought to crisis by questioning the boundaries of the subject? Such an investigation would require not simply a declaration that the subject is unavoidably open and porous, as we tend to see in discourses of cosmopolitanism or tolerance, but also a supplementation of "citizen" with the theoretical work that has to date challenged the myth of individual sovereignty, by which I mean the critiques of the autonomous sovereign subject by affect theory, psychoanalysis, and queer theory.

Political debates in the early American republic provide a surprising window into the role played by subjective attachments in the defining of citizenship. On January 7, 1802, Alexander Hamilton, writing under a pseudonym in his co-owned newspaper, the *New York Evening Post*, excoriated President Thomas Jefferson's proposal to reduce the waiting period for immigrants to become naturalized citizens. Citing the examples of classical Rome and Syracuse, Hamilton warns that the United States could meet the fate that befell them: an inevitable collapse resulting from "a great number of foreigners [who] were suddenly admitted to the rights of citizenship." In the newspaper's pages the following week, Hamilton continued to rage against the proposal in these terms:

> Foreigners will generally be apt to bring with them attachments to the persons they have left behind; to the country of their nativity, and to its particular customs and manners. They will also entertain opinions on government congenial with those under which they have lived, or if they should be led hither from a preference to ours, how extremely unlikely is it that they will bring with them that *temperate love of liberty*, so essential to real republicanism? There may . . . be occasional exceptions to these remarks, yet such is the general rule. The influx of foreigners must, therefore, tend to produce a heterogeneous compound; to change and corrupt the national spirit; to complicate and confound public opinion; to introduce foreign propensities. In the composition of society, the harmony of the ingredients is all important, and whatever tends to a discordant intermixture must have an injurious tendency.[8]

In the two metaphors that Hamilton fuses to make his point, national spirit as a chemical compound and national spirit as a musical composition, the "foreign" is understood in terms of old "attachments" (ties maintained to persons left behind, to the country of nativity, and to its customs and manners) that would likely adulterate the cultural mix or add discordant notes to an existing harmony. Because there is no guarantee that immigrants will bring with them that quintessentially American "temperate love of liberty," Hamilton insists on a waiting period before granting naturalization.[9] His proposal offers a temporal solution for a spatial problem: immigrants can be distanced from their previous home and its cultural mores with the passage of time, fourteen years to be exact. Successful assimilation depends on a temporal break (the spatial break having already happened with the migrant's arrival), and after a period of being adrift in what might be described as an "ousted" temporality, the migrant lands in a second home.[10]

In the Jefferson-Hamilton debate on citizenship, we find an unexpected acknowledgment of the power of affective elements in the formation of political community, nationality, and citizenship, and the capacity of such forces to complicate a smooth transfer of political identity. Yet despite the acknowledgment of this subjective ambivalence constituted by the emotional and personal ties that structure our everyday lives, citizenship for Hamilton remains a binary choice: becoming American means no longer belonging anywhere else. Although it might be argued that the hyphenated American, often understood to be the legacy of increased non-European immigration and 1980s multiculturalism, relaxes this interdiction, what still persists in that formulation, it seems to me, is a notion of "culture" as a transportable set of practices, values, identities, and artifacts that one chooses to keep or give up. This leads to a problematic idea of identity itself as a choice—a view that has been laid to rest over the years not only by Freudian theories of sexuality but also by more recent scholarly interventions in feminist, race, and queer theory.

Moving on to Cole's novel and its own staging of the relationship between temporality and citizenship in a globalized world, I employ a broadened notion of citizenship, using the term with reference not to the legal definition that is successfully acquired through a series of filings, attestations, tests, and interviews but instead, to the subjective performance of belonging that is implied in the formation of any political community. Ranjit Guha's argument that one cannot strictly "belong" to a diaspora is an important insight because it tells us that a "code of belonging" depends on a framing in time and that the concept of diaspora cannot renew itself as a living present with incessant day-to-day transactions. As Guha puts it, "Belonging in this communitarian sense is nothing other than temporality acted upon and thought—and generally speaking, lived—as being with others in shared time, with sharing meant, in this context, as what is disclosed by the community to its constituents as temporal. . . . There is no way for those who live in a community to make themselves intelligible to each except by temporalizing their experience of being together."[11] My reading of *Open City* aims to show how Cole's use of a narrator with an elite perspective further complicates the notion of community formation as insertion into a shared time. Indeed, Julius's autobiographical narrative reveals a certain savviness about the shared time of history, but where the constitutive role of personal attachments and their temporality are concerned, what we get is a subject that cannot fully know its determinations. This indeterminacy in the text is important because it demonstrates the difficulty of reading the narrator simply as a hyphenated American, a Nigerian-American man desirous of joining "we the people" in solidarity with others like him, new immigrants, who are the result of skilled labor transfers prompted by a more recent stage of economic globalization. Identity politics as community building is blocked by the reality that Julius cannot easily make himself intelligible to others and share their time. Because immigration to the United States today is class stratified, thinking of diversity as class differentiated means that the discourse of multiculturalism must account for the uneven access to the gifts of global capitalism by those who are undocumented and unwelcome and those who are documented and tolerated. It means most importantly, thinking of cultural formations by way of a linguistic analogy borrowed from Édouard Glissant: the formation of creole languages gives us a way of thinking about the formation of collectivities that acknowledge the messiness of the subject in cultural exchanges. As Glissant points out, Euro-America was preceded by Meso-America, the "people-witnesses" who have always been here and who struggle to survive and to maintain their identity. And Euro-America is also supplemented today by "Plantation-America" or African America that was born as a result of creolization. Its descendants are still trying to give legitimacy to their "new dimension" of "exchange and mutual exchange" in a world where racism still dominates.[12] Any discussion of migrant reality today must account for such historical sedimentations, the palimpsestic communities that still act on the present conditions of immigration. Glissant challenges us to imagine the formation of new collectivities in a way that brings both the nation-state that receives and the migrant subject that enters its space into a productive crisis, as the nation penetrated by the punctum of the other makes the emergent unpredictable with "radically new dimension[s] of reality," not direct synthesis but "results: something else, another way."[13] Creolization's notion of "open identity" may not offer, as Glissant concedes, much by way of "political or economic power," but as an imaginative practice, as a mode of reading, creolization continually confronts the old and rigid sense of identity; it is "precious for mankind's . . . invention."[14]

In the sections to follow, alongside my reading of the novel are texts drawn from a variety of theoretical contexts in which attachments implicate affect as a political force: critical discussions of the structure and logic of the palimpsest as concept-metaphor for urban space, the work of affect theorists like Lauren Berlant and Brian Massumi on the question of temporality, Freud's discussion of mourning and melancholia producing palimpsests of the mind, and Judith Butler's extension of Freud's analysis into a textual reading of introjection and incorporation as cryptic palimpsests. In the last instance, I look at how analogizing Butler's idea of the queer as nonnormative sexual identity and the idea of the subject as a collection of attachments and losses may allow us to think of *Open City*'s narcissistic preoccupations with melancholia (embodied in the narrator, Julius), and how these affective structures can enable a consideration of the vulnerability of others, including many who float in and out Julius's story—father, mother, grandmother, friends, lovers, tormentors, and victims. Here we might think of how, to use Butler's provocative phrase, "human physical vulnerability is distributed across the globe."[15] Reading avowed and disavowed patterns of desire serves as an affective mapping of other spaces. For instance, Julius's mother's home (Germany) and his father's home (Nigeria) are scenes of conflicts that help us understand Julius's ambivalence about his postcoloniality, biraciality, and class privilege. I also make the related point that when novels like *City* make their primary focus migrant experience and the migrant insertion into US citizenry, other pasts and other places (the Nigeria of Julius's childhood, for instance) can emerge only as fragmentary scenes of attachment or, as the novel puts it, "mostly empty space" with things "remembered with an outsize intensity" floating around in it.[16] This leads me to the final consideration of Cole's novel as a text that stages by way of autobiography important questions about the use of the imagination as a tool of "othering": How do we attach ourselves to things that are not in our "own time," and how do we want to become like others? To borrow a formulation that Berlant gives us, there is a "queer optimism" in people's capacity to be affectively and emotionally "incoherent" because it suggests that "we can produce new ways of imagining what it means to be attached and to build new lives and worlds from what there already is."[17] In *City*, Julius's imagination allows us to enter an uncommon perspective about the inside and outside paradox of nation and globality. Instead of a cosmopolitan citizen imagining the nation as open, porous, and hospitable, rendering himself vulnerable to the other and negotiating a dominant identity that does not seek protection from contamination or mixing, we have the figure of the outsider-on-the-inside looking out to the world from a new place. As the narrator of *City* negotiates the here and now while in the thrall of previous attachments, traumatic events, and even acts of violence that link him to family, lovers, tormentors, and victims, the novel brings the world into the city.

The Polis as Palimpsest and Teleiopoiesis

What is the appeal that the loose collectivity of "New Yorkers" holds for Julius? How is the city imagined? How is the city's history related to Julius's own history, which lies elsewhere and as another plot in the novel? In the novel, we catch Julius entering the New York subway and surveying the crowd around him like a text with the sort of layering embodied in a palimpsest—the city dwellers become part of a "palimpsestuous" collectivity:[18] "The generations rushed through the eye of the needle, and I, one of the still legible crowd, entered the subway" (*City*, 59). To be legible is to be read, and the crowd coalesces into a "we" in the manner of a friendship without fraternization, by virtue of being a living present or the top-most legible writing that lies over the inscriptions of many generations that have lived and died in the city. Cole's readers will notice that the city-subject relationship prestructures the novel as a whole, as it uses its narrator, a flâneur-like pedestrian, as a scripting tool. Here are the novel's opening lines as they constitute the city as a lived space in which the narrating "I" fills itself out by walking—an act that is at once a performance of both spacing and timing:

> And so when I began to go on evening walks last fall, I found Morningside Heights an easy place from which to set out into the city. . . . These walks, a *counterpoint* to my busy days at the hospital, steadily lengthened taking me farther and farther afield each time, so that I often found myself at quite a distance from home late at night, and was compelled to return home by subway. In this way, at the beginning of the final year of my psychiatry fellowship, New York City worked itself into my life at walking pace. (3; emphasis mine)

The novel's exquisite use of photography, art, and music through a mode of mediatic allusiveness lends the overall effect of a temporal layer on the flatness of the pedestrian's pavement and the homeostasis of the sheer mass a city crowd invokes in the reader. The metaphor of the counterpoint in the opening lines of the novel signals such a use of intermedial relations between literature and music. In this instance, time rather than space is the unit of measurement. As a structuring principle for Julius's walks (and the novel we are told is made up of a series of walks) it introduces a "contradictory openness" modeled on the musical fugue—different voices, sensations, and memories intermingle in ways that are often conflicting, contrasting, and interrupting.[19] Julius himself alludes to a "sonic fugue," a phrase that invokes the comforting murmur of many voices at once (5). By definition, the musical counterpoint keeps its elements separate but proximate and brings them together into a harmony that gives the differentiated strands a semblance of unity. In Julius's narrative, it also works to foreground the narrator's unusual detachment from those who are closest to him—his patients, his friends, his lovers, and his family—and his constant attempts to find connections to the multitudes that now live and have lived in the city—New Yorkers past and present. I want to explore in this section and the next how this detachment that operates like a distancing mechanism can be understood as a mode of *teleiopoiesis*, a term that Derrida coins in *The Politics of Friendship* to invoke the notion of bringing something to an end or completion (*teleio*) and invention or making (*poesis*), and although the word does not stem from the same root as *tele*, or "far," he makes this imaginative act into a crossing of distance.[20] Gayatri Spivak's renderings of the concept have given us this compelling formulation: teleiopoiesis is "the reaching towards the distant other by the patient power of the imagination, a curious kind of identity politics in which one crosses identity as a result of migration or exile.... [T]eleiopoiesis wishes to touch a past that is historically not 'one's own.'"[21] My reading of *Open City* argues that Julius tries this distant touching of the past with the figure of the palimpsest. Teleiopoiesis, as we shall see, can also be a reaching for the distant others in one's own life in the manner Freud discusses the subject of mourning and melancholia.

If teleiopoiesis is an imaginative reaching for the past, then the counterpoint is its opposite for the loose collectivity one imagines with people who share one's present; however, Julius's metaphor of the sonic fugue differs from Hamilton's use of harmony as the common nationalist principle of unity in diversity—the former operates within the expanding space of the nation because Julius imagines the *civitas* of the polis as a model for globality. In the evenings spent alone in his apartment, Julius often listens to Canadian and European internet stations. Hearing the murmur of the announcers and "the sounds of those voices speaking calmly from thousands of miles away," Julius imagines himself much like the radio host in a booth far away (*City*, 4). The affective resonance of the murmur finds new objects in his immediate present: "Those disembodied voices remain connected in my mind, even now, with the apparition of migrating geese" (5). The association continues, and watching bird migrations from his window while listening to the radio, Julius wonders whether his own "aimless wanderings" are connected to the "miracle of natural immigration" (4).

These textual examples tell us why the counterpoint has had a good run as an organizing metaphor for the historical and cultural connections of nationalism, cosmopolitanism, and globality and why terms like "fugue" abound in recent critical readings of Cole's *City*.[22] But they also show how Cole's use of the counterpoint in the novel manages to grate against the musical metaphor Alexander Hamilton used for his normative idea of an Anglo-American social order—a "harmony" without discordant notes. The novel's use resonates more with Edward Said's idea of contrapuntal histories in *Culture and Imperialism*, as a counter-dominant principle for the rewriting of world history and world literature from postcolonial and multinational perspectives that aim to run together fugue-like, the contrasting and conflicting stories that unsettle Eurocentric perspectives. For Said, the contrapuntal is a more robust understanding of the political motto, *e pluribus unum*.

It is hard to draw similar optimism from Julius's sonic fugue as a political project. In *City*, the fugue is tied to his withdrawal from the world around him into the solitary experience of the aural and operates as a metonym for his identification with high culture, his elitism, and forms of collectivity that require none of the fraternization one needs for community. These feelings of alienation and subjective detachment often arise at the very moment Julius invokes the collectivity of New Yorkers. Here is an example of the recurring image of the crowd: "Above ground I was with thousands of others in their solitude, but in the subway, standing close to strangers, jostling them and being jostled by them for space and breathing room, all of us reenacting unacknowledged traumas, the solitude intensified" (*City*, 7). In this image of neighborliness without connection, the legible temporality of the present is cut through by yet another temporal layer, the past that Julius calls reenacted but "unacknowledged traumas," or the subject as a palimpsest of attachments to past scenes of loss, suffering, or violence. The narration now hinges chiasmus-like between two axes— one, of shared space and time, a contemporaneity that constitutes the collectivity of the city, "New Yorkers"; the other, an unsettling temporality generated by the subject, also a cryptic palimpsest, the subject of mourning and melancholia, whose collection of traumas and losses although part of the present are not legible or fully named. This tension—between a present collectivity of the city's living, the historical past of its dead, and the lived present of the narrator, whose own past is encrypted in him—is played out in this scene:

> This was not the first erasure on the site. Before the towers had gone up, there had been a bustling network of little streets traversing this part of town; . . . all of them had been obliterated in the 1960s to make way for the World Trade Center buildings, and all were forgotten now. Gone, too, was the Washington market, the active piers, the fishwives, the Christian Syrian enclave that was established here in the late 1800s. The Syrians, the Lebanese, and other people from the Levant had been pushed across the river to Brooklyn. . . . And before that? What Lenape paths lay buried beneath the rubble? The site was a palimpsest, as was all the city, written, erased, rewritten. There had been communities here before Columbus ever set sail, before Verrazano anchored his ships in the narrows, or the black Portuguese slave trader Esteban Gomez sailed up the Hudson: human beings had lived here, built homes, and quarreled with their neighbors long before the Dutch ever saw a business opportunity in the rich furs and

timber of the island and its calm bay. Generations rushed through the eye of the needle, and I, one of the still legible crowd, entered the subway. I wanted to find the line that connected me to my own part in these stories. Somewhere close to the water, holding tight to what he knew of life, the boy had, with a sharp clack, again gone aloft. (*City*, 59)

"This was not the first erasure on the site." Julius's mention of the towers marks the site as the place where the World Trade Center once stood. The year is 2007, and construction has begun on what will soon become the 9/11 memorial, museum, and plaza. We don't need to see the building on the construction site that Julius describes a little earlier as "wrapped in black netting, mysterious and severe as an obelisk" (58). Already, the city is pulsing with the force of those events that seem to be active in the present like an "archaic facies"—Agamben's geological metaphor of sedimentation—that carries within them contiguously, traces of an earlier "ruin."[23] The events of September 11 constitute a recent inscription that separates New York City from a normal temporal rhythm, the city-as-lived-space moving through the continuum of past-present-future, and moves it into the era of terror (58). Julius's gaze now transforms the construction site into a sedimentation of previous inscriptions, into a series of cultural groups that have been serially erased. When the city is read in this temporally sedimented way, the post-9/11 New York City is taken in and absorbed as just one more affectively perceived time on top of the other collectivities and other atrocities, recent and ancient, that form the histories of those who had been here all along and those who arrived here from somewhere else: Syrian, Lebanese, Native Leni Lenape, conquistadors, enslavers, the Dutch. The imaginative touching of these histories that are not the narrator's own is done by way of teleiopoiesis using the figure of the palimpsest: the city reads like a document that has been "written, erased, rewritten." Other traces that presumably lie underneath are also in the present crowding each other, affecting and inhabiting each other's times.

Thinking of past moments as traces resonates with Freud's classic discussion of the memory-trace in "A Note upon the 'Mystic Writing Pad,'" in which he constructs the "mental apparatus" as a writing surface on which memory traces are laid down. In the essay, Freud wonders about the mind's "unlimited receptive capacity for new perceptions" and proposes that this unusual capacity was divided between two different systems (or organs of the mental apparatus): a system Pcpt.-Cs. (perception-consciousness), which receives perceptions but retains no permanent trace of them, so that it can react like a clean sheet to every new perception, and a "mnemic system" lying behind the perceptual system where the permanent traces of the excitations received are preserved.[24] In this stratified topography of unconscious, preconscious, and conscious systems, Freud's distinctions depend on metaphors of surface and depth, latent and manifest. But as Sarah Dillon points out, although scholars have often read the mystic pad as a palimpsest of the mind, a model for the "spectralization of the subject" no less, the surface-depth layered topography of the mystic pad belies a crucial distinction about the permanent traces that are preserved: only the palimpsest holds out the possibility of recollection.[25] Dillon therefore argues that Freud's essays on mourning and melancholia, which theorize incorporation and interjection, are much more useful for thinking about memory than the mystic writing pad. This point resonates with the direction my own discussion is going to take. (See the next section on Freud's "Mourning and Melancholia.") Suffice it to say here that the figure of the palimpsest is a visual tool for representing what Derrida calls "the non-contemporaneity with itself of the living present," because it expresses an understanding of the present that is constituted only in and by the trace of inscriptions from the past.[26] Palimpsests also enable notions of futurity and openness because their surfaces remain receptive to further inscription to come in the future. For Julius, the city is sepulchral in a material sense too (as opposed to the pulsing of historical time). Its permanent traces of excitations (historical atrocities and violence) are preserved in the earth. Buried bodies that lie beneath the city are unearthed from time to time as subway systems burrow into the layers. What is apparent on the surface (the present-day city) is a clean sheet that has wiped itself clean of all these prior encounters. The city's permanent petrified traces may not be mutable like memories, but when they continue to act on the present as "history," they too are like Foucault's genealogical trace—recurring but playing different roles in the different scenes where they are engaged. To be able to see palimpsestuously and spectralize the city's present inhabitants in this way shows that there is an analogy to be made between such representations of urban space and the structure of identity, as well as similar interplays between self's present and the otherness of the past. There is one crucial difference, though. If we consider the analogy between the city and the mind by way of the "trace" in the section I quoted from the novel, we cannot help but notice that the traces of the city are geographically circumscribed within the same space, a "site" that is written over and over again. In contrast, the spectralized subject's traces scatter across the totality of its expressions and thoughts, crosshatching in domains that are not planned in advance. This is the sticking point that limits our ability to "read" Julius as a subject in the novel.

Throughout the narration of his story, Julius, a psychiatrist by training, observes like a cultural critic. He is proud of his ability to "trace out a story from what was omitted" (*City*, 9), and we sense from the recounting of the historical erasures of the city and of his patients' dissimulations that he is good at it. Yet, despite Julius's assertions of belonging to the city-as-collectivity, when he invokes "our city" and "our time," this passage ends with unfinished business. Julius "sees" the generations that have preceded him but says that he cannot find the "line" that connects him to his "own part in these stories." The last sentence of the quote about the boy "gone aloft" holding "tight to what he knew of life" seems misplaced here after the rich palimpsest of historical erasures. The irruption of the singular (a boy on his skateboard near the boardwalk) and the blocked entry of the personal (Julius's own part in these stories) exemplify a structuring tension that gives *Open City* its compelling texture of conflicting desires. There is, it seems to me, an unresolved tension between the desire to see the historical pasts that antedate the narrator's contemporary moment and the desire to understand this contemporary moment as a collectivity in which Julius's own lived story, a "foreign" story, can be embedded.

The boy on his skateboard figures by his solitariness Julius's singular relationship to his own time. Held aloft, he is attached to it and distanced from it at the same time. However, the retroversion employed by the narrator, its constant switching to fragments of his personal past, snatches of memory, constitute a spectralized "I," who, like the entangled inscriptions of past and present, is also constituted in a series of speaking "I"s that have preceded it and all the "I"s it will become.[27] It is Julius rather than the boy, we suspect, who is holding on to his life. We begin to wonder whether the imagined collectivity of "New Yorkers" is simply a cover story, a unification that occludes the part that Julius actually plays in it. Just as the autobiographical subject's "I" also writes, erases, and rewrites its content, the Julius who is inscribed into "New Yorker" remains hidden from us in the passage on historical palimpsests.

To ask about the "I" who is narrating from a critical distance means tracing the history of Julius's entry into the present of "our time." When Michel Foucault proffered a historical method called genealogy, he described the practice as "gray, meticulous, and patiently documentary," operating on a "field of entangled and confused parchments, or document that have been scratched over and recopied many times."[28] Genealogy retrieves and records, he says, "the singularity of events outside of any monotonous finality; it must seek them in the most unpromising places, in what we tend to feel is without history—in sentiments, love, conscience, instincts; it must be sensitive to their recurrence, not in order to trace the gradual curve of their evolution, but to isolate the different scenes where they are engaged in different roles."[29] To look upon sentiments and love as places for genealogy is to read affectively. It is to think of the contemporary in the way Berlant does when she calls for a "proprioceptive history about the present as a relatively affectively formless space."[30] Proprioception is the unconscious perception of movement and spatial orientation arising from stimuli within the body itself. Perhaps this unconsciousness forming within the formless is what the affect theorist Brian Massumi also means when he states that "the present is held aloft by affect."[31] Just as the palimpsest does not automatically reveal previous layers and one has to work to make them legible, Julius's lived present does not make the past inscriptions that are active in it automatically legible. As Julius moves through the city, his body seems to carry a memory within it that he cannot access, but the reader reading (with the patience of the historian) the autobiographical narrative, as an entangled and confused field, may succeed. In the mode of autobiography, we know that the story told by the "I" is never a complete one. In the novel's push and pull of Julius's attachments and detachments, his conflicting aims are presented in the style of a depressive who is cool, cynical, and shut off but also rational and averse. This tension is a hint that many of Julius's attachments may be unacknowledged losses. This raises the question whether his lofty desire for a teleiopoetic solidarity with the historical dead, the seeking of community with others, is possible without a disclosure of his own history. If loss makes us vulnerable and open subjects rather than closed projections of freedom and strength, can the refusal to acknowledge it inhibit the possibility of imagining forms of solidarity that do not require thinking in terms of sovereignty?

In their powerful work on the ethical response to terror after 9/11, Judith Butler shows us how this subjective past may be analogized for the political community when they assert that thinking collectively through the shared experience of suffering means not staying with "loss" (as passive and powerless) but to be "returned to a sense of human vulnerability, to our collective responsibility for the physical lives of one another."[32] For Butler, a nationalist ideal involves not the privileging of one nation's interest at the expense of others but the exploration of new ways of imagining international ties that are attuned to the inequitable global distribution of corporeal vulnerability. As readers of the novel, we have sufficient insight into the city's open pasts; however, the task of turning a closed subject into a vulnerable one requires us to touch imaginatively those sites in Julius's affective map where the illegible parts of a life story can be decoded and the encryptions of unacknowledged losses or lost attachments can be understood. For this task, Freud's writing on mourning and melancholia provides us with some tools.

Mourning, Melancholia, and Attached Losses

In his essay "Mourning and Melancholia," it is the generalizability of libidinal loss that holds Freud's attention, but there is a startling phrase in the essay that brings the concept of mourning into the orbit of concepts like nationality and citizenship: "Mourning is regularly the reaction to the loss of a loved person, or to the loss of some abstraction which has taken the place of one, such as one's country, liberty, an ideal, and so on."[33] The loss of a person is the loss of an attachment, but one can be attached to lost abstractions too, like the country of origin the migrant has left behind. The process of mourning these various losses, as Freud explains it, can unfold in a "regular" (meaning normal) way or in a "pathological" redirection from the expected path, as melancholia. Freud's discussion maintains the distinction between successful mourning—when the subject who has suffered the loss, after an interval of time, finds an internalized substitute for the lost person and moves on—and its thwarted form, melancholia, which has the same mental feature as mourning (denying the loss, withdrawing from the world where reminders of the object abound, even reanimating the lost object), but here the subject is unable to find a substitute and move on.[34] The plot of the subject's stages of recovery gets interesting at the point Freud concedes that, although "reality-testing" shows the subject that the loved one no longer exists, successful mourning is easier said than done: "It is a matter of general observation that people never willingly abandon a libidinal position, not even, indeed, when a substitute is already beckoning to them."[35]

In a later work, "The Ego and the Id," Freud offers a substantial revision of the opposition between mourning and melancholia. He now hypothesizes that all losses require some kind of identification with the lost object, that mourning requires an acceptance of the loss, and that in all stages, mourning has a transformative (desirable) effect on the subject. In other words, melancholia is not necessarily a depressive pathological condition but a kind of internalization that is part of all mourning, a stage one goes through, and the ego is, in fact, constituted by these losses as a palimpsestic archive of "the history of those object choices" and as a "precipitate of abandoned object cathexes."[36] Thus, successful grieving does not imply that one has forgotten another person or that someone else has taken its place. Full substitutability of the lost object with a new one is not the desired outcome; rather, one aims for, as Butler's discussion of vulnerability highlights, an acceptance of the loss and the subject's acknowledgement of its own dependence on and vulnerability to others.

How should we read *Open City*'s references to Freud's writing on mourning and melancholia? These references are, no doubt, a sign that Julius entertains analytical models that are uncommon among his fellow psychiatrists. But if such endorsements of Freud are selective, then as readers we might see this as an invitation by the novel to continue the reading, to use Freud in ways that its narrator will not to render himself legible as a subject of mourning, dependent on and vulnerable to others. If we follow a basic narratological line and look at the way bits of texts are sequenced to deliver meaning, we notice that Freud is used for nonclinical explanations only, a "literary truth," as Julius puts it. The two specific examples that Julius uses Freud to explain are the public response to the events of September 11, 2001, and the case of a patient, Mr. F., whom he treats for depression. These two examples are triangulated in the novel with Freud's writings on mourning and melancholia, and the section in which they all appear is introduced by this line: "It is hard to shake the feeling that . . . there really is an epidemic of sorrow sweeping our world, the full brunt of which is being borne, for now, only by a luckless few." Julius summarizes Freud with two key terms: "introjection," the internalization of the dead by the living, as happens in normal mourning, and "incorporation," the partial assimilation of the dead by encrypting them, only to have them haunt the living from a hidden and sealed-off part of the psyche, as happens in unfinished mourning or melancholia. For Julius, the post-9/11 United States is a case of collective mourning gone awry, or melancholic incorporation: "The neatness of the line we had drawn around the catastrophic events of 2001 seemed to me to correspond to this kind of sectioning off" (*City*, 208). Julius includes himself in this melancholia-ridden "we" as he points out that none of the stories of individual heroism, the presidential firmness of purpose, or the city's resolve to rebuild right away are sufficient evidence that people have moved on: "The mourning had not been completed, and the result had been the anxiety that cloaked the city." The cloaking metaphor also links the numbed city dwellers to the memorial they are constructing, which Julius describes earlier in the novel as a veiled obelisk. Following the reference to 9/11, we get an abrupt transition to the story of Mr. F.: "Set against this bigger picture, the many smaller ones: in the spring, I saw an old gentleman" (209).

The story of Mr. F. is the "smaller" picture set against the bigger one of collective melancholia, national mourning. This patient, we learn, is a World War II veteran who, otherwise in good health with solid familial support, comes down suddenly with a debilitating depression: "When he came in, in his veteran's cap and a blue windbreaker, he had that faraway look of those who had somehow gotten locked inside their sadness" (*City*, 209). The language of locking away, or encrypting, links the patient to the uncompleted public mourning; however, F.'s sadness is for a distant loss that is not legible to any of the doctors treating him. If there is an attached loss, it reads more like a historical trauma, a blind spot that is harder to see and confront. For Julius this kind of substitution is quite common—the scene of trauma for a lost object. Julius's professional treatment for F.'s condition is pharmacological, but the "cure" as we see is accidental, a breakthrough that could not have been planned in advance. In his second session with Mr. F., as Julius is instructing him about the medications, the old man stops him with a raised hand and says, "Doctor, I just want to tell you how proud I am to come here, and see a young black man like yourself in that white coat, because things haven't ever been easy for us, and no one has ever given us nothing without a struggle" (210). The chapter ends with this final sentence as though with this single acknowledgment, the patient has cured himself by unlocking the sadness that has cloaked him for years. When F. speaks, his use of the "we" to identify with Julius as a Black man and the rendering of his speech in a differentiated syntax tells us that the patient is African American. This is teleiopoiesis from the other side, the imaginative reaching out from the descendant of one of those earlier layers of the national palimpsest. By including the new African immigrant, Julius, in the history of his own struggle against racism, Mr. F. does not differentiate the "African American," a historically oppressed racial minority in the United States, from the "African" whose experience of white racism ended with postcolonial rule in Nigeria. For the old man, Julius simply represents a new layer of young Black men who help cure him of the melancholic pessimism that little progress has been made since Jim Crow. This is the sort of encounter that shows the complex negotiations of temporality in the formation of solidarity with those who do not share the same history of incorporation into the nation. In this case, we could conclude that postcoloniality and race can be identical when the postcolonial African is interpellated as the present-day legible layer in a *global* history of racism. Yet we also know that Julius's inclusion in this collective "we" is the result of an officially race-blind immigration policy that in turn resulted from the very political struggles Mr. F.'s generation undertook in their long march for civil rights.

The chapter, as I noted earlier, ends with Mr. F. saying, "Things haven't ever been easy for us, and no one has ever given us nothing without a struggle." In the way sequencing thwarts expectations in this novel, that sentence is still echoing for the reader when the following chapter opens to a violent encounter that cancels out the earlier moment of teleiopoiesis. Julius is brutally beaten by two inner-city African American men who laugh and curse as they kick him as he lies there on the pavement. Robbed of his phone and wallet, bloody and bruised, Julius stoically finds his way back home. The unexpectedness of the attack is magnified by Julius's misreading of the young men's intentions when he first spots them on the street. As he passes them on the sidewalk, Julius thinks that there had been an "acknowledgment" on their part, "only the most tenuous of connections between us, looks on a street corner by strangers, a gesture of mutual respect based on our being young, black, male; based, in other words, on our being 'brothers'" (*City*, 212). These two encounters described consecutively in the novel make the contrast unavoidable, but taken together they seem to say, race and postcoloniality are "neither the same nor opposed."[37]

Julius's response to this attack is in marked contrast to Mr. F.'s vulnerability. When he returns to his apartment to clean his wounds, trembling and gasping from the shock, Julius tells us that "every cliché by which assault could be minimized" hurried to claim space in his head: "These things happen, it was only a matter of time, count your blessings, and yes, it could have been worse—and such bile rose into my throat at these thoughts. Three personal days from work would be enough to restore my equilibrium, I thought" (*City*, 215). These words that combine anger and disgust and the desire to get over it quickly tell us what Julius thinks about the display of vulnerability. It is hard to miss the unmistakable familiarity of some of these so-called clichés; we have heard them used often by victims of sexual assault and rape. When two weeks have passed, the wounds have healed, and all that remains is a pain in his wrist; however, since narrative sequence also conveys meaning in another way, we have to ask whether what follows in the text after the description of the attack is an indication of callousness in the subject (Julius as an unchanging and hardened subject) or the sensory emergence of suffering as the experience of vulnerability (the violence directed at him making him aware of the suffering of others, despite his own attempts to minimize its impact and "restore [his] equilibrium").

Two weeks after the mugging but sequentially presented right after the attack, Julius notices a small security traffic island with an inscription marking a centuries-old burial ground where anywhere from fifteen to twenty thousand enslaved Africans were interred. Most of the burial ground was now under the streets and city buildings, but a Haitian artist constructed a tiny monument on the island to memorialize the dead. As Julius stands there, he thinks, "What I was steeped in, on that warm morning, was the echo across centuries, of slavery in New York" (*City*, 222). He remembers reading about the "traces of suffering" that the bodies bore when subway construction in the city brought many of the remains to the surface: blunt trauma and broken bones. Before Julius leaves this makeshift monument enacted by a fellow New Yorker, he steps across the cordon around the tiny plot and bends down to lift a stone from the grass. As he does so, a pain shoots through the back of his left hand. Julius makes nothing of it, but the narrative sequencing enables a proprioceptive or affective connection—his bodily suffering to the suffering of the ancestors of the two young men who had attacked him in the inner city, and the ancestors of Mr. F., who had sought to fold Julius into that history of suffering.

In *Precarious Life*, Butler points out that there are various ways of dealing with vulnerability and grief. When grieving is something to be feared, and our impulse is to "resolve it quickly," to "banish it in the name of an action invested with the power to restore the loss or return the world to its former order," then we have foreclosed vulnerability, foreclosed the possibility of returning to a sense of vulnerability that expresses "our collective responsibility for the physical lives of one another."[38] Julius's cool, detached interest in the sufferings of others in a historically removed past coexists with the paradoxical inability to think about human vulnerability as distributed across the lived present. This is not, as some might suggest, a form of traumatophilia but rather a struggle between the imagining of the body as bounded and autonomous (that should not be subject to the claims of others) and the body that implies "mortality, vulnerability, agency." As Butler explains, "Bodies put us at risk of becoming the agency and instruments of all these as well." Although we struggle for bodily autonomy, our bodies are "not quite ever only our own"; we are always subject to the other's gaze, touch, and violence and "given over from the very start to the world of others."[39] And building an idea of autonomy that denies one's connections to the others who have been in proximity with oneself (without choosing them), such as the enduring attachments one formed as an infant or young child to caregivers, is also a denial of this social condition of one's embodiment.

Thus, a reading of Julius's unacknowledged losses and primary attachments may be a useful way of understanding how our narrator's self-presentations of autonomy and withdrawal are linked to his inability to establish real connections with people around him, and how an acknowledgment of how his life is "implicated" (Butler's term) in the lives of those who live around him may provide new ways of theorizing vulnerability as the basis for political solidarity. We have been trying to make sense of a novel that chronicles so much historical collective suffering but represents it by way of a narrator who seems unaffected by it, a feature that has led more than one critic of this novel to describe the narrative tone as "affect-less."[40] As readers we find ourselves in an interpretive terrain where we must confront the political implications of Freud's observation in "Mourning and Melancholia" that "people never willingly abandon a libidinal position, not even, indeed, when a substitute is already beckoning to them."[41] Freud, hardly an affect theorist himself, enables a theorization of attachments, their persistence, and their ability to turn affects like shame or grief to new objects and investments, including sexual objects that have, it seems to me, implications for how Julius identifies as a subject who is multiply inscribed by discourses of sexuality, race, nationality, and class.[42]

"Brother!" This term interpellates Julius various times in the novel. When Julius is hailed as brother, his interlocutors are always fellow immigrants: an African cabdriver, a Barbudan museum guard, a Liberian refugee, and a Moroccan café owner in Brussels. "Brother" indexes in the novel a pan-African identity in the diaspora constituted in part by the common loss of a home or, simply, migrancy from the African continent. The dissociative principle is at work too. At times Julius greets other men of color saying, "Hello, my brother," but any attempt by others to initiate such a connection is obstructed by the class differentiation of this African unity-in-diversity. One day a cabdriver takes offence at Julius's coldness and says, "Hey, I'm African just like you." Julius apologizes but is inwardly angry. "I was in no mood," he tells us, "for people who tried to lay claims on me" (*City*, 40). Julius the cultural critic is too savvy to be unaware that his palimpsestuous New York is fractured by these contradictions. One day, as he stands on a boardwalk looking out toward New York Harbor and Ellis Island, the historical differences of the hyphenation of African and American comes to mind: "Each one of these past moments was present now as a trace. From where I stood, the Statue of Liberty was a fluorescent green speck against the sky, and beyond her sat Ellis Island, the focus of so many myths; but it had been built too late for those early Africans—who weren't immigrants in any case—and it had been closed too soon to mean anything to the later Africans like Kenneth, or the cabdriver, or me" (55). Julius is capable of insight like this: that the palimpsest is always unsettled by a genealogical principle that is also at work, and that "foreign" and "immigrant" are not always identical, just as "brothers" does not include the present-day African American whose history lies within the older, coerced migration of slavery and is understood to be distinctly "American" by the postcolonial African brothers.

We have seen how "brothers" when used in the novel is haunted by historical traces that establish undeniable differences in its constitution by economic migration in the twentieth and twenty-first centuries (like a postmodern Negritude) and its constitution by the descendants of those who underwent the coerced transportation of premodern slavery. Any new mobilization of this term that brings those two histories together can be imagined only by virtue of new forms of creolity and nonhyphenation. Thinking the history of the city and the history of the United States this way makes political citizenship into a palimpsest. In other words, political identity is not simply a lateral choice, as Hamilton imagined it, of one identity substituted for another, the Nigerian or German or Barbudan for a common language of the American, but, rather, it is a layering in which the different histories of the so-called African diaspora do not allow for easy substitutions. Race as a term of identity constitution often elides such historical layering and makes us forget these differences. As Julius realizes while looking out at Liberty Island, migrancy is not a neutral term today, as racial and ethnic diversity is increasingly class differentiated. It is to this question of class differentiation as well as gender differentiation that I turn in the final section of this chapter. The novel makes some harsh disclosures at the end that force us as readers to retroactively question the detachment of the narrator. Indeed, we realize that Julius's inability to insert his living present into all the stories of the past that he sees so clearly is tied to his inability to imagine himself as a palimpsestuous subject, to render himself vulnerable to his past, to the play especially of the primary gender differentiation that all of us carry within us as sexed subjects. I argue that when we begin to focus on Julius's past, and the scenes that are recounted of his time in Nigeria, a personal history emerges that is not historically overlaid like the United States we encounter in the novel by way of its metonym, New York City; rather, it is as though the narrator as an elite, biracial, and heterosexual subject shaped by the attachments and losses of his childhood is unable to connect these intimate scenes of subject formation to the violence of state-sponsored phallocentrism, in the Nigerian case. The task remains for the reader to find the links between Julius's fragmented recollections of his Nigerian father, his German mother, and his grandmother, and the stories of postcolonial Nigeria and postwar Europe.

Reading Nigeria through Objects of "Outsize Intensity"

The insight that the ego may be constituted by prior losses is what allows the psychoanalyst Melanie Klein to posit that the experience of grief later in life, as an adult, can "revive" the subject's "early mourning," as for the child's loss of the mother's breast and all that it stood for—namely, love, goodness, and security: "All these are felt by the baby to be lost, and lost as a result of his own uncontrollable greedy and destructive fantasies and impulses directed against his mother."[43] The key point Klein makes is that the child in the normal course of growth manages these destructive feelings and overcomes loss by preserving an internal mother who reflects the happy experiences he has with his external (real and visible) mother. I will frame my reading of Julius's relationship with his mother in terms of an unacknowledged loss, a grieving for a lost object that is manifest when Julius revisits scenes involving this primary love object. In so doing, the novel not only invokes the destructive aspects of mourning, which take the form of a violent gendered fantasy, but also its blocked reparative or productive aspects. For Klein, mourning can be a "productive" form of suffering that reinstates the love for the lost objects, deepens the relationship to them, and produces a new capacity for appreciation—suffering may bring out new gifts like "painting, writing or other productive activities." Some people are "enriched" in a different way—"more capable of appreciating people and things, more tolerant in their relation to others—they become wiser."[44]

In *Open City* we confront the paradox that the novel's focus on migrant reality and globality (the story of Julius as a general story of the new American) makes it almost impossible to think postcolonial space in politically and historically palimpsestuous terms. Of course, it is possible to read that space through Julius, but within these limitations. As Julius reconstitutes his self in New York City, scenes of subjection that formed the conditions of his childhood and youth in Nigeria continue to haunt the adult. At these moments, Julius too becomes a spectralized subject in whom attachments from the past persist and continue to act on the present, but in ways that are not transparent to him. As narrator, Julius is of course aware of this active role of past in abstract terms and offers his own theory about how they appear in the present:

> We experience life as a continuity, and only after it falls away, after it becomes the past, do we see its discontinuities. The past, if there is such a thing, is mostly

empty space, great expanses of nothing, in which significant persons and events float. Nigeria was like that for me: mostly forgotten, except for those few things that I remembered with an outsize intensity. These were the things that had been solidified in my mind by reiteration, that recurred in dreams and daily thoughts: certain faces, certain conversations, which, taken as a group, represented a secure version of the past that I had been constructing since 1992. But there was another, irruptive sense of things past. The sudden reencounter, in the present, of something or someone long forgotten, some part of myself I had relegated to childhood and to Africa. (*City*, 156)

Here, Julius gives us a good starting point. The present when experienced as "a continuity" (what I referred to in the introduction, and elsewhere, as the past-present-future continuum) becomes meaningful only when it "falls away," when it is distanced from a contemporaneity. For Julius this past appears both as conscious memory, which is like a rear view of the past experienced from the present—Nigeria as a space in which significant events and persons float, which recur as remembered conversations and faces in his daily thoughts and dreams. These memories of "outsize intensity" taken together allow for the constitution of a fantasy: "a secure version of the past" that Julius has been constructing since leaving Nigeria. Then, there is a second kind of memory, "the sudden reencounter, in the present of something or someone long forgotten" that he had "relegated to childhood and to Africa." This sense of the past is the "irruptive sense of things past," a nonconscious memory that shocks and reactivates the past, at once reconstituting the world of the present differently. Massumi has called this kind of memory "an actively present germ of the past."[45] What Julius offers in this passage is a texturizing of narrative retroversion that taps into a distinction much like the one Massumi posits between "conscious memory" that is retrospective and goes from the present to reactivate the past and "active memory" (what Julius calls "irruptive"—a sudden surge, like the irregular migration of birds to a new place) that comes from the past to energize the present.[46] In what follows, I want to address the affective textures of these gendered past attachments by tracking them through the two kinds of memories Julius has about Nigeria: one, mostly childhood memories in which the empty space of the country emerges through persons, events, and things remembered with what he calls an "outsize intensity." In this category are the memories that solidify by way of recurrence (memories of his family and schooling) and constitute a secure fantasy version of the past. The other involves memories that emerge as an irruption, when something or someone long forgotten reappears and creates a new sense of the present. The most significant irruption of this kind is the withheld (or erased) memory of Julius's relationship with a young Nigerian woman, Moji, whose chance encounter with Julius in New York City brings with it devastating disclosures about him. Moji's arrival in the narrative, unaccompanied by a backstory or previous mentions in the fabula, does not enjoy the narrative anticipation associated with what D. A. Miller calls an "open secret."[47] There are no early clues about Moji's existence in the novel or any noticeable narrative ellipses where we imagine her story is being withheld. Once her relationship with Julius is established, the status of his story as one told by a reliable narrator is called into question.

In *City* Julius's charged memories of his Nigerian childhood invite us to understand their "outsize intensity" as a result of the long affective persistence of sexualized and gendered attachments that can be connected, as Freud suggests, "to the loss of some abstraction which has taken the place of [a loved person], such as one's country." This is the allegorical mode in which Julius's attached losses, especially those of his family members (through death or abandonment) are also losses of abstractions like Nigeria. The Freudian love triangle again analogizes the problematic of mourning and melancholia in the discourse of citizenship and nationality. Both scenarios, the sexual and the political, exhibit similar yearnings for the resolution of a triangulation for a subject caught between a lost object for which it yearns and a new object that beckons to it with the promise of resolution and restoration of fullness. Julius's memories of his family, of a dead Nigerian father, an estranged German mother, and a grandmother who has broken with the family, are a series of attachments, real people that Julius has lost in some way, but they are also displacements of the abstractions that substitute for the places Julius associates with the lost objects—Nigeria-Germany-Brussels. All three places compete to establish their own historical palimpsests in the novel, but although Brussels gets its due because Julius visits the city over the course of the novel's events, the Germany and Nigeria accessed through his mother's and his own memories, respectively, make the emergence of concrete historical layers almost impossible. In such cases, events take on outsize intensity, and one such event, which I discuss below, Julius's childhood memory of an afternoon when he drank a bottle of Coke without permission, is replete with substitutions that suggest it is an allegory of the melancholic structure of heterosexual identification.

The second kind of memories, in which falls the irruptive function of the young woman Moji, appear without conscious recollection. These fall squarely within the psychosexual desires of the narrator as a subject who is a collection of his losses, a cryptic palimpsest that helps us understand how and why he tells the story about himself this way and not another. For such a reading, one more level of theoretical help is needed. To that end, I draw on Butler's critique of normative heterosexuality as a melancholic structure and the way gender identity always retains a permanent palimpsestuous structure. It is never fully settled, always carries the hetero and the homo, and is always open to queer potentialities. Normative gender identity is palimpsestuous and melancholic because it never arrives at a clean slate—the successful mourning for, or a real coming to terms with, the loss of the parental loved object, especially the mother.

Both melancholia and mourning, as we have seen, involve identifications that the subject initiates with the lost object, but they can also be read as two different modes of gender differentiation. In *Gender Trouble*, Butler's exploration of how heterosexuality is established as the norm borrows from Nicolas Abraham and Maria Torok's reworking of Freud's distinction between *introjection* (the identification associated with mourning) and *incorporation* (the identification associated with melancholia or incomplete mourning): "Incorporation denotes a fantasy and introjection a process."[48] Incorporation is consistent with fantasy because fantasy masks something in order to maintain the status quo; fantasy seeks to change the world in a way that keeps the subject uninjured and invulnerable. Thus, incorporation is essentially narcissistic and is a resistance to change on the part of the subject. By contrast, introjection is a process that facilitates successful mourning because the subject acknowledges the loss rather than going on in a fantasy world in which it pretends the lost object is still alive, or that it was never lost, because it was never loved.

Now to the way Butler makes these two forms of identification into modes of gender differentiation. In Lacanian theory, the repudiation of the maternal body is the precondition for entry into the symbolic, and mourning is, therefore, central to all subject formation. Just as the child experiences the emptiness and fills the void left by the loss of the mother in the initial stages "with sobs and cries, then as calling, ways of requesting presence, as language," mourning requires the acknowledgment and representation of the loss. Mourning, for that reason, is not narcissistically driven but rather oriented toward the social, a community. Butler's discussion of gender-identity formation challenges the Lacanian picture of successful mourning by the child using language and emphasizes, instead, instances where it is not clear that the subject has successfully displaced the libido from the lost object through the formation of words. Butler points out that, whereas the grasping of the symbolic order involves displacement or metaphorical activity in which words figure the absence and surpass it, gender identity is a melancholic structure that depends on incorporation rather than on introjection—fantasy and literalization through body parts rather than successful substitution with language.[49] Normative gender identity, Butler argues, depends on a refusal to acknowledge the loss of the mother and thus a failure to displace into words. The loss of the mother is then literalized as a disavowal of that original desire and the pleasure associated with her ("I never desired her!"). The love associated with the loved and lost mother is incorporated in a way that determines and prohibits that love at the same time through compulsory sex differentiation.

What Butler's analysis shows in conjunction with the other readings of Freud I have discussed above is that multiple identifications (introjection and incorporation) can reconstitute so-called gender identity into a nonhierarchical configuration of shifting and overlapping palimpsestuous identifications that call into question the primacy of any univocal gender identity. For the melancholic heterosexual female, "the loss of homosexuality is refused and the love [for the mother] is sustained or encrypted in parts of the body itself, literalized in the ostensible anatomical facticity of sex." For the melancholic heterosexual male, the love for the father is stored in the penis and in making the woman-as-object, this love is safeguarded by the denial—"He never loved another man, he *is* a man."[50] There is one key difference in the structure of disavowal: the loss of the homosexual object requires the loss of the aim and the object (total denial), while the loss of the heterosexual object requires only the loss of the object but not the aim (one acknowledges the loss but redirects the desire and finds another love to replace the lost one). It is this unresolved nature of incorporation that Butler finds potentially subversive for gender identity.

In this section my reading of *City* undertakes an analysis of the autobiographical narrative as an encrypted text that, like the subject that is possessed of a psychic space that can be cleared and replaced with new objects, "comes to exist by installing within itself lost objects along with the social norms that regulate the subject's disposition to the address of the other."[51] In *Precarious Life*, where Butler takes up the question of mourning in greater detail, they provide a way to think about how the experience of mourning is not an experience of privatized grief, or of depoliticizing, but rather an experience that can furnish a sense of "political community of a complex order" by bringing to the fore our relationships of dependency, relational ties, and ethical responsibility:

> When we lose certain people, or when we are dispossessed from a place, or a community, we may simply feel that we are undergoing something temporary,

that mourning will be over and some restoration of prior order will be achieved. But maybe when we undergo what we do, something about who we are is revealed, something that delineates the ties we have to others, that shows us how these ties constitute what we are, ties or bonds that compose us. . . . At another level, perhaps what I have lost "in" you, that for which I have no ready vocabulary, is a relationality that is composed neither exclusively of myself nor you, but is to be conceived as *the tie* by which those terms are differentiated and related.[52]

What would it mean to read Julius's losses, the ones that are explicitly interjected and the ones that are encrypted through incorporation as losses of real people, as a lost relationality, a tie by which these terms "I" (Julius) and "you" (mother, father, grandmother) were differentiated? The death of his father when Julius is fourteen and the estrangement of his mother when he is seventeen are not mourned as losses. Julius seems almost unaffected by this symbolic orphaning. In fact, both parents hardly "speak" in the novel. They appear as apostrophized figures. Whenever Julius seems most willing to acknowledge a real loss, it is of a person that he hardly knew at all—his German Oma.

Julius's assertion that Nigeria appears by way of things of "outsize intensity" could operate as a caption for a chapter in *Open City* that focuses almost entirely on a childhood incident with a bottle of Coca-Cola. One afternoon the nine-year-old Julius is home alone and sets his mind to breaking a house rule. Bottled drinks, being a "controlled substance," were not to be drunk without his mother's permission (*City*, 132). Overtaken by an insatiable thirst for a Coke, Julius spends some time contemplating an act of disobedience. His attempt to masturbate fails. The sequence plays itself out when after a series of deflections, he goes to the fridge, picks out a bottle, uncaps it, drinks it, replaces it with a warm bottle from the storeroom, and goes about his day.

The fillers between this sequence of actions are where the affective texture and significance of the performative are to be found: "I swore that I would never forget the intensity of what I was feeling at that moment. I solemnly promised myself, electrified by the self-consciousness of oath taking, that, once I became an adult, I would drink Coke with impunity." The thought of doing this every day almost drives him, Julius says, "mad with excitement." His heart "raced at the thought of such a vengeance." It is the mention of "vengeance" that connects the bottle of Coke, that quintessential commodity fetish object, to the maternal sexual object. While it is the thought of disobeying and transgressing his father's rules that generates the initial sexual excitement, the real object of the transgression is his mother, who has "abandoned" him for his father: "But these rules were all my father's. He had clear ideas about how not to spoil a child. The enforcement, though, had fallen to my mother, and if I resented the rules—which I only rarely did, as they were the only conception I had of childhood—if on rare occasions I ever resented the rules, I did so on my mother's account, and never took into consideration my father's part in it. In this way I created a kind of innocence for him in my mind" (*City*, 133). The anger directed against the mother for "siding" with the father thus constitutes paternal (symbolic) power as neutral or innocent and partly disguises the literalizing (melancholic) nature of the act: by drinking the bottle of Coke, Julius is swallowing the loss of his mother's love. At the same time, it is the Oedipal rebellion against the father's law by which the son imagines his sexual adulthood and freedom from the father—the ability, as young Julius imagines it, to drink Coke with "impunity." Finally, we see an act of melancholic mourning when the son's failed act of masturbation cannot substitute the primary sex object with another imaginary one: "My genitals lay squished in my palm." Later that evening, as Julius watches his mother drive up to the house, he tells us that it was toward her, "the enforcer," that he "wordlessly directed all the afternoon's anger" (135).

The achievement of heteronormativity happens, as Butler explains, when "the loss of the heterosexual object results in the displacement of that object but not the heterosexual aim."[53] If the Coke incident records Julius's inability to displace the desire for his mother, who is lost to him, the mother remains encrypted as a loss that is not mourned. We know this because the reasons for Julius's long estrangement from his mother are never explained. As the years passed, Coke no longer held any appeal for him, but Julius is willing to speculate that his temptation to overinterpret the events of that day (the outsized intensity of what he was feeling) probably held an explanation for his rejection of his mother. As readers of the Coke incident, we notice something our narrator cannot: the language of entitlement, vengeance, and power associated with the breaking of the rule, albeit unobserved, is done without shame. In tying the desire for sexual freedom and adulthood to an act of disobeying and disavowing the mother, Julius successfully links sexual pleasure to a form of entitled male power. Unsuccessful mourning now takes the form of a gendered violent fantasy. The intensity of this incident involving an everyday object is a good example of what Freud identified as the substitutability of objects for the same affective aim. A few months later, driving in the back of his parents' car to his first day at a military school, we see the shift that has taken place. Julius recalls feeling "an unexamined loyalty" to his father and a "growing antipathy to his mother" (*City*, 77). The novel hints through this sequencing that Julius's identification with his father may be connected to the role of male power, soon to be embodied for Julius by the elite men churned out by the military schools to be the future leaders of Nigeria.

The novel's redefinition of heterosexuality and the family romance in the context of a much broader network of relationships is where the novel's allegorical coding kicks in. The reattachment to his father by way of rejecting his mother brings a renewed association with the father's land—Nigeria. It is the country that Julius's German mother loves "but to which she could never belong" (*City*, 77). When Julius discloses his shame on being named after his mother (Julianne), he seems to hold the mother's genetic trace responsible for hybridizing (delegitimizing) his own connection to Nigeria. The implications of biraciality for an elite subject in modern Nigeria are, however, complicated. "These are the rich little maggots who swallow our country whole," says his tormentor, an instructor, Lieutenant Musibau, as he hauls Julius away for a public caning at the school. Class privilege is not easily diminished by Julius's European heritage in a school for the children of the postcolonial elite. Julius turns the public flogging, an act of brutal unjustified violence against his body, into a display of fearlessness. It was his schooling that built, as Julius describes it later, his "callous self-confidence" (84). I note the word "callous" because a young woman, Moji, will use it years later to describe Julius when she confronts him in New York. Meaning "hardened in the mind" or "unfeeling," callous comes from the Latin *callosus*, meaning "thick-skinned," and *callus*, "hard skin." There is Julius's body, a surface of skin and flesh exposed to the other's touch, violence. The caning intended to shame and humiliate Julius creates the opposite—a textural change described as though the resistant surface of Julius's skin absorbs that shame and converts it into a hard confidence. We see an example of what Butler might be indexing when they say that suffering can result in the denial of vulnerability and a prolongation and redirection of violence—a hardening of the self toward the other.

The internalization of shame is thus part of the successful production of the subject in any given cultural context; however, the household of the Freudian family romance can be historicized as the original desire for the mother or father produced in the elite households of late capitalist Nigeria. Furthermore, saying mourning and melancholia is universal is not to say that it operates the same way cross-culturally or that it has a formulaic way of determining social life. Rather, we might think of the affective structures of mourning and melancholia as dominant frames within which social relations take place, a part of every social form or political belonging that exists and operates somewhere. There is some irony here: the inability to read a Nigerian family in the manner of the richly historicized contexts of modernist texts, like Chinua Achebe's *Things Fall Apart* set in the rural space of a not-yet Nigeria, or Buchi Emecheta's *Joys of Motherhood* set in Lagos during the Second World War, tells us that the globalization of the Freudian family romance is an imaginative leveling symptomatic of the formation of an undifferentiated middle class under oil-rich postmodern Nigeria's insertion into the global economy.

I now move to the second kind of memory that Julius reckons is available to him only in its random and unexpected occurrence. In these instances Nigeria emerges unplanned and unexpectedly, as happens when Julius runs into his old acquaintance Moji in a New York City supermarket. He recalls her, he says, only vaguely and is therefore unable to reciprocate the warm greeting, as she addresses him by his full name. Julius wonders in what capacity he had known her—a friend, an old friend, an acquaintance? Because Julius's adult heterosexuality is not developed as a narrative strand in the novel, readers have to go with the few scattered references to an ex-girlfriend (Nadege) who leaves him before the narration begins and a brief sexual encounter with a woman he meets while holidaying in Brussels.

After the initial moment of befuddlement, Julius remembers who Moji is: the sister of a close friend from military school. In the narrative Julius goes on to describe subsequent meetings with her in the city. There are even suggestions that a casual friendship has formed between them. This is why the novel seems to perform an irruptive act of its own on the reader when, a few weeks later, Moji confronts Julius with the accusation that he had raped her years ago. This disclosure, which comes with little warning, reminds us that this novel is first and foremost one person's, Julius's, telling, and it is *he* who makes the disclosure to the reader with these cryptic words: "Each person must, on some level, take himself as the calibration point for normalcy, must assume that the room of his own mind is not, cannot be, entirely opaque to him. Perhaps this is what we mean by sanity: that whatever our self-admitted eccentricities might be, we are not the villains of our own stories." The irony is not lost on us as readers when Julius ends by asking, "And so, what does it mean when, in someone else's version, I am the villain?" (*City*, 243). Our narrator, a professional authority on affective disorders and a savvy critic of national-global cultures, has so far merited our sympathy and our readiness to believe the best about him. We have had to assume that as the narrator of his own life, his mind could not be fully opaque to him. Julius also adds a professional footnote to the disclosure that follows by saying that Moji's accusation to him was expressed "as if, with all of her being, she were certain of its accuracy":

> Moji looked over the river, narrowing her eyes. Then she turned to me and said, in a low and even voice, emotional in its total lack of infection, that there were things she wished to say to me. And then, with the same flat affect, she said that, in late 1989 when she was fifteen and I a year younger, at a party her brother had hosted at their house in Ikoyi, I had forced myself on her. Afterward, she said, her eyes unwavering from the bright river below, in the weeks that followed, in the months and years that followed, I had acted like I knew nothing about it, had even forgotten her, to the point of not recognizing her when we met again and I had never acknowledged what I had done. This torturous deception had continued until the present. But it hadn't been like that for her, she said, the luxury of denial had not been possible for her. Indeed, I had been ever present in her life, like a stain or a scar, and she had thought of me, either fleetingly or in extended agonies for almost every day of her adult life. (244)

Moji's description of Julius as a stain or a scar left on her life impresses the point that her rape, although a single bodily act, continued to traumatize her long after the fact, as a memory carried by her body, affectively texturizing almost "every day of her adult life." When Moji tells Julius that he has had the "luxury of denial," we wonder how deep this disavowal goes. Were Julius's prefatory remarks an admission that this denial had been so successful that even he could not reach the site where it had been encrypted all these years? The most damning thing that Moji says to Julius is that while she still carried the "hurt," he had lost "none of his callousness." "I don't think you've changed at all, Julius," she says. "Things don't go away just because you choose to forget them" (245). The contrast between the texturizing metaphors is gender differentiated. The scar and stain carry the memory of violence imagined through vulnerability. One is the mark left by the healing of wounded skin while the other is a permanent mark that ruins the thing on which it is left. The callus in Julius's callousness is the mark left on a body that reacts to the violence by hardening itself against it till the dead skin no longer has any sensation. This is a texturizing that denies the body's vulnerability.

Once this disclosure is made, our own reading performs a retroactive rearrangement like the affective function of irruptive memory. Did we miss clues that were already there in the narrative? Were there earlier textual references that signaled what was to come in the future? A possible list of such retroactive reconstructions on the part of the reader might include Julius's obsessive attempts to find his lost grandmother, Oma, who was raped by Allied soldiers occupying Germany after the war; the abrupt shutting of a window when Julius hears women chanting during a Take Back the Night march; his sexual desire for "wounded" women with physical disfigurations; and so on and so forth. But without a confession from Julius, Moji's story remains an open wound in the narrative. Even if we were to believe that the confrontation with her attacker may have brought an end to Moji's grieving, the measure of undecidability that allows us neither the satisfaction of dismissing Julius as a rapist nor the satisfaction of supporting Moji's testimony through her own backstory leaves the novel, like the city, with a radical openness.

Perhaps Cole's point is that we desire easy fixes and no easy fixes are possible. Part of Moji's address to Julius is given to us in the mode of free indirect discourse, the effect of which is to let some of her most damning words stand on their own without being changed by Julius's reporting. To make something of this narrative texture, we could use Berlant's insight (by way of Barbara Johnson) that free indirect discourse projects a "merged and submerged observational intersubjectivity"; it is a rhetorical mode in which the narrator partially merges with a character's consciousness. The effect of this is the impossibility of separating the body from which the observation originates and the body it is referring to. Berlant suggests that such a rhetorical texture forces the reader to "transact a different, more open relation of unfolding to what she is reading, judging, being, and thinking she understands."[54] But even this rhetorical gesture of openness by the narrator leads nowhere. In the end, the novel moves away from Moji, the victim of rape, to Julius's everyday life. We are back in the lived present of his reflections on books, musical recitals, bird migrations, and the monumental city. But like the twinge of pain that Julius feels from time to time as he moves his arm (the residue of the mugging in the inner city) the novel's ending on this uneasy note stages, it seems to me, an openness rather than a fix. This is a novel that does not work with the pieties of cosmopolitanism. The ghostly figure of Moji haunts Julius's story from a narrative crypt and forces the question of sexual violence onto the palimpsestic city that has been, for Julius, only the scene of mass atrocities and loose collectivity.

In a recent collection of essays titled *Cosmopolitanisms*, Bruce Robbins and Paulo Lemos Horta argue that it is time to rethink old European models of cosmopolitanism because "wherever and whenever history has set people in transnational motion, sometimes very forcibly, it is to be expected that many of them and their descendants will show signs of hybrid identity and increasingly divided loyalty."[55] Their point is that existing norms of cosmopolitanism are still wedded to an ideal of national identity that, like Hamilton's, do not allow for the possibility of multiple loyalties or attachments to multiple collectivities. In her contribution to this collection, Leela Gandhi makes the point that any notion of divided loyalties must introduce elements that cannot be accommodated by the logic and structure of cosmopolitanism, especially its tendency to paint the objects of cosmopolitanism's regard with the same brush when it comes to the structure of agency. Ethical programs of self-regard, along with kin concepts of hospitality and cosmopolitanism, convey, she argues, perhaps quite unintentionally, "the ethical passivity of those at the receiving end of violence in all historical variety." Whether it is the other of alterity theory, the guest of hospitality theory, or the stranger of neo-cosmopolitan theory, they all inspire a form of ethical action or ethical heroism of "reformed host/cosmopolitan subjects."[56] Such ethical programs based on other-regard are, she states, "nothing if not victim-oriented"; they are always asking how we can protect those who are vulnerable to us and do not quite engage the resources and reversals of victim consciousness. *Open City* forces us to confront this possibility: Can we produce an ethics of suffering in which, as Gandhi puts it, "solidarities have to be formed (nauseatingly enough) with perpetrators?"[57] What would it mean to keep an imperfective aspect (Julius as the perpetrator of past violence seeking inclusion) that haunts the formation of political community and prevents it from becoming a finite process in the name of easy collectivities like "New Yorkers" or "Black brothers"?

Questions like these have always nagged those active in anti-colonial and decolonial struggles. Negotiating between the experience of powerlessness of the colonized and their desire for violent struggle enacting revenge and reversal posed ethical challenges to modern intellectuals like Mohandas Gandhi, Frantz Fanon, and Desmond Tutu throughout their political lives.[58] Today, as the war-driven refugees and economically deprived migrants who approach the borders of the European nations and the United States are represented as criminally or culturally dangerous interlopers rather than as vulnerable guests, it seems crucial to imagine alternatives to the binary structure of affective attachments implied in the idea of citizenship. *Open City* engages affective states that provide opportunities for nondualistic thought and nondestructive forms of connectedness with those who are not only victims and powerless but also perpetrators of the very structures from which they are running away. In so doing, the novel allows us to engage imaginatively with the subject's restlessness and its multiple loyalties by way of a repetitive return to the scene of lost attachments and the performative act of mourning. Within the limited narration performed by an autobiographical "I," the novel asks us to consider the lived present of the nation, the synchronicity of the "we" as a site of converged histories that must be accounted for, strand by strand, to reveal the class, race, and gender differentiations that come in the shape of heterotemporalities that unsettle the continuum of a national past-present-future.

CHAPTER THREE

Networks
Sheer Space as Synchronous Experience

These days, networks are everywhere, offering useful descriptions of a wide range of phenomena. From social circles to drug cartels, from economic processes to the movement of refugees, network models have percolated into disciplinary knowledges, popular culture, and the language of everyday life. The word itself may be a cliché, yet despite its familiarity and recognizable visual forms, a network is hard to explain. As a diagramming tool, its popularity may owe something to the ability to make complex interconnections in the world visible and seemingly manageable by organizing such links into bounded shapes and forms. However, the visual simplicity often belies an epistemological complexity, especially of the ways in which networks constrain and limit the knowledge of the phenomena they depict. Sometimes networks seem boundless, self-sustaining, and self-regulating because they lack a central node that sits in the middle. Appearing to create their own shape and reality without the controlling hand of economic, political, or cultural laws, they are like webs without spiders. Ultimately, in their visual and textual manifestations, networks constitute their own "network effects," or ways of mediating our temporal and spatial apprehensions of linked phenomena, whether they be the connections between material objects themselves or the social relations in which these objects are located along with other human and nonhuman beings.

One of the most compelling effects of a network is its ability to turn time into space. This is because, even as networks express fluidity and randomness and a capacity to expand, they also, paradoxically enough, bring a semblance of order and fixity to phenomena. Networks change how we perceive the phenomena they map. First, their configurations turn geography into abstract space whenever connectivity, rather than location, is the organizing logic. Then, differences that might exist—in the manner in which events unfold or the time it takes to get from one node to another or the frequencies of circulation and movement from one point to the next—are flattened and minimized. A spatialized mapping of interconnected nodes constitutes a visually unified whole, a super-site with a synchronous temporality that in turn supports this totality. Simply put, we can *see it all* in one glance.

The flattening effect also results from the equivalences created by a network assemblage, within which all manner of objects, such as events, processes, people, institutions, and goods, are hitched together to become similarly structured parts of a path, a hub, a hinge, or a node. The resulting interconnected whole can now be lifted off the surface of the earth as a visual object that exists as if it is independent of the geographical location or the temporal unfolding and sequence of the events it represents. It is not without reason therefore that networks have become ubiquitous concept metaphors in the analysis of globality, for which they instantiate the "flows" of ideas, goods, money, and people in information networks, commercial networks, financial networks, and social networks. If networks are accompanied by other metaphoric entailments, such as the language of flows, then the resulting abstracted mobility dissimulates differences created by speed, friction, culture, crises, or malfunctions. In other words, a flattened space of interconnections depends on prioritizing an indifferent synchronicity, the notion that everything exists all at once, over historical or temporal inflections that striate or layer the network's seemingly seamless and smooth flows.

Let me illustrate this synchronic effect by way of a visual example: a diagram by the late artist Mark Lombardi titled *Oliver North, Lake Resources of Panama, and the Iran Contra Operation, ca 1984–86*.

In a series of drawings that were exhibited in a 2003 retrospective, *Global Networks*, at the Drawing Center in New York City, artist Mark Lombardi traces the various connections that underlie several notorious financial and political scandals that made the headlines in the 1980s and 1990s. Figure 1 shows his diagram of the Iran-Contra scandal that involved the collusion of government actors and intelligence operations with nonstate players like banks, corporations,

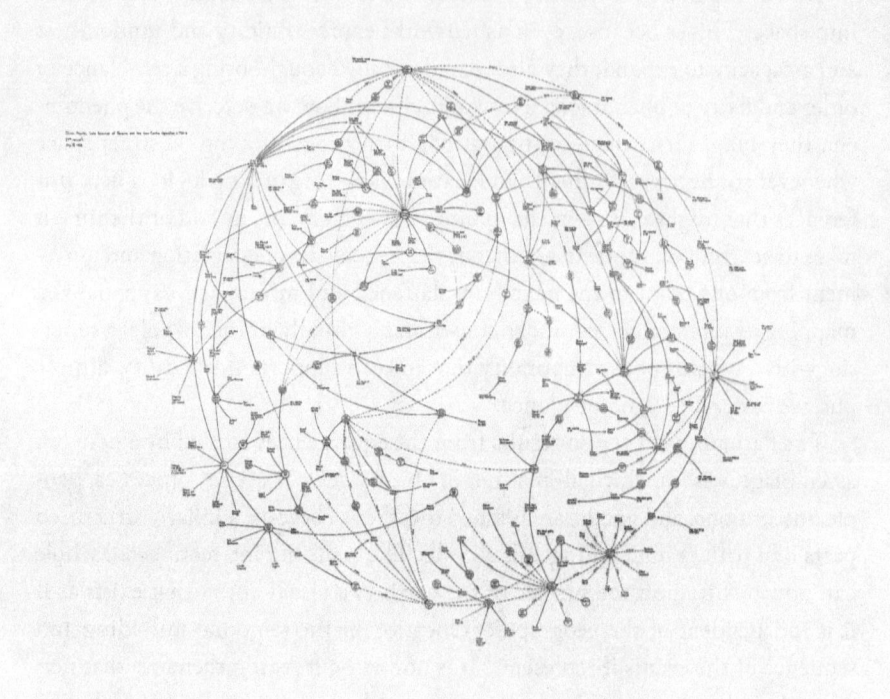

Mark Lombardi, *Oliver North, Lake Resources of Panama, and the Iran-Contra Operation, c. 1984–86* (4th version), 1999. Colored pencil and graphite on paper. 63 × 82 7/8 inches (160 × 210.5 cm). Image courtesy of the Lombardi Family and Pierogi Gallery; photo credit: John Berens. Detail opposite.

militias, terrorist groups, and organized crime. In the drawing, lines connect various nodes to establish relationships between actors and organizations: a line with a single arrow indicates a type of influence or control, a line with an arrow on both ends is a mutual relationship or association, and a broken line is the flow of money or loans. Terms like SWAPs (financial agreements to exchange cash flows based on interest rates, foreign currency exchange rates, and commodity futures) indicate the presence of virtual and nonhuman actors in the assemblage. The diagram is a skeletal narrative of the Iran-Contra affair and the parts played specifically by the Reagan administration, groups like Hezbollah, and money-laundering schemes linked to illegal arms sales to Iran and the cross-border shipments of drugs in Latin America. The end game was to aid the Contra militants bent on overthrowing the Sandinista government of Nicaragua and to use Iran's influence to secure the release of US prisoners held by the

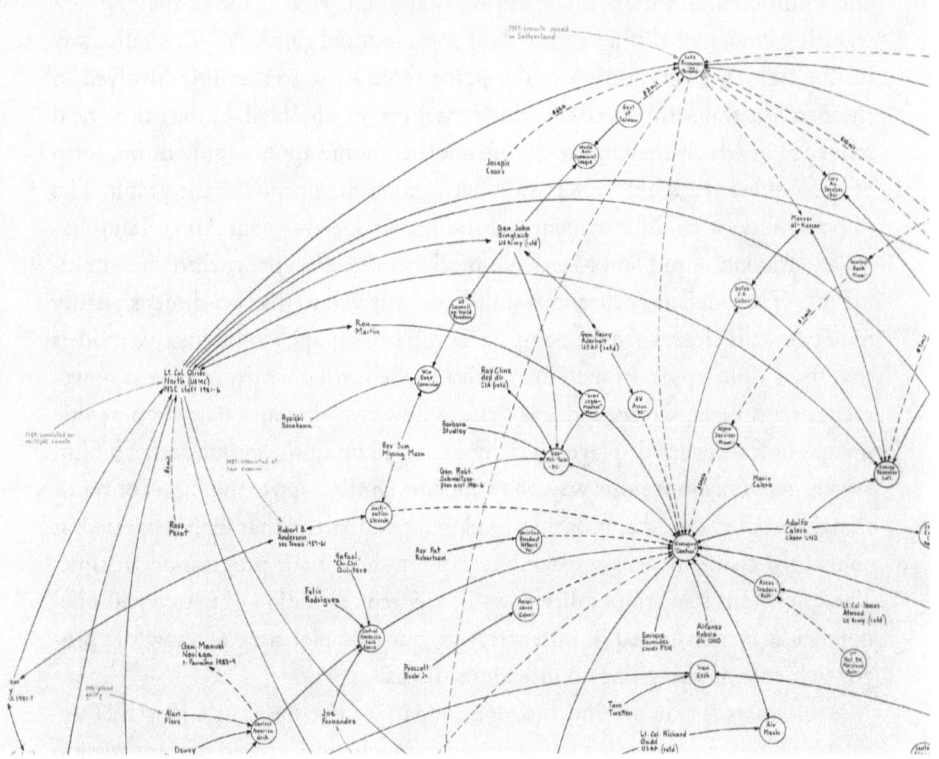

Hezbollah in Lebanon. Looking at Lombardi's diagram, we notice that the network has no real center. The nodes and hubs that represent shell corporations like Lake Resources are on top of the sphere, while Oliver North, one of the main players in the affair, is on the upper left represented as a very busy hub. Somewhat centrally placed, in the top half, is a beneficiary—the "Nicaragua contras." More than any single player or organization, what stands out in the diagram is the disorienting detail of the network itself—the sublime aesthetic effect of its scale and totality.

The sublimity of this and other drawings among Lombardi's work is an effect of their ability to abstract by deterritorializing. Despite the real referents provided by names of people, places, and entities, we cannot overlay this image back on a map or trace the named locations within the boundaries of the United States, Lebanon, Israel, Iran, Panama, Nicaragua. An abstract space of flows rather than strict geographical place seems to determine the network's shape. The whole thing seems to stand alone, floating above the ground, freed and unmoored. Yet there is the unmistakable spherical shape of the network standing in for globalism, a sort of dark conspiratorial globality. What falls away in Lombardi's diagramming is any perceivable sense of the time involved in these transactions, the speeds at which these events unfolded, or the calendrical sequence in which they followed one another. Time appears only in the form of bookended years like "1984–86" that Lombardi appends to the graph. The impossibility of reading sequence, duration, or speed—what Anna Tsing has called "friction" amid flows—is what produces the effect of synchronous simultaneity.[1] That such a synchronous simultaneity is tied to the two-dimensionality of networks is clear when we compare Lombardi's graphs to interactive models that show time lapses. In such interactive models, what we experience as movement or a time-lapsed sequence is akin to how two-dimensional photographic images or frames are displayed serially and sped up in the animation of a film. When networks move this way, they concomitantly expose the limits of traditional spatiality-based approaches to global phenomena that map separate but connected elements across space but cannot show their progression in time. The important role temporality plays in any representation of networked phenomena is demonstrated in interactive graphs that plot time to show the progression of something like an infectious disease.

As diseases spread around the globe today "at the speed of a jet airplane," calculations of a pandemic's impact depend much on the speed of transmission rather than the geographical origin of a virus or the projected area it could cover.[2] In the midst of the COVID-19 pandemic in the early months of 2020, the *Washington Post* ran a series of data visualizations showing a mathematical model that governments and health agencies used to estimate how contagious the coronavirus was and how far it could spread.[3] The *Post* model calculated the rate at which a disease could spread through a "susceptible population" (people without vaccinations, masks, or quarantines) to get the disease's basic reproductive number or R_0. COVID-19's R_0 was 2.3, meaning that one person with the disease would spread it on an average to 2.3 others. (The higher the R_0, the faster the disease is in taking off and infecting others in a population.) A second measurement, the R_e, or the "effective reproductive number," described the growth rate of an epidemic in progress. Once this value falls below 1, the epidemic stops spreading because it has run out of people to infect; people have either recovered or died from it. What was most striking about the COVID-19 models was the assumption that the spatial reach of the epidemic was determined by the speed of the viral transmission; the actual distances between China and Italy or China and the United States were insignificant in such projections. As we may remember from the 2020 pandemic, spatialized practices like border controls, travel bans, containment measures, and quarantines, moderately effective in the earlier stages of the outbreak, were incorporated into model projections only as factors that would slow the progression of transmission, not stamp it out once and for all. These strategies, the models assumed, only reduced the pace of the outbreak till the health systems were able to catch up.

Similarly, researchers studying the contagion of SARS in 2002 have argued that it was mass, rapid, international travel that transformed SARS from a local outbreak into a global pandemic. The high degree of mobility of infected, asymptomatic individuals through the networks of international airlines increased the risk of transmission.[4] As the recent outbreak of COVID-19 made clear to us, populations today are not completely isolated. All it takes is one person to get on a plane or leave an affected group to take the virus to a new population. Researchers have argued that this makes recent pandemics like COVID-19 vastly different from the more "spatially contagious diffusion" (spread from major regional epicenters to smaller places) of a disease like AIDS.[5] What we see instead is the global spread of COVID-19 occurring between global cities like Hong Kong and New York and then the cities becoming interchange sites for the spread of the virus nationwide—sites determined mostly by the routing networks of air travel.

I have discussed two vastly different networks—one charting the transactions involved in a conspiracy-scandal and the other tracking the progression of a contagion—to show that even if each network has its own way of organizing the world and the connections and pathways along which persons or commodities or viruses move, both need the supplementation of other "narrative" elements like sequencing, rhythm, tempo, frequency, repetition, contiguity, and topology (the relative positionality of various nodes or locations on a network as opposed to measurable distances between them) to give us a more complete understanding of the events or processes they represent. Caroline Levine makes a related point about narrative networks (the textual representations of the social as "multiple contending forms"): however clarifying and practical it might be to isolate a single network, it is also misleading to treat any one of them as totally separate from other kinds of networks. At any time, a mass of people participates in "overlapping interaction networks," some of which are codified as "small-scale local interaction," while others involve the recoding of these local interactions at more abstract levels into networks of economic exchanges, bureaucracies, military alliances, religious communities, legal systems, and so on. Therefore, for any comprehensive understanding, we have to pay attention to a multiplicity of networks and their differences and ask whether they are local or expanded over great distances, whether they are dense in their relationships or diffused, whether they have a center with peripheral connections, or whether they are rhizomatic with multiple hubs but no discernable center.[6]

As networks have emerged in their impressive privilege as concept metaphors in theories of globality, it is clear that their utility springs from their topological aspects—features that can be studied without regard to matters of measure or quantity. Without the measurements of distances, for instance, it is relative position that implies sequence and constrains the network's evolving shape. For instance, in the global spread of SARS in 2003, it was Hong Kong's status as a global city situated as an interchange between North America and China (and greater Asia) that made it the main node for the transmission of the disease.[7] Topology as used in mathematics involves a plasticity implicit in the way shapes exist and preserve their basic form even when they are twisted, bent, stretched, or deformed. Thus, a topological imagination is central to the sort of modeling associated with groups of separate but connected shapes, which together create interlinked positions of those shapes and objects. This picture of multiple interconnections can then be understood as "one single supersite" that is always undergoing a "translation of placement."[8] The ability of networks to convey continuity and fundamental contours despite various kinds of transformations makes them as important for the risk analysis of financial markets as they are for epidemiological modeling. Both depend on the number of conversions and trades (or contacts) between capital (or an infected person) and relative positions of those they infect. In other words, bridging and connectedness are what matter most. Because situations and positions depend on the layouts of connected nodes and pathways, less visible in these systemic graphs we call networks are the sorts of narrative elements that I referred to earlier: elements that either enable a network or cause friction in its functioning. Such elements may also be constitutive exclusions: processes that are excluded or disconnected from the network but play an important and often unacknowledged role in its creation.

In the COVID-19 outbreak of 2020, the need to institute remote working and technological connectivity made visible existing inequities of the social order in the United States. The sector of the essential workers that had no option but to take their bodies to work also reflected the racial and class indicators of those who were most likely to die from the virus.[9] This class-divided network society also encountered a temporal paradox, when President Emmanuel Macron delivered a video address from the Élysée Palace, asking for a collective chrono-*civilitas*: "We are not fighting an army or another nation," he said. "But the enemy is there: invisible, elusive, and advancing." All of the public commitment, all of its energy, all of its strength must be concentrated, he went on to say, "upon a single objective: slowing the forward movement of the virus."[10] The pandemic exposed that, all our global connectivity aside, political leaders still draw upon specific national histories and conceptual repertoires for their calls to action. And yet it is a curious call to arms, aimed at "slowing" a virus. I offer this as an example of how technological networks, when understood solely in terms of speed or in terms of synchronous simultaneity, hold within them the possibility of other temporalities that create bumps, delays, and lags in the synchronicity. Since networks privilege mobility and flows, reading for the ways in which friction, slowdowns, and recoding have agential roles can help us think about the multiplicity of temporalities (many of which we hardly notice) as well as the temporality-related challenges of globality.

Because narrative forms like the novel allow the representation of various networks at the same time, they are profoundly useful cultural sites to study networks as spatiotemporal configurations. In a cyberpunk novel like Hari Kunzru's *Transmission* (2004), for instance, the connections and bridges that build the various networks in the story are represented by different codings, such as media networks, contagion networks, financial networks, cultural networks, labor networks, technological networks, and so on, but the novel's narrative itself is also a network, constituted on the one hand by linguistic units like words, sentences, and narrative units that are connected most obviously by their placement next to each other in a principle of contiguity, or *parataxis*. On the other hand, a narrative also creates intersecting nodes such as those materializing when characters, unbeknownst to anyone but the narrator, pass each other in the plot, or when tiny actions trigger cascading consequences, or when independent stories run in parallel to each other but are brought together in a single junction by a crisis. The self-consciously threaded structure of interlocking lives, converging fates, and crisscrossing protagonists—a web of life without a controlling spider— is what the film critic David Bordwell has called "network narratives."[11] Bordwell first identified this "genre" in a series of essays on Alejandro González Iñárritu's *Babel* (2006). It tells us something that this director's "signature element" is to be seen not only in cinema but in many print narrative forms with global themes. A formal principle in which several protagonists are given more or less the same weight as they participate in intertwining plotlines on several continents, and in which the story lines affect one another to some degree in a relatively short time span, is aimed mostly at showing a larger pattern underlying their individual trajectories.

The conceptual performance the novel stages is that of networks and connectivity, and this is invoked most obviously in Kunzru's allusion to "transmission" in the novel's title, at once invoking two separate but linked meanings—as the contagion of an infecting virus and as the transfer of messages in an informational network. The two discourses intersect in the novel's central crisis: the spread of a computer virus over the cyber networks. The contagion-as-crisis trope demonstrates why the network is so popular as a concept metaphor for all kinds of systems but especially its usage as the abstract technological circuitry of cyberspace and as a technological metaphor for the interconnectivity of globalization. Fredric Jameson summarizes these two relayed meanings succinctly: "Globalization is rather a kind of cyberspace in which money capital has reached its ultimate dematerialization, as messages which pass instantaneously from the nodal point to another across the former globe, the former material world."[12] This relay, I argue, has consequences for how we imagine the political and ethical questions that result from these nodal connections. With newly imagined links come new responsibilities as well as new antagonisms and new solidarities. Does imagining the social in terms of a technological network, or global capital in terms of a world-connected cyberspace, create new possibilities for political agency and social justice, or do such analogies serve only to occlude the hierarchies and inequities that already underpin the notion of a network?

My reading of *Transmission* focuses on whether the synchronous simultaneity of a network is inevitably punctured by heterotemporalities such as the differential capacities of individuals, groups, and nations to respond with the same speed to the "simultaneity of the crisis."[13] The stakes of such a reading are several, but the most significant one, as I see it, is that an emphasis on temporality exposes why we would do well to exercise skepticism when technological networks are taken to be not just analogons for the world-system (as it is in Jameson's quote) but also the very medium and glue of our social existence today. I contend that subscribing to notions of the network-as-the-social (most famously in Manuel Castells's work on "network society") promotes a sort of technological determinism that mistakes the connectivity of networks for the functioning of global capitalism as such. Such a conflation elides the political and economic reality of the present day that a large part of the world is not connected through any technological network. And even in the advanced nations where connectivity seems the norm rather than the exception, practices of networking hardly turn out to engender the abstract space of equality touted as a result of the network's flat ontologies, such as, for instance Thomas Friedman's best-selling accounts of contemporary globalization that anticipate the technological utopia of a "level playing field."[14]

The discussion in this chapter also forms a hinge in the overall trajectory of the book's argument about the importance of reading temporal disjunctures in accounts of globality. In the first two chapters, I looked at specters and attachments as concept metaphors that perform crucial narrative anachronies constituted by the persistence of the past. This chapter looks at an anachrony made possible in the present when the world is imagined in a sort of "timeless time" (Castells), where measurable distance is overtaken by the speed of transmission. If our penchant for networks is a cognitive response to a desire to grasp connections across vast swaths of space, then we should not ignore the political problems that networks also imply or the symptoms they substitute for in our everyday lives. It is not hard to see that there is something comforting and fascinating at the same time about networks. They are comforting because they project a notion of connectivity and integration in a world that is increasingly disaggregated in many spheres of human activity. Who hasn't felt the disaggregation of encountering global supply chains that disembed capital from their sites of production or the disaggregation of laboring groups whose work moves away from the site of their labor power (the body) in virtual migrations, or the disaggregation of production as commodities are made with materials from very remote and far-flung sources? If these forms of disaggregation are represented as networks, they appear to be less about hierarchies, vertical power relations, or direct cause-effect links. They seem to be more about patterns of lateral movement, horizontally oriented circuits of flows, and spreading hubs and nodes. Because they seem self-sustaining and self-regulating, networks always enjoy more descriptive than explanatory power. Less real representations of social relations, they are better understood as indicators of a widespread desire for the sort of ontology that proponents of globalization like Friedman and Castells promote—a flat ontology that is comforting and fascinating at the same time in their visual mastery. I investigate the ideological implications of the network as a model for social description, and to that end, my consideration of the limitations and possibilities of networks as a form for cultural analysis will depend on a reading of Kunzru's *Transmission* that unpacks its thematic investment in the concerns of internet or cyberpunk fiction. As I see it, the novel is a compelling instantiation of all three of the metaphorical entailments that I have discussed above: the technological network (the internet or cyberspace), the web of social life (the network society), and the economic system (global capitalism).[15] Because Kunzru writes *Transmission* in the style of corporate satire, the novel's inbuilt skepticism about networking and networkers, and its use of a hacker protagonist whose depredations create a global crisis (an electronic pandemic), gives us an opportunity to examine the language in which the networks are critiqued and to understand language itself as a site of contestation—as a common resource that is being appropriated for "informational capitalism."[16]

Transmission stages the three kinds of networks as distinct levels of the text. The novel resists a flat ontology in that the narrative structure strives to differentiate between what appears and what recedes in the text as a multilayered object, as a texturized play between foreground and background. The use of background and foreground tells us something about the author's narrative choices, about what the novel seeks to show up front and what it relegates to the level of the barely seen. In so doing, Kunzru draws attention to the unavoidable structural differentiation that narration provides as a principle of literary "worlding": everything cannot appear at once, especially when networks privilege flattened, surface-only topographies. As Benedict Anderson showed us so persuasively in his classic discussion of nationalism, there are epistemic changes afoot when a new mode of temporality signals its appearance simply by the use of the word "meanwhile" in the realist novel.[17] In the sections to follow, I will begin with a reading of *Transmission* that looks at its use of network as a technological abstraction—cyberspace and the internet. In this analysis, the notion of the topological (as opposed to measurable space) provides a key theoretical lever for thinking about narratives as networks and to explore Kunzru's use of the network as an allegory to represent the cultural impact of teletechnologies in our lives. Subsequently, I ask why narrative networks have become such fascinating objects for literary critics (and social scientists like Castells) and respond to that question by reflecting on what it might mean to think of the novel as a network in which the human subject cannot be figured as an agent—as its weaver or spider-producer. The network's narrative sprawl is achieved, I argue, by means of parataxis, deployed both as figure and as style. Using parataxis as a way to explore the novel's representational limits, I show in a third section that narrative constraints on time and space are best understood as limits of the human sensory apparatus itself. These limits tell us why the popular notion of "network society" and its appropriation of the linguistic commons are mistaken about the idea that we are indeed in a "timeless time." In the fourth and final section, I address the broadest implications of the use of networks as systems, especially as a metaphor for the current globalized economic system. Here, I draw attention to the loss of analytical precision and dissimulated ideological investments that come into play when metaphoric entailments like flows, nodes, links, and hubs are brought into an analysis of capital. In the discussions in this chapter, up front and central to each specific rendering of the network is the question of temporality. How might an accounting for temporality as a chronopolitics ensure that the network is not simply a visualized dead end of a global sublime? Would the temporal rhythms forced on us by a viral electronic pandemic—its accelerations, surges, peaks, and slowdowns, for instance—reveal the potentialities and possibilities for imagining another world, in the same way that we intuited in 2020 that there is no "normality" to which we will ever return as a result of the COVID-19 pandemic?[18] How does *Transmission* operate as a "portal" that takes us not to another space but to our world in a future time, a future for which we may be willing to fight today?

Webs without Spiders: The Internet as Technological Network

Transmission opens with the familiar hail of a phishing email, "*Hi. I saw this and thought of you.*"[19] Then the novel's unidentified narrator steps in to say:

> Maybe you got a copy in your in-box, sent from an address you didn't recognize: an innocuous two-line e-mail with an attachment.
> *leela.exe*
> Maybe you obeyed the instruction
> *to check it out!*
> and there she was; Leela Zahir, dancing in jerky QuickTime in a pop-up window on your screen.... There you were, doing whatever you normally do online: filling in form fields, downloading porn, *interacting*, when suddenly up she flounced and everything went to pieces. (*Transmission*, 3)

The conceit is obvious: an unwary reader opens the novel to encounter on its very first page Leela.exe, a computer virus that is introduced like a character in the story. Named after the rising Bollywood star Leela Zahir and resembling her in pixelated form, the virus has already done its damage, infecting hundreds of thousands of screens and causing damage in the billions to global businesses; however, the virus cannot operate like most novelistic characters. The dancing Leela with her clinging sari diverts attention from the "machinery at work under her skin" (4). As though proving this point, Leela.exe is introduced in opening lines of the novel but disappears soon after from the main action of the novel, just like a computer virus that is visible as a simple icon on the screen but is in fact maliciously working deep in the software code. What the hapless hacked user would "see" as Leela is only a "surface effect" because the "real action" is taking place in the "guts of the code"—as "a cascade of operations, of iterations and deletions, an invisible contagion of ones and zeroes" (4).

When the virus disappears into the background in the opening chapter of the novel, the story rolls out its main players, one by one, in parallel plots happening at the same time: Arjun Mehta, a programmer in New Delhi, is heading off to the job interview that will turn into a computer security job in the United States; Guy Swift, the owner of a London-based public relations company, is on a flight back to the UK after meeting with clients in Asia; the real Leela Zahir, Bollywood actress, is on location with a film crew in the Scottish Highlands; and Gabriella Caro, a freelancing publicist and Swift's girlfriend, is just waking up in her bed. These characters also circulate in the novel for much of the time like "surface effects" without intersecting at a nodal point in the plot, leaving the reader powerless to track individual storylines when they are dropped, picked up, or multiplied into clusters that never connect to each other, never, that is, till the virus upends all their lives at once.

In the same way that a narrative network is put together by bits of text, units of the story, cut and pasted together in the foreground, Kunzru renders the medium of cyberspace, in which the virus lives, into a virtual network that can appear only as an irretrievable, invisible background. The background is invisible because the virus appears only as a pixelated figure on the frozen screen, like the symptom of a deep-lying infection. In playing with the idea of a form of appearance, the novel reminds us that a "network" is not ontological; it is more about conceptual grasping of an abstract technology that we visualize diagrammatically as a structure of links, nodes, routers, and hubs. The technology is immaterial not only because its material supports (hardware and software) are tucked away from our eyes but also because data transmission is a different kind of messaging system. Our everyday experience of cyberspace tells us that we cannot grasp the internet as space of measurable linear connections between near or distant points. The internet is more akin to topological points created by the transmission of messages between hyperlinks in web pages, links that lead to other links and machines in the network. Such a technological network is impossible to map because of the size and scale of its user base and of the endless possibilities and randomness of the movements (by users) from one node to another. There are no predictable paths or circuits in these scale-free networks. Although we can conceivably map a network of computer users across the globe, we cannot map their itineraries through cyberspace.

There is no better way to demonstrate an affordance of the novel as a print form than by recognizing the novel's impossibility in representing this kind of cyberspace in its totality and scale. Kunzru offers a tongue-in-cheek transmedial experiment in *Transmission* with this blurb to begin the virus's story: "A chain of cause and effect? Nothing so simple in Leela's summer. It was a time of topological curiosities, loops and knots, never-ending strips of action and inside-out bottles of reaction so thoroughly confused that identifying a point of origin becomes almost impossible" (*Transmission*, 4). Describing cyberspace as a topological rather than topographical (or mappable) domain implies that it is a "place" without a center or an origin—a spiderless web that has no weaver, scale, or walls to which it is attached.[20]

If topology is the structuring principle for the network as cyberspace, what does it mean for the novel to attempt a representation of this space? What happens to a narrative if we actually imagine it as "loops of knots" and "never-ending strips of action"? Could the breaking and rejoining of narrative segments convey cyberspace's spatiotemporal forms through an older medium (print) that the digital has in effect supplanted? As I indicated earlier, the space of the internet cannot be cognitively mapped as a network of linear connections between distant points with sequence and directionality; rather, cyberspace involves a radical topological juxtaposition of pages in what feels like synchronous time, even though we can only access these pages sequentially, one after another. Web links access pages that are separate and discrete, of various scales and density. They appear on the screen like various views; they can be overlaid on each other but without any taxonomic order that might organize them into a hierarchy or cause-effect relationship. As Kunzru's lines of text meld into a sequence, what is conveyed through the narrative jumble is not only the media affordances of print narratives but also a cautionary note about the euphoria of the technological sublime in the era of digital technology: in the age of teletechnologies, the reader, the human being still thinks and performs space and time as extension and sequence. This does not change.[21]

Parataxis, the linguistic figure that exemplifies the breaking and rejoining of narrative, places side by side or one after another phrases, clauses, and sentences in a loose connection. It is conjunction rather than cause-effect predication or hierarchical subordination that is prioritized. Some sort of pattern recognition is needed to make these elements relatable to something else.[22] I do not mean to suggest that the idea of narrative fragmentation is specific to the notion of the network. Indeed, there is hardly an era of literary history regarding which critics have not asserted something on the order of the literary fragment as a symptom of the time. In *Transmission*, however, parataxis works in a very specific way. The electronic network is a paratactic form, appearing in narrative as pieces joined together. The imaginative work of cutting and pasting demonstrates that, like the consciousness, narrative, too, apprehends time as sequencing and space as expansion. Using the reading of a text as an analogy for reading the world, we confront the possibility that if we cannot imagine the network except through parataxis, we cannot also imagine the abstractions of any totality (such as the globe or planet), except in bits and pieces. Parataxis is a quintessentially flattening figure when it is used without something else, like a virus, to remind us that it is a surface effect. The networks that construct a flattened world use the paratactic structure of serial appearances or overlaps without hierarchical structures; without logical subordination, there is little backgrounding or foregrounding of information, as everything is made to appear at once, a synchronous effect of the texture of the narration itself. We see parataxis at work when the novel gives us a tongue-in-cheek globe-girdling view of a "quiet day" before all hell breaks loose with the virus:

> Around the world, the twelfth of June was a quiet day. Bombs went off in Jakarta, Jenin and Tashkent. An old single-hulled tanker sank off Manila, releasing its load of crude oil into the South China Sea. In Malawi a man was diagnosed with a previously unknown retroviral infection. At London's Heathrow Airport, two Ghanaian boys were found frozen to death in the undercarriage of a Boeing 747.
>
> As Guy ate bitter sandwiches with Yves, sunrise on Friday was sweeping across the Pacific. Over the Gulf of Mexico a U.S. Navy F-16 fighter made brief contact with an unidentified flying object, and at the bottom of a ravine in Tasmania a mother of two was found trapped in her Ford Cortina. . . . Arjun was still awake in his room at Berry Acres, staring at his screen. He did not sleep and went into work early, sitting on the bus listening to soundtrack from Crisis Kashmir, the one where Leela Zahir plays a soldier's daughter caught up in a web of terrorism and international intrigue. (*Transmission*, 119)

Just as identifying a point of origin is impossible in the technological network, parataxis creates the impression that there is no one actively selecting the various elements in the passage above. While three of the novel's main characters are mentioned here, there is no plot connection between Guy, Arjun, and Leela. Instead, they are randomly distributed elements without causal links to any of the other people and events that appear alongside them in the paragraph. The point of it all is to signal a synchronous simultaneity—a "quiet day" in June. But the common time is satirized: "quiet" for whom? Here too, the network appears as a web without a spider. Like the soldier's daughter in the film *Crisis Kashmir*, these random elements too are "caught up" in a narrative network that seems unpredictable and inconsequential because intended actions cannot guarantee specific outcomes. In the novel it is the virus, rather than the human characters, that sets the time line. The novel's networks rarely feel like sites of planned or directed action (after perhaps Arjun's initial hack and release of the virus). The ensuing chaos ruins the lives of the novel's main characters; they are all collateral damage of the electronic pandemic. This is why, it seems to me, the novel then offers us unplanned, nonhuman, unforeseeable elements like "noise" and "glitch" as unprogrammed transmissions, systemic interruptions that could bring about positive outcomes.

The poet Bob Perelman has argued that parataxis can be a catalyst for good, because it demands "new reading habits" or an impetus to create connections in what seem to be random and disconnected elements. By so doing, Perelman's reading subject draws attention to "the act of writing, and to the subject's own position within a larger social frame."[23] In *Transmission* we are likewise reminded in the novel's paratactic moments, of a narrator who puts these fragments together behind the scene. No one can see the "whole" world all at once. Given these sketchy representations of human agency within paratactic structures, the political implications of imagining our social lives today as human-technology assemblages can be posed as a series of questions. These are questions that *Transmission* seems happy to answer, albeit in a satiric mode.

In the wake of the internet's deterritorializing potential, its ability to disembed the human subject's location, origin, identity, and agency, what does it mean to think, as some sociologists of globalization tend to do today, of society as a network? When communicational and informational technologies, which are the machineries of reproduction rather than of production, are seen as generators, or predecessors, of social relations rather than as the effect of the latter, we have a metaleptic reversal: media's ability to appear as though it is the cause rather than the effect of a decentered, postindustrial, multinational, or global stage of capital that has been underway since the mid-twentieth century. As such, discussions of society as a network can distract us from the economic by assuming that we all now live in this brave new world of unlimited freedom of exchange, mobility, and extended associations. The imaginative flexing of the computer-as-network allows a cybernetic metaphor to operate as a shorthand not only for the world as a globally integrated circuit of nodes and flows but as a form of social organization—the networking of human beings in a virtual connected space where bodies are displaced from their locations and identities to produce deterritorialized subjects. In the next section, I discuss recent uses of the network as a model for the social and read these theoretical formulations in conjunction with the novel's parodic use of parataxis as a way of foregrounding the frictions and lags in what is revealed to be only seemingly synchronous and simultaneous.

In the Network Society, Speed Is King

When network theorists like Manuel Castells assert that networks are descriptions of specific features of contemporary society, two ontological assumptions are at work: one, that networks have replaced or will soon replace what we have previously known as social structure, and two, that the explosive advances in information technology have ensured that the organizational forms of networks (usually associated with corporate structure and capital flows) have trickled down to every aspect of social life and have changed the very ways in which human beings think about time and space.

In his magisterial three-volume study, *The Information Age*, Castells describes the development of the so-called network society as a technological revolution that is "reshaping at accelerated pace, the material basis of society."[24] While Castells grants that changes effected by technologies are strategically decisive in each historical period, he maintains that what has happened from the 1980s onward is the unprecedented transformational power of information technology in restructuring the capitalist system.[25] In contrast to the views of others like Fredric Jameson, for Castells, technology is the cause rather than the effect of global capital because, in the new informational mode of development (or mode of production), knowledge generation is the source of productivity, and information technology "diffuses throughout the whole set of social relationships and social structures, so penetrating and modifying power and experience."[26] For Castells, "history is just beginning," and in this "new existence," information will become the "key ingredient of our social organization," as "flows of messages and images between networks constitute *the basic thread of our social structure*."[27]

Thinking of the social as an abstract space of flows (rather than of location or social structures) produces a flattened ontology where the network stands above social relations and creates its own reality, a process that is self-sustaining and self-adapting. The appropriate figuration for the network as a social form is the Deleuzian rhizome. A rhizome is best understood as a contrast to the sort of thought facilitated by a tree diagram with structures and hierarchies. What it is more like is Lombardi's sprawling networks: a rhizome has no top or bottom and goes off in different directions. Connections can be made from any point to any other point. Points can be similar or different, and a part of the rhizome can break off and stand on its own. You can enter and exit it at any point. Thus, to think rhizomatically, one has to give up beginnings and endings (a narrative time line) or layers with tops and bottoms (hierarchies). Instead of a logic that proceeds in forks or branches (this or that), one proceeds in a loose conjunctive manner (and . . . but . . . so). This flat ontological surface of the network imagined as rhizome again has its verbal analogue in the rhetorical figure of parataxis, which too is capable of infinite expansion by placing sentences, clauses, and phrases one after another with minimal or no use of subordination. When structure and causality are replaced with contingency, plurality, and fragmentation, then the social order no longer has a necessary basis. As Jonathan Joseph puts it, "Just as globalizationists support the idea of the 'hollowing out of the state,' so the network theorists advocate what might be called the 'flattening out' of society."[28] This also means that we have moved beyond key features of industrial modernity, including class, the family, collective representations, the nation, and the state. Similarly, thinking of the social in terms of networks and flows implies that we have moved beyond traditional ways of theorizing postindustrial society, most notably, through analysis of class, gender, power politics, state, and place—in effect, the idea of social structure as such. What we are left with, instead, is a theoretical package that involves very little emphasis on collective struggles or forms of mass politics.[29]

Castells is, of course, aware that there are large chunks of the world that have not entered any form of this new network society, but he thinks of these exclusions as mere instances of "technological retardation" caused by cultural and social factors.[30] In other words, people who think outside the virtual channels of telecommunication are not keeping up with this connected society; this includes not only the rural poor and the underclasses of the global North and South but also those of us, who, as Gayatri Spivak puts it, "might believe in that archaic instrument called the book." Network society has no place for "those who believe that it might take time to train the imagination," because in the world of telecommunication "speed is king."[31] But Castells goes further. For him, if the network is the basis of social organization as such, then the subject's mode of perception is also going to change. Here is a key section where Castells describes how telecommunication transforms our ways of thinking: "I propose the idea that timeless time, as I label the dominant temporality of our society, occurs when the characteristics of a given context, namely, the informational paradigm and the network society, induce systemic perturbation in the sequential order of phenomena performed in that context. This perturbation may take the form of compressing the occurrence of phenomena, aiming at instantaneity, or else by introducing random discontinuity in the sequence. Elimination of sequencing creates undifferentiated time, which is tantamount to eternity."[32] In Castells's formulation we see the unmistakable logic of parataxis operating as the "elimination of sequencing," the creation of an "undifferentiated time" that, for him, is *the* "dominant temporality" of our society. In other words, split-second capital transactions, flex-time enterprises, the blurring of the life cycle, instant wars, the culture of virtual time—these are all fundamental phenomena that for Castells introduce "random discontinuity" in the sequence and "systemically mix tenses in their occurrence."[33] There is some unabashed technological determinism in these assertions, especially the proposition that telecommunication is a form of literacy that human beings acquire in an *unmediated* way. Castells does not think technology has any *specific* cultural component attached to it. Nor does he think that telecommunication is necessarily in the service of global capitalism, but rather, he believes it to be a tool that human beings have on hand to use when "networking logic" becomes the basis of social structures.[34]

These axioms are more commonplace than we may realize. One of the key ways in which globalization theory invokes a notion of "timeless time" is in its adherence to the vocabulary of "flows" and "circulations"—both of which, as I will show later on in this chapter, are entailments, or extensions, of the network metaphor. The notion of "flow," especially, imagines a world as a circuit of sped-up and self-regulating mobility. Flow also naturalizes teletechnologies and their social networks as inevitable and progressive, as shaping how human beings experience or even perceive the world. But is it the case that how human beings perceive, or sense, the world has actually changed, or is it that we, for instance, narrate the world, tell its stories, in different ways?[35]

The novel as we have seen is metaleptic in that it is an old medium representing a new technology. Therefore, the novel is a useful form to test the notion that our minds change with the technological networks, or as Castells puts it, that we can indeed eliminate "sequencing." When *Transmission* represents the electronic network and tries to mimic its circuits, speed, spatial compressions, and energetic flows, the novel attempts to foreground an abstract complexity that is often beyond the "capacity of the normal reading mind."[36] But does this mean that we have, as a society, actually entered Castell's "timeless time"? The speed of reading, and the limits placed on language itself, as the narrative mimics a network will surely tell us something about the human mind and its irreducible difference vis-à-vis the time-space affordances of the teletechnologies of communication. As my discussion of parataxis and the background-foreground distinction in the novel shows, we cannot see everything at once or without sequence. Kunzru specifically addresses the question of human thought in the network society by satirizing various attempts to control and appropriate human language—the medium in which we think and through which the social is imagined and experienced.

In *Transmission*, it is Guy Swift, the globetrotting media consultant, and his use of language that satirizes the value placed on "data" and "information": "'Humans are social,' [Swift] would remind his clients in pitch meetings. 'We need relationships. A brand is the perfect way to come together. Human input creates awareness and mines the brand for emotion. In a real way, the more we love it, the more powerful it gets'" (20). Swift embodies the ideal of a network in which speed is king (a point emphasized by his surname, which alludes to his Hermes-like role of messenger for the new world order). Through this character, a creator of marketing brands for companies, Kunzru taps into one of the key economic roles of social networks, a role that Castells, for one, does not acknowledge when he proclaims that the flows of messages and images between networks constitute the basic thread of our social structure. This is the paradox that when data becomes a form of value, human labor is no longer realized in a material product.

The abstraction of value can be grasped at the linguistic level in the novel's satire of the product that Guy Swift's firm, Tomorrow*, sells—deep branding. When Swift gets his first close-up in the novel, he is presented in a heavily mediated way, through quotes or paraphrases from the brochure he circulates to his clients, *Guy Swift: The Mission (GS:TM)*: "The future is happening today, and in today's fast-moving future the worst place to do business is the past. I strive to add value by surfing the wave of innovation. I will succeed." The narrator then takes over and satirizes Guy's mission statement in a summary:

> Tomorrow* was, he liked to say, different from other agencies. It produced results.
>
> Results*
>
> In a glittering career Guy had raised awareness, communicated vision, evoked tangible product experiences and taken managers on inspirational visual journeys. He had reinforced leading positions and project-managed the generation of innovative retail presences. His repositioning strategies reflected the breadth and prestige of large portfolios. His communication facilitation stood out from the crowd. Engaging and impactful, for some years he had also been consistently cohesive, integrated and effective over a spread spectrum. (*Transmission*, 19)

It is difficult to miss in the brochure's hyped-up language of self-valorization that Guy Swift is the brand value: speedily transportable and representable by the acronym "GSTM." The brochure achieves its persuasion-oriented hype by manipulating the common resources of everyday language into "communally desirable social information."[37] Asterisks and boldface type denote the transformation of a common word into a pending trademark or logo, and affective terms like "awareness," "engaging," and "inspirational" are blended in with the corporate-speak "product," "strategies," "project-managed," "retail," and "portfolios." It would seem that one of Swift's major achievements is transforming supersensible things into commodities: communicating "vision," evoking "tangible product experiences," and taking clients on "visual journeys." These are Kunzru's tongue-in-cheek representations of linguistic neutralization and the immaterial labor that is involved in the production of data as a value-form or commodity. It is key to the novel's satiric effect that all marketing talk sounds as empty of content as possible. In the network where speed is king, the brochure soon morphs into a form of sped-up communication, teeming with acronyms and nominalizations that, by changing adjectives and verbs into "things," also mimic the added value of the company's main product, deep branding, by transforming these words into achievements rather than starting points. "What I do," Guy tells his Middle Eastern clients at one point, "is take a business and transform it from being an abstract thing into an entity that consumers can feel emotional toward" (169). But what the brochure actually shows us is how Guy Swift takes common verbs, adjectives, and nouns and makes them into abstractions that represent value. This inspirational message that he writes down for himself, in a first-class cabin during a business trip, sums it up: "We knew how to network, how to manipulate the flows of money and information to produce **results**" (206–7).

If a character like Guy Swift in *Transmission* is satirized by means of the utopian techno-speak we associate with theorists like Castells, is it possible that an outmoded and outdated print medium like the novel also lends itself as a narratological critique of timeless time and flattened ontologies? If Castells is right, and we as a networked society have actually entered "timeless time," then the speed of reading, and the limits placed on language itself, as the narrative mimics a network will surely tell us something about the human mind and its irreducible difference vis-à-vis the time-space affordances of the teletechnologies of communication. When a novel, an older narrative form born in the era of print, now undertakes the task of representing the newer technologies of world making that have already dispensed with the very material supports (paper and ink) on which it depended, its cultural function, far from being obsolete, is, in fact, cutting edge—the temporal lag of the novel is at the heart of its critical function as a saboteur of the technological sublime. The dissonance of incorporating the network into the very substance of the novel is a way of distancing readers from the very thing (technological networks) that they, arguably, inhabit today. The novel grates against the unifying totality of the network when it confronts its readers with confusing narrative sequences, scalar leaps, and jump cuts between scenes—interruptions and breaks that belie the seamless totality, endless expanse, smooth flow, and speed of the network. This disruption in the reading experience, it seems to me, makes the novel more than a medial anachronism that is out of place and out of date. Rather, the novel's narrative drag is a form of resistance that makes its medial affordances (the limitations and potentialities of its medium) into a question about the affordances of human mental capacity in the electronic age. In other words, Kunzru's novel is a full-fledged undertaking of "narrative" as a response to the "network," both as epistemology and as ontology. When the language of the network takes over the sociological analysis of the globe today in globalization theory, and the world is increasingly imagined as a borderless space of nodes and flows and of sped-up communication, *Transmission* works against this naturalizing of a technological sublime by asking whether it is desirable to imagine the world as a network. Whose interests are advanced when the world is imagined primarily in the language of mobility and flows? Who cannot emerge as a historical subject in a world imagined as a network society?

Kunzru has often spoken of his fascination with networks. Some of the connections he makes between networks and the abstractions of the global economy are worth repeating here. In a 2013 interview, he says, "The essential nature of value in a market economy fascinates me, especially when we're talking about highly abstracted objects." Pointing to the emergence of high-frequency trading as a creation of value that is no longer tied to what Marx called "socially necessary labor," Kunzru sees the takeover of economic "life" by an abstraction: "We have what looks increasingly like a parasitical double world that is preying on the socially useful functions of markets in order to hive off profit for the people who have access to and control of the tools."[38] Kunzru believes that literary fiction has a role to play in demystifying through "narrative knowledge" and that it does a better job with understanding networks: "Never more than now, when so many of the powerful, ubiquitous aspects of our daily life are these network phenomena [that are] distributed and made up of many parts, some of which are physical, some of which are made up of data, some of which are people . . . [reification or] fixing things down becomes an important task. . . . Novels are particularly good at dealing with these and describing how it is right now just to navigate through this networked world. . . . Fiction is a network form."[39] Kunzru's response to a "parasitical double world" of finance that preys upon the unwitting participants of the market is to use satirical realism, humor, and irony as tools of demystification. But whereas Kunzru suggests that novels are useful because they reify or make "something concrete and particular out of an abstraction," I have found more compelling *Transmission*'s exposure of the spectral world of abstraction that hives off profit from "socially useful functions."[40] Its mimicking of various techno- and marketing idioms reveals the narrative form's affordances, its specific limitations and possibilities, vis-à-vis the postindustrial world of virtual media.[41] The novel's formal innovations and its relentlessly satiric thrust challenge an unqualified valorization of mobility and networks of globalization. In that the network is both a virtualization of the social and a sign of the dominance of electronic capitalism, the novel's incorporation of network elements thematically and narratively is a mode of critical intimacy that inhabits and critiques the form of the network at the same time.

Earlier we saw how Kunzru used parataxis as the verbal analogon of the internet's topological space. But parataxis in the novel is not only visible at the level of the sentence or the paragraph; one of the key narrative innovations in *Transmission* is its mirroring of the syntactic and verbal fracturing at the level of the sentence by larger-scale narrative breaks that resemble the cinematic jump cut—when the camera switches between scenes and shots without the transition of a fade-in or fade-out. These editing cuts, memorable in films like *Babel* or *Syriana*, are reminders that the globe is grasped visually, too, through modes of parataxis; we do not see the whole thing at once. Paratactic juxtapositions of this kind create breaks that belie an appearance of seamlessness or flows. Let us look at how Kunzru converts one of the exemplary spaces of flows (like airspace) into differentiated or hierarchical space:

> As the bus trundled over the Yamuna Bridge, past the huge shoreline slum seeping its refuse into the river, he [future Arjun] ran several variations of this basic fantasy, tweaking details of dress and location, identity of companion and soundtrack. . . . Lost in his inner retail space, he stared blankly out the window, his eyes barely registering the low roofs of patchworked thatch and blue polyethylene by the roadside, the ragged children standing under the tangle of illegally strung powerlines. High in the sky overhead was the vapor trail of a jet, a com-

mercial flight crossing Indian airspace en route to Singapore. In its first-class compartment sat another traveler, rather more comfortably than Arjun, who was squashed against the damp shoulder of a man in a polyester shirt. Did Guy Swift sense some occult connection with the boy on the bus thirty thousand feet below? Did he perhaps feel a tug, a premonition, the kind of unexplained phenomenon that has as its correlative a shiver or a raising of the hairs on the neck or arms? No. Nothing. He was playing Tetris on the armrest games console. (*Transmission*, 11)

Here the text interrupts an abstract space of flows (airspace) by slicing it horizontally into several zones. In the same narrative frame, we get the contrast between those who are part of the network but exist at different levels of access and speeds (up-down, plane-bus, first-class cabin–public transport) and those whose mobility is arrested by internal borders of class and caste (the displaced poor, migrant workers, and urban slum dwellers visible from Arjun's bus window). Kunzru brings both network and mobility as global imaginaries under scrutiny. The passage does this by distinguishing between Guy's unfettered border crossing in airspace and Arjun's crossing of class, cultural, and national borders as a tech worker.

We might think of Arjun as a worker caught in a labor flow that moves software programmers and tech workers from poor countries to the iconic centers of the US tech revolution like Seattle and Silicon Valley. Similarly, Guy Swift might exemplify the informational flow of consultants or transnational elites who commute between global cities. However, Kunzru's novel, while it trucks with representations of hypermobile people and objects, stops short of celebrating this mobility by including elements of friction within the speed-driven and peripheral circuits that lie outside the more visibly integrated circuits. For instance, the novel's juxtaposition of ubiquitous "nonplaces" (spaces of flows like airspace) to the equally ubiquitous places of arrested movement (urban slums that don't belong to a hypermobile world) suggests that a mode of stop and go, rather than hypermobility, is the novel's take on the real condition of most people in the contemporary world. This narrative slicing of vertical space through spatial parataxis resonates with Michel Serres's characterization of the globe as a message-bearing system with different lanes. Guy Swift in the sky draws attention to the space that Serres deems the "province of airline companies and of international purveyors of information by means of orbiting satellites." (Today one could add the military-industrial complex with its drones to this list.) Serres's semi-theological topology of the "new, single, global city" produces a fundamentally divided space: "upper quarters" for the "wealthy and well appointed" and "nether zones" of "abysmal poverty."[42]

When we encounter Arjun at his destination in the United States, the novel begins to satirize the trope of mobility as such. Like the trundling bus of the earlier example, the novel homes in on a figure "trudging along the margin of a wide California highway. One foot in front of the other, each pace bringing him a little closer to the point, marked with a low concrete barrier, where the Taco Bell lot ended and the Staples lot began." Anyone on foot in suburban California is one of four things, the narrator tells us: "poor, foreign, mentally ill or jogging." For the soccer moms zipping by in SUVs, he was "a blur of dark skin, a minor danger signal flashing past on their periphery." And to Arjun, the pedestrian, the soccer moms were "more cosmological than human, gleaming projectiles that doppplered past him in a rush of noise and dioxins, as alien and indifferent as the stars" (*Transmission*, 37).

Kunzru's satire measures the alienation of this tech worker as an extrusion of the network society. Moving on foot is a sign that Arjun is not fully incorporated into the technological networks of the upper strata. The repeated cookie-cutter environment of California suburbia appears as a sort of nonplace when contrasted with Silicon Valley, the fantasy space of flows for tech workers. By keeping Arjun stuck in one of the lesser circuits that services the Valley region without intersecting with the production lines of its highly skilled labor pools, the novel makes the astute point that some of the most visible hubs of flows in a network render invisible the lesser circuitry on which they also depend. A. Aneesh explains this structural invisibility as a deliberate obfuscation: "The existing institutional setup of the modern nation-state, despite a long partnership with transnational capitalism, still depends on a categorical closure between the citizen and the alien. To protect the citizen, it must restrict the alien's field of operation and mobility."[43] As guest worker, Arjun remains in a perpetual transit zone, the inhabitant of crowded hostels where the on-off rhythm of work generates its own labels. When not working, the tech workers refer to themselves in subcontractors' parlance as workers in a "body shop," who are "on the bench" or "on the beach" (*Transmission*, 44). The subcontracted worker is an integral part of labor pools moving from poorer to richer countries, but the novel's point is that, rather than thinking about these circuits as flows, they are better understood as forms of interrupted operations, where access to workers is ensured but their employment is "flexible" and dependent on the needs of the company at any given time; they can be partial, part-time, overtime, piecemeal, or temporary workers who are not added to a US company's payroll. The novel deflects the movement of these labor pools not toward the expected destination of a global city but toward a shadow zone existing within the banal everyday of a California suburb, where the workers cross a frontier (rather than a border) and where wages can be depressed without public outcry.[44] As Arjun explores America through ten-block walks, his pedestrian, feet-enabled mobility is a jab at jet-setting elites like Guy Swift in their first-class cabins. Spaces of flows, Kunzru wickedly reveals, are set out in lanes, and they differ by speed, altitude, and class. The novel's narrative friction interrupts the abstract borderless spaces, seamless transitions, and multidirectional hypermobility we normally associate with networks.

The geographer Mike Crang records his skepticism about sociological analyses of the so-called interstitial spaces of social life by asserting that they have their own blind spots with regard to economic class: "The studies of nonplaces are often studies of elite spaces. . . . What is a nonplace for one may be a place of employment or exploitation for another."[45] Similarly, Castells's idea that the dominant aspects of social life are increasingly operating on the basis of exchanges between electronic circuits linking up information systems in different locations ignores fundamental dichotomies between the space of flows and the space of place.[46] The space of flows is characterized by what Castells calls timeless time, but as we have seen through our reading of *Transmission*, the narrative network cannot but appear as a space of hierarchies and borders. In the novel, these "nonplaces" of mobility (airports, airspace, hotel lobbies, Silicon Valley, high-rise condos, Dubai) are shown to be places of managed mobility through which global inequality is visible. This single passing image of Dubai, for instance, is a good example: "In the distance a city skyline was approaching and half-built skyscrapers soon started to appear at the roadside, their skeletons crisscrossed by plastic lines hung with the drying dhotis of Indian laborers" (*Transmission*, 166).

We might now add that the novel represents the multidimensionality of networks (the technological, sociological, and economic) by using three distinctive levels of narration. At one level the novel assumes the shape of the technological network we refer to as cyberspace. The attempt to represent this spatial matrix ends in expected failure, for the novel cannot materially embody this kind of network. This failure, however, is the basis of the crucial insight that the novel's expression requires the cut-and-paste of serial strips (parataxis) and the structuring and sequencing of language in order to be understood. At another level, the level of its linguistic expression, the novel parodies a neutralized and reified use of English associated with communication in the globalized network society.

In parodying the registers of techno-speak, the narrative challenges the degree to which we can imagine ourselves in a posthuman world of network society without the subjectivity of the language animal. Finally, at the third and most abstract level, *Transmission* incorporates a computer virus as a character in its fabula. By sensing the life of this virus in the deepest recesses of computer code, but unable to register it except through its effects, the novel gestures to a totality that lies beyond the capacity of the reading mind and renders the network as an analogon of the whole economic world-system of present-day multinational capitalism.

The Time of Capital

The release of Arjun Mehta's virus, Leela-exe, generates a narrative "friction" ("glitch" or "noise" in a transmission) that disrupts the seamless surface of communication. The impact is widespread as public and private networks go offline and crash. With this plot development, the novel announces that it is not in the camp of utopian fiction that endorses the power of electronic media to reshape the world for good. When the Leela virus brings down computer operating systems all over the world, not everyone bears the brunt of the fallout in the same way. Arjun is dismayed to find that his company (the main target of his hack) designs new antivirus software for immediate sale as if to say that in electronic capitalism when data is the value form, crisis can become profit. However, the virus brings Guy Swift's firm, Tomorrow*, to near collapse as it corrupts servers and sabotages much-needed contracts. The narrator delivers the news about the fate of the network society's most celebrated denizen with some relish. We learn that Tomorrow*'s Shoreditch offices in London have been sold and that "the old sweatshop now houses a direct-mail company." The retreat into the past is Kunzru's satiric thrust at the network that makes speed into king. Tomorrow's owner and CEO, Swift? He leaves his glass-fronted, Thames-facing, wirelessly smart apartment for a "single-story stone cottage" designed to "withstand battering by the Northumbrian wind and rain" in a bleak countryside that "has changed very little in hundreds of years" (*Transmission*, 257–58). As Guy Swift goes off the grid, his girlfriend Caro kills herself. The actress Leela Zahir contacts her now-notorious ardent fan, Arjun Mehta, and the two seem to vanish together from the material world. The end of the novel finds them ghosts in the machine, traceable only through bits of data *about* them—blogs, websites, essays, postings, images, video, and so on—that are constantly generated and circulated by their online fans and followers.

The novel's most abstract use of the technological network as a metaphor for the globalized capitalist system may owe something to the historical banality of the technology itself. In contrast to the compelling literary representations of machinery, steamships, trains, and planes of the nineteenth and twentieth centuries, the technological networks of computers, mass media, and information processing of our age cannot be visualized as awesome spectacles in themselves. Fredric Jameson has suggested that perhaps it is this lack of visual and emblematic presence that increases these newer networks' metaphorical potential. Appearing less in their own right, they can appear as embodiments of something else, as allegories or "distorted figurations" of the fascinating and mesmerizing networks of power and control that are difficult for the human mind to grasp—the "whole world-system of a present-day multinational capitalism." Thinking of the network as "representational shorthand"[47] for the complex and often invisible object worlds of global capital lets us imagine an occult zone in which capital is dematerialized in an ultimate sense: here we have not just money but its abstraction as finance capital, with postmodern avatars like derivatives, commodity futures, and SWAPs that need neither production (as capital does) nor consumption (as money does). Accompanied by its new electronic supports, this multinational capital is further dematerialized as bytes and "messages" that pass instantaneously from one node to another across the globe and jump from place to place like a virus. But is the technological virus, which, as we can see, is *already* a metaphorical rendering of the biological virus (since the eighteenth century, an "agent" that causes an infectious disease), more enabling or disabling when used as a linguistic figure for thinking about the temporal rhythms of global capitalism?

In *Transmission*, the virus Leela.exe, never able to appear as itself, takes the form of a dancing pixelated figure on computer screens. By keeping the virus as an active agent in the background, Kunzru adds a layer to the text—a layer of the code where much of the viral action is happening but that can never quite be penetrated or rendered visible. With this occlusion, the network itself becomes a second-order surface behind which another complex process is unfolding, a process that at times may be initiated by a human agent, but that never remains under the control of its creator. A central argument of my book is that literary representations of contemporary globalization, for the most part, do not conceptually penetrate the abstract layer of the social in which capital operates, and that some of the terminology that theorists of globality use, like "flows" or "circuits" (also a metaphoric entailments of the cybernetic metaphor of "network"), actually tend to distort human agency and make social and economic life into a reified thing in whose processes (beyond our comprehension and control) we are caught. Yes, networks are webs without spiders, but only if we are looking at certain ways of being a spider. The question of human agency in a network requires us to rethink both the human and the agentic at the same time, and this conundrum is placed before us by the novel's creation of a spectral layer in the narration that is distinct from the technological network in which the virus appears. Simply put, Kunzru prevents the conflation of technology with capital. He lets us imagine a level of abstraction behind the flat surface of networks and flows. By doing so, the very act of abstracting is made into a human endeavor—not an indication that something has gone dark, beyond our perception, but that we know that it is there. We only have to find better and better ways to grasp it in all its complexity. One of the common characterizations of agentic movement in the network is provided by language of flows, but this comes with its own problems.

The conflation of the network with phenomenal forms of mobility (of people and things) is partly responsible for that way in which, as Mary Louise Pratt puts it, "flow" now exemplifies the "official, legitimating language of globalization." "Flow," she points out, is not a "value neutral term, but a positively valenced term (contrast 'drain') used detached from any ethical dimension."[48] Pratt's main criticisms of this widely used metaphoric entailment of the network resonate nicely with Kunzru's critique:

Flow creates a flattened ontology—a horizontal equilibrium of leveling forces by which the world resembles a contour map rather than a relief map—without top or bottom, without hierarchies of hills and valleys. The metaphor does not allow us to distinguish between one kind of movement and another: between the travel of globe-trotting elites like Guy Swift, the migration of transplanted workers like Arjun Mehta, or the smuggling of the refugees caught in the dragnet of immigration laws at the novel's end. It does not also make visible the immobile, or resource poor, who cannot enter the flows and circuits of global exchange. "'Flow' bypasses the question of directionality."[49] Who benefits and who loses in global flows? Do global flows track which way the movement of resources and people tend to go? Which flows tend to be unidirectional movements from rich to poor countries, and vice versa? The metaphor of flows tends to naturalize economic processes and occlude the role that state policies, immigration laws, or institutions play in mobility. Similarly, "transnational culture" becomes a neutral term for the diffusion of cultural phenomena like Hollywood films and the English language, without addressing how even global markets of cultural exchange depend on power differentials. "'Flow' obliterates human agency."⁵⁰ Flow is an intransitive verb that does not account for who *sends* and who *receives* or who *decides* to move or who *refuses* to move.

Transmission provides a critique of this ubiquitous trope of hypermobility most obviously in the lampooned figure of the jet-setting Guy Swift, but also by means of a constructed fictional world where all mobility is shown to be a differentiated process within an abstract and deterritorialized space. In this space of flows instead of journeys with resting places, origins, and destinations, we simply have repeated patterns of circulations. For instance, the abstraction of the space of flows is belied by those who move and those who are arrested by borders of race and class. In the novel, transnational global flows are lanes of mobility of different speeds with upper and lower circuits of movement. Finally, by allowing its readers to sense that the story line and the object worlds of the network are surface effects behind which something else is happening, Kunzru presents a deep structure where a powerful, but invisible, virus is at work in ways that will affect the fates of all its main characters. This multistoried structure, as I will show, offers us a way of imagining capital as a totalizing but abstracted activity that is happening away from the surface phenomena of circuits and flows.

Away from the surface phenomena is the destructive work of the virus as a nonhuman agent, but the virus is more than a Frankenstein-like monster that comes back to annihilate the life and career of its creator (Arjun Mehta) and those who operate within the media technology sector (like Guy Swift, Gabriella Caro, and Leela Zahir). The virus also acts like another powerful economic monster—the abstraction we call finance capital. Like the phantasmagoric realm in Jacques Derrida's *Spectres of Marx*, the novel too allows its readers occasional glimpses into a vast, worldwide, disembodied, spectral domain that lies behind the story line and the object worlds of the network. By analogy, *Transmission*'s contagion crisis may be read as capitalism (as an economic rather than technological network) that spreads not like a slow wave or an expanding network but like clusters formed by the infections of virus-like capital that leaps from place to place, like a free-floating epidemic that has to play itself out. The virus is a common trope today among cultural theorists looking for better concept metaphors to grasp the invisibility of capital's movements, its transformation into algorithmic data, and its accelerated global movement as "bytes" of data. For McKenzie Wark, "capital is the virus of abstraction" because it enters into any and every kind of social relationship, corrupts it, and "makes it manufacture more relations of abstraction."⁵¹ In his discussion of finance capitalism, Jameson turns to the metaphor of the epidemiological virus as a way to understand the abstraction of capital in a new historical phase. Finance capital, as he sees it, has to be "something like a stage in the way it distinguishes itself from other moments of the development of capitalism." Drawing on Giovanni Arrighi's insight that capitalism does not develop in a straight line but might well "organize itself in a spiral," Jameson eschews teleological determinism as well as the "mythic overtones of the various cyclical versions." He attempts instead the formulation of a cyclical scheme that posits capitalism's movement as "discontinuous but expansive," that with each "crisis" mutates into a "larger sphere of activity and a wider field of penetration, of control, investment, and transformation."[52] Thus, discontinuity can be positioned "not only in time but also in space," and it has to add the "historian's perspective," which must attend to "national situations" and the "uniquely idiosyncratic developments within the national states" as well as greater regional groupings. In other words, the capitalist process cannot be captured in the flattened ontology of an expanding network representing a larger and wider sphere of activity. The leap from geographical space to geographical space involves two temporalities—both "local teleologies" and "spasmodic historical developments and mutations." Thinking about the development of capitalism as an epidemic, or a "rash of epidemics," allows us to grasp a systemic logic that undermines and destroys what is already in place (whether precapitalist, traditional, agricultural, or industrial societies and economies). But like epidemics that play themselves out as herd immunity increases or there is no one left to infect, the capital-virus leaps to "new and more propitious settings" in which preconditions are favorable to renewed development.[53] It is important to note that Arrighi's spiral model that Jameson is characterizing above incorporates long periods of time and leaps. The "long twentieth century" that stretches from fourteenth-century Renaissance Italy to sixteenth-century colonial Spain and from seventeenth-century colonial Holland to the twentieth-century United States is in three stages and takes six centuries to unfold. But each of these stages has in common a time when capital is ready to take flight to move onto its new hot spot and new cluster. In each of these long historical stages, capital shows the same internal movement—a phase 1 when capital is invested in trade, a phase 2 when it is invested in agriculture and manufacturing, and a third phase of financial expansion when the "withdrawal of profits from the home industries" leads to a "feverish search" for new markets. This is the stage of economic globalization we are in right now—although trade, agriculture, and manufacturing remain sectors of capitalist investment in national economies, "capital has itself become free-floating." Now, separated from geographical context, capital is no longer, as Jameson puts it, "cotton money," "textile money," or for that matter "oil money" or "tech money."[54] It no longer lives in factories or on various sites of production but lives in an entirely new context—the floor of the stock market. Some of the novels we have read show this supplanting. The cybernetic revolution represented in *Transmission* has overtaken that earlier historical moment in Kincaid's novel (chapter 1) when Lucy overhears Lewis on the phone with his stockbroker and wonders whether "that" has anything to do with the lives they lead. The network as a technological metaphor is thus a cultural expression, an attempt to grasp a problem of abstraction that is even greater in degree than the abstraction of money. As telecommunication technologies seem to abolish space and time by making capital transfers virtually instantaneous across national spaces, transactions of immense quantities of money at a blink of an eye speed have made such processes incalculable and unrepresentable (a problem addressed in the next chapter). If Jameson is right and the speed of teletechnologies has intensified the abstraction of finance capital, then the cultural expressions that attend these economic changes have also aimed for new artistic perceptions (like parataxis) and perceptual categories (like network).

In *Transmission*, reading globalization as a sort of electronic network (cyberspace) in which money capital is completely dematerialized and passes instantaneously from one nodal point to another means that the crisis set off by Leele. exe the computer virus is the Arrighian moment of feverish search for new markets, the moment in which the logic of capital leaves behind its factories and workforce in ruins and takes flight elsewhere. It is interesting that even the crisis in the novel reads like that crucial moment of transition in Arrighi that exhibits, as Jameson puts it, paradoxical (dialectical) turns whereby "winners lose and losers sometimes win."[55]

Guy Swift's magnum opus is an insidious anti-immigration project called PEBA, or the Pan-European Border Authority, a wing of the European Union intended to "harmonize the immigration and customs regimes of all the member states" (*Transmission*, 122). Swift, our inveterate border crosser, imagines a virtual border post (using biometrics and social tracking) to stop the undocumented and the poor from coming into the EU. His sales pitch to the EU is cooler, less ominous: "What my team has come to realize is that in the twenty-first century, the border is not just a line in the earth anymore. It's so much more than that. It's about status. It's about opportunity. . . . Like we say in one of our slides, 'the border is everywhere. The border . . . is in your mind'" (235).

Swift's software will transform Europe into a nonplace—"the world's VIP room," reserved for the highest levels of frequent flyers and income brackets (239). But the project is doomed because it, too, does not escape the Leela virus.

The day the virus peaks in its infection worldwide coincides with PEBA's first coordinated action, called Atomium—a sweep aimed at taking five thousand *sans papiers* off the streets overnight and deporting them to their countries of origin in express time. In the wrong place at the wrong time when the virus hits, Guy Swift is accidentally caught up in the sweep. He finds himself in the back of a van filled with East Africans and Chinese migrants making its way through Brussels to a deportation hangar at the airport. It is a classic case of mistaken identity, but as the narrator tells us with obvious glee: "How Guy Swift, young marketeer, British national and vocal speaker of English came to be identified as Gjergi Ruli, Albanian national, suspected pyramid fraudster and failed asylum seeker in Germany, was one of the more bizarre stories to result from the infection of the Schengen Information System by what is known as the Variant Eight Leela, the so-called transpositional worm" (*Transmission*, 263). Jet-setting consultants get a taste of their own medicine as the shuffling action of the virus produces a number of false positives in the system. Deported to Albania, Swift pawns his Rolex to get on a smuggling boat that is carrying a Bangladeshi family to the Italian coast. There, washed ashore on a tourist beach after being dumped by the smugglers, he is apprehended and held by the Italian border police till his identity is finally verified.

As the network becomes a dominant and inevitable model for economic organization in our age, the place of the human and human agency is unclear. This is why the novel's reminder—that when the space of flows requires the management and arresting functions of borders, it is the human body that is caught in the dragnet—is an important one. Even in this age of virtuality and mobility, we seem to be returning to some fundamental forms of inequality and class struggle. When Arjun releases the Leela virus as payback for his dismissal from his job, he cannot calculate the outcome. The unforeseen mutations and variations of the virus as a machinic life form are a metonym in the novel for actions and events that exceed the intentionality or advance calculations of the human subject. However, to read the virus as a metaphor for capital also means acknowledging that, in the end, there is the physical human body that acts as a mediator in the movement of the virus, in its infection—as its creator, as its unwary host, as its manipulator and facilitator, and as its exterminator. The disappearance of the virus-creator Arjun reminds us that, indeed, *it is the human body that is the continuing glitch in the global network*.

Isn't this the lesson that the recent COVID-19 coronavirus outbreak has brought home to us in such a terrifying way? In an essay penned during the pandemic, Arundhati Roy asks, "Who can use the term 'gone viral' now without shuddering a little?" A common metaphor used to describe the transmission of speedily and widely circulated internet messages is now feeling the force of a real (literal) event, and a metaphor's vehicle has temporarily recalled its tenor's borrowing privileges. Roy offers a metaphor of her own in the title of her essay: "The Pandemic Is a Portal." Portals are gateways or doors to other places, but in sci-fi, a portal also means a gateway to another time ("a time portal" like a wormhole). More recently, portals have come to mean the main sites or terminals on the internet from which users can go to multiple other sites. The discursive nexus between the epidemiological and the technological looks like it is here to stay, and Roy's contention that "the virus has moved freely along the pathways of trade and international capital" suggests that economic networks in fact enabled the global spread of the virus. I take that to mean that the COVID-19 pandemic is not simply a metaphor for capitalism but a byproduct of the system, a system that by enabling capital's penetration into every nation, city, and household has in turn created the pathways for an almost synchronously simultaneous infection—it took only a few weeks for the virus to move into every corner of the world. But, as Roy also points out, unlike the flow of capital, this virus merely seeks proliferation, not profit, and has thus "inadvertently to some extent, reversed the direction of the flow." Even Kunzru's dystopian novel could not imagine a shutdown of the scope we witnessed in March and April 2020. Like the Leela virus, COVID-19 has, as Roy reminds us, "mocked immigration controls, biometrics, digital surveillance and every other kind of data analytics," but it has struck hardest as Roy says "in the richest, most powerful nations of the world, bringing the engine of capitalism to a juddering halt." In this mass shutdown, Roy sees potential, a time of reflection, temporary perhaps, "but long enough for us to examine its parts, make an assessment and decide whether we want to help fix it, or look for a better engine."[56]

A biological virus has brought the global economy to its knees, but the power of the false dichotomy between "saving lives" and "saving jobs" tells us that there are always new ways for economic experts to spin the yarn of the logic of capital. This logic continues to have dissimulating power; it is still capable of persuading workers even in the midst of an economic shutdown (because human bodies cannot be risked) that the same bodies are not the engine of value creation. When the crisis hits, however, the invisible support systems of the so-called networked society are no longer glimpsed like the construction workers' *dhotis* described in *Transmission*, fluttering bits of cloth on the scaffolding of high-rises in Dubai. They are now more like the masses drifting on makeshift boats toward Europe.

These are the extruded masses of the recent pandemic, on the streets, running the "essential" services, while the wealthy and middle classes stay and work from home, an irony hard to miss when such a designation could not raise these workers' minimum wages before or after the pandemic. The masses who are now patching up the broken agricultural supply chains were the same ones threatened with deportation a few months ago. In India too, the picture is bleak: now driven out by their employers and landlords and forced to march as "migrant workers," until a few weeks ago they were Indian citizens from another state. Here at the phenomenal level, the fake reality of a technological network standing in for a social of timeless time is torn asunder—we are not all networked. At another level, there is the painful awareness that the neat diagrammatic controls of imagining the world as a network has forced a spatialized imaginary that hid the chronopolitical implications of the connections it traced.

In *Transmission*'s ending, Kunzru leaves us with the feeling that when epidemics play themselves out, they will catalyze the world to a new equilibrium. This is where the novel comes closest to a notion of incalculable future outcomes. The novel's irreducible plurality with its interweaving multileveled and multistoried form guards against the possibility of a single plot destiny or cause-effect outcome that would help us look into the past or the future and draw straight lines to either one from the present. This formal divergence expects us to consider whether the intensified integration of global capital today does not also allow for unforeseen connections, surprises, and possibilities. That fictional imagining has become reality as this pandemic reveals our world to be a doomsday machine, in which as Roy puts it, there is no possible return to normality, no possible way to stitch our future to the past. What we are faced with (unless we want to delink and retreat to a hovel in Northumbria like Guy Swift) is to break with the past and use the opportunity to imagine the world anew. And in this world imagined anew, it is not the relinking of broken supply chains that will matter anymore but whether in choosing to walk through this portal, we want to drag along with us the failed experiments of our world, a world that has finally exposed the fragility of its globalist economic fantasy and the corroded base of what seemed to be an unshakeable edifice.

CHAPTER FOUR

Markets
Capital and the Resource of Time

The language of "networks" and "markets" is so seamlessly fused in contemporary descriptions of the global economy that it is hard to see what the latter term shares anymore with its premodern meaning—the market as a fixed place for people to buy and sell goods. Networks, as we have seen, exchange a sense of place for mobility and time. They intoxicate us with their ability to enact movement across an abstract space while also feigning a worldwide simultaneity, a sense of time according to which the individual could be "in any place at the same time and participate in everything happening elsewhere."[1] It is as if the present is everywhere because one can easily communicate with people all over the world. However, the tendency to talk about markets using the language of telecommunications is not surprising in light of the expansion of market forms under globalization. Markets, as we understand them today, are concept-metaphors for the highly abstract economic transactions that are increasingly virtual and time determined. As such, the very notion of global markets indicates a hollowing out of the present—a present that is hard to occupy because of the speed at which the transactions take place and because such accelerations project the illusory synchronicity of a connected globe. Markets have also made their way into personal subjective time, or the lived present of biographical time that is the basis of everyday life. This cultural process, often captured in phrases like "the financialization of daily life," suggests that we are now able to apprehend a social imaginary that provides ideological support to the new markets and that ensures, as the sociologist Randy Martin puts it, that "finance, the management of money's ebbs and flows, is not simply in the service of accessible wealth but presents itself as a merger of business and life cycles, as a means for the acquisition of self."[2]

This chapter looks at three contemporary novels that illuminate the temporal experience of the market from two distinct scales: that of subjective everyday life and that of the macro level at which "free" markets created by neoliberal reforms have found their way to the poorer countries of the Global South, as national trade barriers came down in the 1980s and socialist states retreated from their caretaker roles in providing public welfare and public goods. In this macroeconomic "history," we hear a tale about the growing abstraction of a self-regulating system as national markets join the circuits of international commodity trade and the virtual markets of financial capital. In the virtual markets of high-stakes speculation, a fraction of the world's elite transacts with the future and successfully raids the present. The temporal capture I describe here is exemplified in the way new financial markets handle risk by means of instruments like derivatives and dynamic hedging, which create speculative products that allow the value of future returns to be converted into present value.[3] Joseph Vogl sees their key role to be the transformation of uncertainty: "If the price of future risks can be converted into current payments then future uncertainty can be calculated and compensated for in the present."[4] Such a commodification of the future as a valued calculation of risk inevitably makes any present economic value increasingly hard to perceive (or calculate) even as it also reproduces the paradoxical (and unverifiable) truism that markets will always perform efficiently in the long run. This faith in the long run continually runs afoul of our own experience over the past three decades in which it has been abundantly clear that unexpected busts have rapidly overtaken the rewards of expected booms.

Our experience of the market today shows the merging of the financial system and the subjective-social experience into a vanishing point that is not a goal-oriented future but an "endless series of anticipations."[5] Here, the story is of the market's social and ideological hold over cultural life as it has evolved fully into what Charles Taylor calls a "social imaginary." This imaginary, which once shaped the ideas of influential modern thinkers like Adam Smith, David Ricardo, and Karl Marx and of dominant social classes like the bourgeoisie, now makes financial logic self-evident in our descriptions of every realm of social life.⁶ In the contemporary era we encounter a paradoxical state of affairs that operates at the two different levels I have identified: on the one hand, there are the computer-generated algorithmic abstractions that rule our economic activities in ways that we will never fully understand, while on the other, economic reason in the form of transactional and monetary relationships insinuates itself into every aspect of private and intimate life, encouraging us to take up a new kind of entrepreneurship: investing in ourselves and directing our lives into temporal cycles determined by the financial world. For literary scholars, the growing abstraction of the financial system and its capture of daily life holds particular interest. When the market becomes multileveled, hypertrophic, and abnormally large, does it lend itself to narrative treatment? Can literary art provide a "solution" that connects disparate sectors of the market into a unified whole so that they can be grasped in all their contradictions?

The works of the three authors I discuss in this chapter, Mohsin Hamid, Aravind Adiga, and Don DeLillo, respond to these questions in compelling ways, and they do so by repurposing allegory as a narrative genre that delivers a multileveled structure of meaning. I will show how the allegorical mode effectively tackles the scale variance we face when analyzing the market as a macroeconomic abstraction of global transactions and as the more microscopically and ideologically charged social imaginary that insinuates itself into everyday lives. Central to my discussion is the premise that while specific stories of the biographical and the everyday in these novels differ depending on where the neoliberal transformation of an economy is taking place, the novelistic representations of these changes by Hamid, Adiga, and DeLillo show how we have underestimated the power and resilience of allegory as a structural genre that has immense cross-cultural potential. My readings of these novels will foreground the temporal regimes embedded in the allegorical form, the premise being that it is in such structures, rather than the topographical descriptions of the stories themselves, that the novels undertake a critique of transnational capital—how it makes time into an infinite and inexhaustible resource. On the one hand, market time is rendered into more and more abstract and hence inaccessible forms of exchange, while on the other, at the level of the subjective, of biographical and everyday life, individual experience, under the pressure to accelerate, is sensed as an "extended present" that has no use for the past and is driven by the desire for the new. I borrow the term "extended present" from Helga Nowotny, who uses it as a way to signal how neoliberalism removes real choices pertaining to one's future and replaces them with something along the order of "flexibility," a term that in its corporate usages shows how effectively private resources can be appropriated from their employees' everyday lives. When work and free time, paid and unpaid time, are increasingly blurred in ways that accelerate the lived present of everyday life, or when transactional relationships and temporal availability dramatically shift how subjects experience the bar between work and home, the resultant feeling of "not having enough time" effectively abolishes the future as a planned goal and replaces it with the time of an extended present.[7]

When these heterotemporalities converge in Hamid's *How to Get Filthy Rich in Rising Asia* (2013), Adiga's *White Tiger* (2008), and DeLillo's *Cosmopolis* (2003), we encounter a much more complex repurposing of allegory than those previously attributed to twentieth-century writers such as Thomas Pynchon by critics like Maureen Quilligan (whom I will discuss shortly). These novels don't use allegory as if its cultural power is diminished under the dominance of modern realism, or as if its narrative meaning involves an unsophisticated symbolic practice with limited aesthetic potential. Rather, these novels stand forth as *neoliberal allegories* that produce a new critical view of market culture in which we see the combination of two notably divergent views of how allegorical meaning works. I suggest that neoliberal allegories work on two axes: they incorporate Quilligan's notion of "horizontal" meaning or narrative wordplay in which meaning accretes serially; however, they also work on an axis she believed to be "absolutely wrong" in her analysis of the genre—allegory conceptualized as a multileveled genre having a "vertically organized fictional space."[8] Quilligan's analysis is a direct challenge to the model that Fredric Jameson presents in his recent work, *Allegory and Ideology*, that details allegory's multileveled structure and argues that the genre's most recent versions are symptomatic of a time when the "illusory surface of existential life" (of which the "synchronous simultaneity" of global networks and flows may be a good example) makes it difficult to represent how the "tectonic plates of deeper contradictory levels of the Real shift and grate ominously against one another." In other words, wordplay generates illusory surfaces while allegory's nonliteral levels access deeper contradictions that cannot be expressed in the surfaces of social life. For Jameson, allegory in the global era does not function as a two-level parallel plot that uses a code to establish a one-to-one correspondence between a "primary narrative" and a secondary one that becomes the "meaning" of the first. It is a narrative mode that strives to set "incommensurable forces . . . in relationship with one another in a way which, as with all art, all aesthetic experience, can lead alternately to ideological comfort or restless anxieties of a more expansive knowledge."[9] Thus, not just two levels, but four, maybe more.

Jameson's rendering of allegory as "fourfold" identifies as many levels of meaning starting from the "simplest" elements to its more complex forms: the *literal* or the historical level, which coincides with the primary story of the text, such as an actual history of economic restructuring in different national contexts (the Pakistan, India, and United States of our three authors, for instance) and classes of individuals like entrepreneurs, who are receptive to these changes. The *allegorical* second level, which forms a dual narrative with the first, is where the historical-literal story reduces itself to certain elements (like a character's obsessive desire to accumulate wealth or certain keywords associated with abstract ideas) and establish points of sustained comparison to something else, such as the economic doctrine of neoliberalism. The emergence of a third level, the *moral* or individual level, where we perceive the construction of subjectivity and the biographical progression of a protagonist, tells us that first two levels are insufficient to represent the social imaginary. Finally, there is the *anagogical* or collective level, where we sense the "political unconscious" that is "always latent in conceptions of our own personal destinies."[10] At the anagogical level, complex relationships come into play: this level might overshoot the subjective level and pose as the absent cause of the character's actions, or it might return to the literal-historical level and represent the more abstract economic relations of the capitalist mode of production that prevails in that national context. The "bet" of fourfold allegory in Jameson's analysis, "lies in its promise to hold all four levels together in an original and somehow inseparable unity, albeit a unity of differences."[11] Indeed, neoliberal allegories are so conscious of the interlacing of the systemic and subjective, of finance capital and everyday life, that such a unity is part and parcel of the three novels discussed here. My analysis of the different levels of allegory is less interested in seeking out gaps between them, as in showing the temporal structures that are specific to each of them and relatable to the temporal regimes of the others. The stakes, as I see them, are both epistemological and political. Unless we render the tectonic shifting plates of the economic market as events with temporal and spatial dimensions, we cannot grasp how the economic occupies our experience of time and remakes it into temporal regimes, for it is in that shift that time itself becomes a resource that can be "occupied" by capital. Political visions that remain fixated on spatial reoccupation and wealth redistribution tend to underestimate the potential of chronostrategies that could change the very relationship of everyday time to the time of capital.

The shift I propose reframes the ways we think of temporality in relation to capital, first, through an analysis of those time units that constitute what is called the lived present of everyday life, and then, through an analysis of economic practices like entrepreneurship and speculative risk that I see as complex deployments of time aiming to control, colonize, or defer the future endlessly. I propose that we read narrative texts like novels, not for their social realist rendering of our contemporary world as much as for their conceptual performances with market time and their use of contrasts between the time of work and so-called free time in representations of biographical and everyday life. Furthermore, as multileveled narratives, novels bring to the fore ways of representing time that cannot be perceived in the everyday or measured by the human mind, such as the abstract time of market risk. Novels play with background-foreground distinctions and in so doing reveal points of conflict between levels, such as when the national-historical mobilizations of great public institutions like the state and the economy are confronted by the temporal perspectives of their suffering citizens and workers. When levels grate against each other in this way, they can interrupt the visions of neoliberal economic restructuring with the perspectives of others who are bystanders or expendable victims in its wake. This is why I have focused my reading of allegory as a mode of temporal unfolding that delivers the multilayered time and space of global capitalism through a shorthand—neoliberalism—as the most recent version of systemic penetration by the market into realms that were previously marked as "free" or "intimate" or "common."

By rewriting stories of individuals in terms of an explicit rather than a subtle "master code" (neoliberal economics), the three novels I discuss in this chapter reveal how *Homo economicus* (the European historical subject of possessive individualism) involves a colonization of what we are fundamentally, what *is* human, even if this notion of the human is contingent on the social imaginaries that are already in place. Social theorists' understanding of this seismic political-economic shift that neoliberalism entails in the late twentieth century is captured by the title of Wendy Brown's recent study *Undoing the Demos: Neoliberalism's Stealth Revolution*. In this book Brown details how a "neoliberal rationality disseminates the *model of the market* to all domains and activities—even where money is not an issue—and configures human beings exhaustively as market actors."[12] The stealth of this revolution, she argues, is attributable to the manner in which neoliberalism "interpellates" us to act like "market subjects" in domains where wealth generation was not a priority, such as, for instance, in education, health, fitness, family life, or neighborhood. The private-public distinction that was fundamental to the demarcation of civil and political life from the eighteenth century onward is no longer an economic boundary. The buyer-seller relationship becomes the basis of all social relations, or, as Brown puts it trenchantly, "in contrast with classical economic liberalism, we are everywhere *homo oeconomicus* and only *homo oeconomicus*."[13]

In what follows, I begin with Hamid's novel, *Filthy Rich*, where I look at wordplay in allegory as a novelistic technique that generates different levels of meaning. Here, I depart from Jameson's emphasis on simile in place of metaphor and argue that wordplay (especially metaphorical wordplay like personification) is an important axis of meaning in allegory because it creates a spatiotemporal network of meaning that traverses the text by way of linguistic differentiation. Furthermore, *Filthy Rich*'s wordplay also generates through its glossing of terms like "entrepreneur" and "self-help" personification as a chronostrategy that emphasizes questions of neoliberal restructuring in the time of ordinary living. In *Filthy Rich* one worthy response to these questions involves the novel's use of biographical narration as a tactical entry into the dimensions of personal time and individual life spans.

The remaining two sections of the chapter focus primarily on the vertically organized levels that Jameson's model identifies. My discussion of Adiga's *White Tiger* looks at allegory as a mode of historical analysis in the neoliberal age. Adiga's narrator, "the White Tiger"—an entrepreneurial figure like Hamid's protagonist only more rapacious—dismantles and repurposes the self-help book, a genre often associated with the ideological advocacy of free enterprise and possessive individualism. "Don't waste your money on those American books," exhorts the narrator of *White Tiger*. "They are so *yesterday*. I am tomorrow."[14] The pronouncement that something is "so yesterday" indexes the narrative's allegorical reference to the time structure of the market's creative destruction; however, the novel is not only interested in the one-to-one matchup of the character as the personification of economic doctrines like neoliberalism but also the White Tiger as a version of the *Homo economicus* emerging from the historical transition that liberalizing India underwent since the 1980s. The novel taps into a temporal complexity whereby an extension of a present is constituted precisely because there is no value put on historical consciousness. Market time is the novel's ideological dismissal of the past as something not worth being understood or accounted for in the present—or for that matter, the future. What Adiga effects through the Tiger's blatant dismissals, and the reader's reversals of these dismissals through satire, is to bring into play the discounted and dismissed past as a time that bursts into and shapes the present. Here the "shock" of allegory (to use a phrase from Walter Benjamin's discussion of history as allegory) provides the temporal structure that brings the layer of the literal-historical into a productive intersection with both the individual-moral as well as the anagogical-political layers. Benjamin's theory of allegory facilitates a consideration of a shock dimension—"allegory appears suddenly and without prior preparation."[15] In Adiga's novel, over and over again, despite the Tiger's drive for a tomorrow that propels him toward the goal of wealth (the moral-individual level), the historical past empties into the present, revealing older hierarchies of domination that are not yet over. In a move that resonates nicely with Benjamin's metaphor of constellations, *White Tiger* creates a "present" in a neoliberal Indian landscape that is disturbingly unsettled by the narrator's biography and the country's history as a postcolonial nation. Finally, the novel's brilliant prestructuring of nocturnal narration and diurnal silence presents a reversal of "natural" circadian rhythms (like Scheherazade's perilous one thousand and one nights) and belies the so-called synchronous simultaneity of global networks. The White Tiger's success as an entrepreneur who has to "watch his business all the time" is ironic (*Tiger*, 7). As the owner of a taxi service that ferries workers to an outsourcing call center in the Indian city of Bangalore, the Tiger's fantastic notion that his company "virtually runs America now" is only further evidence that the natural temporal rhythms of human life cycles can be dictated by transnational capital from another time zone.

The discussion of market time as the time of global financial capital is the focus of the third and final section of this chapter. Here, the subordination of everyday life to capital time moves beyond the temporal availability of a call center, Adiga's Bangalore that works for the United States during the night. For DeLillo, the intensified, accelerated market time is the continuous 24/7 functioning of the tele-connected global financial market. Like the nocturnal narrator of Adiga's novel, DeLillo's protagonist in *Cosmopolis*, Eric Packer, is an insomniac, a currency trader for whom sleep fails "not once or twice a week but four times, five."[16] The time of finance capital is 24/7 and operates, as Victor Li puts it, as "a future-oriented worldview" that remains troubled by the times that cannot enter this temporal regime and are therefore to be dismissed as "anachronistic and obsolete."[17] It is true that the value of the hours the billionaire Eric Packer spends sleepless are worth many times over those of a worker in the White Tiger's call center; however, both index a temporal regime of availability that in a different economic era might have been called "overtime." *Cosmopolis* addresses the most abstract layer of economic time through its focus on algorithmic machine time and the sorts of data that are beyond the reach of the human mind and the daily time in which the narrator's biography unfolds. For DeLillo's protagonist "nothing existed around him. There was only the noise in his head, the mind in time" (*Cosmopolis*, 6), and it remains to a chorus-like figure, Vija Kinski, Packer's "chief of theory," to translate this affective condition into the terms of a financial market for which time is already posthuman: "Time is a corporate asset." It "belongs to the free market system" (79).

Taken together the three novels show us the powerful temporal structuring of everyday life, which the novel plots using biographical time, as that realm is penetrated by the regimes of time fixed and governed by the market. Tracking this restructuring of the everyday transnationally through three contemporary novels written a few years apart, between 2003 and 2013, allows us to link their historical contexts. As my readings show, the common use of allegory gives us an alternative way to read the feudal, the industrial, and the post-Fordist not as stages of development that different nations go through but as local configurations of what is ultimately a single system connected globally. This was the lesson, I believe, Jameson intended to convey in that infamous essay written many years ago about "third-world allegory."[18] Clearly, Jameson's longstanding admiration for the genre is now more palatable when it is presented in terms of allegorical systems that are related to the "dimensions of their respective social formations" and forms of otherness that allow demographic access to those billions of others with whom we have to coexist in the era of globalization.[19]

Biographical Time of the *Homo economicus*

Hamid's *How to Get Filthy Rich in Rising Asia* parodies the so-called self-help book, a genre that embodies the paradox of market society's contractual model: free individuals giving away the labor of their bodies and minds while still endeavoring to preserve a vision of themselves as autonomous, choice-driven, self-regulating entities. For the market, subjects are first and third persons at the same time, acting as agent in one and objectified by market forces in the other. If the market is now in the pores of cultural life, we might think of the self-help book as a cultural form that embodies exchange in its self-reflexive structure: narrative mimics the buyer-seller relationship in the linguistic exchange of the narrator and the reader. But where we might expect to see reciprocal acts creating a social totality that then governs their individual actions, in Hamid's parody of the self-help book the narrative contract that creates the illusion of a free and autonomous reader (who helps herself by reading the book) is thrown into disarray by the creation of a third party—a "you" that is neither the narrator nor the reader but an empty slot in the narrative that can be occupied by both. I will say more about this later.

In what is still regarded as one of the most comprehensive and thoughtful studies of the structural genre, *Allegory: The Theory of a Symbolic Mode,* Angus Fletcher gives us an imagined encounter with the allegorical agent: "If we were to meet an allegorical character in real life, we would say of him that he was obsessed with only one idea, or that he had an absolutely one-track mind, or that his life was patterned according to absolutely rigid habits from which he never allowed himself to vary. It would seem that he was driven by some hidden private force; or viewing him from another angle, it would appear that he did not control his own destiny, but appeared to be controlled by some foreign force, something outside the sphere of his own ego."[20] Fletcher's notion that an allegorical character is obsessed with a single idea and has a "one-track mind" is a wonderful encapsulation of how the trope of personification works. Fletcher's inclusion of a "hidden private force" that seems to control this character from "another angle" outside the "sphere of his own ego" and endows it with the doubled and split nature of subjectivity (as subject and object of power, as self and other, as I and you), succeeds in adding another level (of the anagogical or collective) to that of the moral-subjective. We can now ask what pulls the strings of this obsessed subject. Yet the allegorical narrative of *Filthy Rich* eschews the relatively static, primary-secondary, one-to-one correspondence that often accompanies personification, as in the entrepreneur or *Homo economicus* embodying or being pulled by the doctrine of neoliberalism. Instead, the novel develops its plot of the narrator's biographical life as if it were patterned into a program of getting filthy rich in twelve steps, by deconstructing the meaning of terms like "entrepreneurship" and "self-help" and showing them to be diminished words that are now being actively resignified by another source—neoliberalism. The modern meaning of "entrepreneur" as a go-getter who undertakes a risky enterprise is what organizes the plot of the novel and directs its action. Terms like "self-help" and "entrepreneurship" generate a series of associated action words like "get," "move," "work," "focus," "learn," and "strategy" that move us along the various steps of the program, with chapter titles like "Move to the City," "Get an Education," and "Focus on Fundamentals."[21]

On first pass, Hamid's novel is a perfect primer for an imagined reader who wishes to master instrumental reason, to *become* the very human being that neoliberalism posits as universal to all human societies: "We are everywhere *homo oeconomicus* and only *homo oeconomicus*" (Brown). Indeed, the series of pointers in the twelve chapters, the "steps," are so general that they seem to work without much cultural translation. As Koray Çalişkan and Michel Callon have pointed out, models of instrumental rationality are sufficiently abstract to have "universal scope," but to guarantee their universal applicability to a wide diversity of observable realities, one simply has to posit that the ends being pursued are culturally defined.[22] On a second pass, we notice that entrepreneurial principles get a curious makeover when Hamid transforms some of the key action verbs into instructions. Moving to the city involves living in a slum, getting an education means joining the student wing of a political party, learning from the master means marketing illegal goods, and then there are instructions that would make any neoliberal guru nervous: "be prepared to use violence," "befriend a bureaucrat," "dance with debt," and "patronize the artists of war." Hamid's execution of a series of metaphoric substitutions succeeds in depriving entrepreneurship of its sensuous fullness. In Hamid's fictional Pakistan, a country under military rule and a player in the US military theater in South Asia, the market is violence, it is bureaucracy, it is war, it is debt, and so on and so forth.

"Allegory is in the realm of thought what ruins are in the realm of things."[23] The principle of resignifying words makes up one side of Benjamin's well-known formulation; the other side, that of empirical ruins, is the focus of the next section. Hamid's wordplay generates an allegorical experience of reading that resonates with Benjamin's linguistic insight that allegory works in the wake of the ruination of meaning, when ordinary words become allegorical emblems in a profane world that is "robbed of its sensuous fullness, robbed of any inherent meaning it might possess, only to be invested with a privileged meaning whose source transcends this world."[24] The notion that allegory involves animating words with new meanings brings me to the key point about allegorical wordplay in Hamid's novel: it turns on its ear Jameson's recent observation that in allegorical meaning, it is metaphor that arrests time and constitutes stasis.

In *Allegory and Ideology*, Jameson argues that metaphor (as opposed to simile) denarrativizes narrative by arresting its temporal movement and preventing access to other levels of meaning: "The horizontal momentum is disrupted, we pause on a vertical association and linger in some metaphorical perpetual present (or eternal present, out of time), which brings to a halt that onward rushing temporal momentum that the simile only tends to accentuate. Simile redoubles the power of narrative, while metaphor arrests it, transforming epic back into a lyric stasis."[25] Jameson's view that metaphor creates stasis instead of temporal momentum and impedes our movement through the various levels ("pause on a vertical association") is questionable, given Maureen Quilligan's persuasive point that wordplay is "basic" to allegory. If we follow her cue and look at Hamid's use of personification, often regarded as one of the most trustworthy signals of metaphor in allegory, we see anything but stasis. Instead, the novel uses personification to unify the four levels of allegory that operate together in the text—the literal level of the narrator's story as a successful entrepreneur, the allegorical level of the self-help book as a guide to entrepreneurship, the moral-subjective level of the self-fashioning of an "I" and a "you," and the anagogical or collective level, the political unconscious, of the market as a neoliberal social imaginary driving a new mode of production. The novel's literal-historical level is the sparsest one, because the events of the narrator's life are listed without the empirical realities that would allow us to concretize the abstract landscape of a Pakistan that is rendered without proper names, dates, or recognizable historical events. Such emptiness at the literal-historical level lets personification emerge even more fully as the connective tissue between the subjective-moral and the other two levels.

Both personification and its related rhetorical figure of prosopopoeia involve a comparison that is in the mode of metaphor rather than simile; they do not claim an object or action is "like" another object or action but that is literally the same object or action, with the added caveat that the object being described is not human but being described as human. When allegory makes inanimate nouns animate, we get further exfoliations of plot and move away from phenomenological descriptions of abstractions like neoliberalism to an ethics, the way an ideal life should be lived. Therefore, personifying neoliberalism in the figure of an entrepreneur, a more recent iteration of the *Homo economicus*, reminds us of Karl Marx's defense of the trope in the first volume of *Capital*: "Individuals are dealt with here only in so far as they are the personifications of economic categories, the bearers of particular class relations and interests." Marx's point was that if one's standpoint viewed the development of the economic formation of society "as a process of natural history," then one cannot "make the individual responsible for relations whose creature he remains."[26] To put it differently, personification for Marx is not the valorization of the individual as agent but a literary exercise that deconstructs the mysterious transformative relationship between commodities and people in the market. Similarly, Hamid's narrator is a caricature in his obsessive single-mindedness, and satire exposes this figure to be a representation of the political and economic class interests whose creature it is and who are the sources of its cultural power. In the life story of the novel's unnamed entrepreneur referred to as "you" (a further emptying out of the figure into an emblem), Hamid allegorizes a neoliberal program that operates without the constraints of civil institutions and civil society that we would expect in wealthy nations, and in so doing, this programmed path to wealth reveals much-needed detours as neoliberalism ends up increasing rather than decreasing the hold of coercive institutions like the army, the police, the bureaucracy, and the black marketeers.

As the chapter titles unfold in succession, the entrepreneur-narrator of *Filthy Rich* does not "pause on a vertical association" as Jameson suggests, but makes it part of the unfolding of the story itself. We get a series of vertically organized levels that start with the entrepreneur's family moving to the city from a village. The novel then scales upward and outward into social institutions that control the socioeconomic mechanisms: schools, religious groups, criminal networks, small businesses, bureaucracies, political parties, the military, the government, and above them all, the real master pulling the strings of neoliberalism—the market. In a chapter titled "Dance with Debt," the narrator confides in the reader in language that evokes the power of the market as an unseen force, "Leverage is flight . . . a glorious abstraction, the promise of tomorrow, yes, a liberation from time" (*Rich*, 180). The operative metaphor here is of cybernetic teletechnologies that are seemingly more appropriate to Don DeLillo's New York than a poor South Asian country: "Over the coming months your business is quantified, digitized, and jacked into a global network of finance, your activities subsumed with barely a ripple in a collective mathematical pool of ever-changing current and future cash flows" (183). Hamid's narrator never leaves Pakistan, but the point is that once he reaches the level where his business gets a loan from a bank that leverages itself on the international financial market, he has become part of the cosmopolis that DeLillo's novel uses as a powerful allegory of the market.

Anna Kornbluh's insightful analysis of Marx's use of personification gives us another way to think of how the allegorical narrative of *Filthy Rich* establishes a much tighter correspondence between the moral-subjective level of the narrator's story and the anagogical-political level of economic restructuring under neoliberalism: "Personification as a conspicuously brandished endowment of the commodity body with a soul here figuratively records and performs the phenomenological and corporeal transformations precipitated by exchange."[27] What Kornbluh's link between the commodity and market-determined exchange suggests to me is that if neoliberalism authorizes new forms of value and exchange, then personification can disclose this material transformation of the commodity body, even as it shows the objectification or reification of a personal life into an investment. If reification is how capital turns an activity into a thing or object, then personification reverses that process by turning objects into speaking things, an exchange in which meaning may be reversible. To put this in context of Hamid's novel, we are motivated to look for a closer link between personification and the ideological power of neoliberalism itself as the will to transform everything into commodities and everyone into entrepreneurs.[28]

As I have discussed earlier in this chapter, Wendy Brown understands neoliberalism to be much more than a set of ideas or a resetting of the state-economy relation. For her it is a "normative order of reason" that has developed since the 1980s into a widely disseminated form of global governance that "transmogrifies every human domain and endeavor along with humans themselves, according to a specific image of the economic."[29] Individual human agency is defined as an essentialized, economizing behavior or instrumentality, where individuals are decision makers who choose between alternative means to maximize their utility with a minimum of effort. David Harvey makes this connection between the market and individual freedoms when he argues that neoliberalism is, in the first instance, "a theory of political economic practices that proposes that human well-being can best be advanced by liberating individual entrepreneurial freedoms and skills within an institutionalized framework characterized by strong property rights, free markets, and free trade." The state has a role to play in creating and preserving this institutional framework, but beyond that the state should not venture.[30] Such a theory also sees all human societies "as collections of choice-making individuals whose actions imply trade-offs between alternative ends and the various means to attain them."[31]

Thus, it is the autonomous "I" (the possessive individualist) that is the first target of Hamid's satire. This is a self that represents the illusory and ideological underpinning of "self-help" and autonomy, the building blocks of *Homo economicus* at the individual scale but also the ideological basis that provides the rationale for neoliberalism's dismantling of welfare and socialist economies with their safety nets and caretaking states in the name of individual "freedom" and "liberty." Hamid's first rhetorical ploy is to satirize the very genre (self-help) in which the novel has clothed itself: "Look, unless you're writing one, a self-help book is an oxymoron. You read a self-help book so someone who isn't yourself can help you, that someone being the author. This is true of the whole self-help genre. It's true of how-to books, for example. And it's true of personal improvement books too" (*Rich*, 3–4). The linguistic strategy that shores up the deconstructive ploy is the use of the second-person throughout the book. The sleight-of-hand, whereby someone else's life, achievements, and advice can be ingested as "self-help" by an ideal reader, works partly because of the dialogic principle of the "I"-"you" exchange. When a narrator speaks in the first person, the reader is an engaged but silent listener—the "you"—for whom the narrator's speech is intended. However, unlike a real conversation between two people, the reader cannot respond and take the place of the "I." When Hamid's narrator speaks entirely in the second person (a technique that Hamid also uses in his earlier novel, *The Reluctant Fundamentalist*), the reader is put on the spot and realizes that she cannot occupy the role of an active "I." This realization breaks the dialogic illusion that, as Hamid suggests, makes neoliberal interpellation work its magic: "The idea of self in the land of self-help is a slippery one. And slippery can be good. Slippery can be pleasurable. Slippery can provide access to what would chafe if entered dry" (4). The idea that the "self" or in this case, the standard use of the I-you dialogue in self-help books, works as a lubricant for the thrust of neoliberalism goes to the heart of what we have called the economizing of the social, where human society is analyzed as a collection of choice-making individuals whose actions imply trade-offs between alternative ends and the various means to attain them. Neoliberalism screws you but lubricates this violation with the offer of possessive individualism.

Hamid's novel in tandem with the other two discussed here suggests that the global dispersal of marketization has given rise to a new literary mode that might rightly be called "neoliberal allegory."[32] This mode satirizes the ideological branding of the "free market" as the creator and guarantor of individual freedoms, the conflation of free markets with democracy, and the conflation of the *Homo economicus* with the citizen-subject. In so doing, these allegories also add a component that has received less attention: they provide insight into the temporal structures that are commensurate with the various levels at which the allegories operate. They allow us to see, one, how financial markets have enabled versions of the future to raid the present and, two, how neoliberal marketization of everyday life has created an extended present from which it is difficult to imagine a future in which the subject's own biographical life span has any significance. Yet in that novels are ultimately multilayered allegories, Hamid's text reveals other temporalities that shift and grate against one another and therefore resist the capture of the everyday by the time of capital. For instance, in comparison to the living labor of human beings, capital offers temporal availability that far exceeds that of the organic and biological sphere. Perhaps this is why the most unexpected move in *Filthy Rich* comes in the tenth chapter, when the how-to book about getting rich reverses course and becomes a story of downward mobility, bankruptcy, and dispossession.

This is not to say that the novel is unaware till this late in its narration about temporal conflicts. Early in the novel while recounting his childhood, the narrator describes his father's labor as a cook in terms of "units of backbreaking toil" measured in "hours and days and weeks and years." The father accepts his situation because he cannot see labor as anything but an exchange of "an allocation of time in this world for an allocation of time in this world" (*Rich*, 7). There is presumably no surplus value to be made here; in the life of the narrator's father, a poor migrant worker, to work is to live and die at the same time in equal measure. The novel juxtaposes the expropriation of the father's life span to the narrator's own fantasy of a good life spent acquiring wealth. On getting rich, the narrator too hitches his biographical life to the market but in a way that allows him to flex the exchange relations between time and money. It is to Hamid's credit that *Filthy Rich* makes market time out to be indifferent to gender: the reader is sensitized to the fact that a woman cannot tell a story of entrepreneurship in the same way—the single woman with no economic means is under pressure to use her body as labor power. Running alongside the narrator's story is that of an unnamed "pretty girl" who is his first love interest and who, like him, leaves the slum in quest of wealth. While their parallel tracks rarely intersect in the story, the narrative calculates lost time for both of them. Neither has time for intimacy or friendships till a chain of events—the narrator's heart attack, a lengthy hospitalization, and the embezzlement of his funds—reverses the course of the story.

In the penultimate chapter, the narrator finally tells us that the game is up. He confesses to certain "false pretenses" under which he has been doling out "economic advice" in what is now revealed to be a self-help book written by a failed entrepreneur (*Rich*, 201). Chapter eleven finds him at eighty years of age, bankrupt and in frail health with limited savings, barely enough to rent him a room in a two-star hotel and pay his medical bills. As the narrator describes his daily routine, we sense that he is mostly relieved to have been separated from his fortune and that he enjoys a life that expects no financial rewards for his contributions. His motivations now stem from "lingering desires to connect and to be of use, from the need to fill a few hours of the week and from curiosity about the world beyond" (204). One day, the narrator encounters "pretty girl" in a pharmacy, and they sit down to tea and talk about "what ex-lovers meeting again after half a lifetime usually discuss" (210). At this point, the narrative tempo slows down to keep pace with the advanced age of "you" and "pretty girl." The remaining years and months of their lives are detailed in lyrical prose as time frees up for them to take in new experiences of the world and of each other: "She sees how you diminish her solitude, and, more meaningfully, she sees you seeing, which sparks in her that oddest of all desires an I can have for a you, the desire that you be less lonely" (213). We now understand what the narrator means when he announces how it suits him to have few possessions because "having less means having less to anesthetize you to your life" (191). The final chapter, ironically titled "Have an Exit Strategy," awaits the narrator's final performance—he goes further than any narrator does by describing his own death. The ending may seem sentimental, but the conceit works because it is the time of one's own mortality that is incalculable and endlessly deferred by the market when it constitutes an extended present with its vision of endless satisfaction of wants, a stockpiling of acquisitions without end.

The philosopher Bruno Latour has argued that thinking of capitalism as an economic "system" creates only helplessness because it makes the economy seem absolute, limitless, transcendent, and immutable. Any "radical critique" of such a "system" should avoid, he contends, falling into the trap of jumping to another superior level. Instead, critique should follow the "exact same paths" through which any "market organization" spreads, amends, modifies, and corrupts.[33] Hamid's novel, it seems to me, is a critique that follows the path of a cynical economic reason that does not respond to the sentimentality of everyday suffering; however, Hamid does not dispense with the idea of an economic totality (for what else must we think it when neoliberalism aims to transform at the infrastructural and the subjective level). In the allegorical impersonation of a self-help book that makes it speak against itself, as an "other" speech, *Filthy Rich* unifies the collective and the subjective levels of allegory without losing sight of how they grate and shift against each other. In the next section I discuss *The White Tiger*, another novel that repurposes allegory to challenge forms of neoliberal rationality. Adiga's rapacious entrepreneur dispenses with all niceties when his successful enterprise comes about through murder and fraud. Here, the "shock" of allegory is delivered by way of this calculating violence and by a historical displacement that demolishes the postcolonial confidence of the neoliberal project in a developing nation, a confidence embodied by the frightening White Tiger himself.

The Allegorical Shock of History

In *White Tiger*, the double representation of allegory is achieved by the act of speaking otherwise—through the satiric possibility of ventriloquism or a "speaking other." Here, we might think of personification as a form of impersonation by means of which a figure displays the inner thoughts not of an object but of an adversary. Allegory as prosopopoeia lends voice to an idea or an abstraction like the market, or conversely, it can transfer the voice of the market to someone else, placing it in a vastly different figure, as a ventriloquist would. When an unashamedly cynical character voices the shibboleths of the free market and represents murder as an entrepreneurial act, such a transference exposes, in turn, the cynical, exploitative, and predatory nature of neoliberal reforms in poorer countries. The clichés of neoliberal economic doctrine thus issue from an unlikely and illegitimate spokesperson: Balram (also known as the White Tiger), whose self-identification as a successful "entrepreneur" is made on the basis of his ascendancy from the position of poor domestic servant to owner of a taxi-service business. In this act of "speaking otherwise," the servant appropriates the language of his employer, the underclass the language of economic success, and the criminal the mantras of the entrepreneur. In Adiga's novel, when Balram, acts as the mouthpiece for entrepreneurial success, we encounter neoliberal mantras as profoundly destructive and monstrous as criminality. To these mantras the novel adds another level of meaning that emerges at the literal-historical level—a dark national past that has been replaced with the fake contemporary of a shining new India.

In *White Tiger*, the temporality of the market represented as a "creative destruction" of rural collective life (the anagogical level of the mode of production) is allegorized in the figure of a driven entrepreneur who heads for the city, but that perspective is accompanied by a literal-historical level that reads this individual's fate as that of a nation. On the one hand, we have Balram's anticipation that he is living in a new age in which the motive is profit and innovation, and competition must drive out the old and usher in the new. On the other, there is the story that is readable literally on the surface: of India, a nation undergoing a seismic shift, where an economic structure is incessantly destroying the old one from within, incessantly creating a new one.[34] This historical prestructure is embedded into the epistolary form in which the novel's narrative unfolds for its reader.

The novel is written in the form of a long letter penned by Balram over several nights and addressed to the Chinese premier, Wen Jiabao, whose visit to Bangalore, India's silicon city, in 2005, was heralded by local media as an occasion for the two nations to put aside their historic rivalries and welcome a new "Asian century."[35] The impending event frames the literal-historical level of Balram's story in *White Tiger*—the march of postcolonial India toward regional and global dominance in the twenty-first century. Hearing a radio announcement that Jiabao's mission was to meet Indian entrepreneurs and hear the story of their success from their own lips, Balram offers his own life story as an example.

Unfolding in a sequence of nightly narrations, in seven chapters running sequentially from "first night" to "seventh night," the story's opening header does much to ensure a unity of the novel's literal, moral, and anagogical levels:

From the Desk of:
"The White Tiger"
A Thinking Man
And an entrepreneur
Living in the world's center of technology and outsourcing
Electronics City Phase 1 (just off Hosur Main Road)
Bangalore, India. (*Tiger*, 3)

The discrepancy between the story of the entrepreneur and that of a nation is ironic and hard to miss. The heading alludes to India's neoliberal restructuring beginning in the 1980s as it went from a socialist welfare state that restricted foreign investors to the "world's center of technology and outsourcing." We learn that Balram is the proprietor of a taxi service that owns twenty-six vehicles and proudly claims on its website, "We drive Technology Forward" (301). Adiga's joke is a pun on "drive." A forward-looking (driven) entrepreneur makes his money driving call center workers around at night, not exactly a great example of technological "innovation." Instead, Balram is a quintessential facilitator of temporal availability: he makes it possible for young Indian men and women to spend their nights working for the tech sectors of Western countries. There is no missing the satiric thrust of Adiga's critique of India's disproportionate investment in the technology sector when the Tiger politely informs the premier, "Apparently, sir, you Chinese are far ahead of us in every respect, except that you don't have entrepreneurs. And our nation, though it has no drinking water, electricity, sewage system, public transportation, sense of hygiene, courtesy or punctuality, does have entrepreneurs. Thousands and thousands of them. And these entrepreneurs—*we* entrepreneurs—have set up all these outsourcing companies that virtually run America now" (4). The jarring juxtaposition exposes a neoliberal lie. On the one hand, we have the ruins of the postcolonial Nehruvian socialist state of the 1950s, a newly independent modern India that had promised to provide basic infrastructural support and amenities to all its citizens. This is the state that neoliberal economic restructuring undermined by doing away with poverty alleviation and welfare-oriented policies. On the other hand, out of these ruins emerges Balram's vision of a land teeming with entrepreneurs, mostly resource-poor and rural people who are expected to inherit the new century. The novel's allegorical plotting depends on a recurring wordplay alluding to entrepreneurship at the individual level and economic development at the national level. Corresponding to these two levels are different structures of temporality. "Like all good Bangalore stories, mine begins far away from Bangalore. You see, I am in the Light now, but I was born and raised in the Darkness" (14). At one level, Balram's biography as a rags-to-riches story is a teleologically driven plot that unfolds over several years, from a poor childhood in a North Indian village to the life of a small business owner in Bangalore city. At another level, which holds together the literal-historical story of liberalizing India and anagogical level of its political unconscious, it is the collective historical past of India that enters into the "shining" illusory present, as a shadow cast over it, as the darkness of unfulfilled promises, bringing with it the cannibalizing violence of a jungle (of which the White Tiger is the most exceptional animal of prey).

The mapping of India into competing areas of darkness and light is a wicked take on the "India Shining" slogan of the Bharatiya Janata Party in the 2004 national elections, when the right-wing nationalist party tried without success to showcase India's globalizing urban economy as a world in which all Indians benefited equally. Balram's phrasing thus draws attention to what lies hidden outside the penumbra of the political spotlight and outside the media appetite for feel-good numbers and data about economic success—the darkness of the impoverished rural. It is this rural that appears from the shadows of neoliberal reforms and that gives this novel its most brilliant allegorical shock effects at the literal-historical level.

When Balram's birthplace, the village of Laxmangarh, makes its appearance, the narrator directs his sarcasm at this recent dissimulation of the rural in the national story:

> I am proud to inform you that Laxmangarh is your typical Indian village paradise, adequately supplied with electricity, running water, and working telephones; and that the children of my village, raised on a nutritious diet of meat, eggs, vegetables and lentils, will be found, when examined with tape measure and scales, to match up to the minimum height and weight standards set by the United Nations and other organizations whose treaties our prime minister has signed and whose forums he so regularly and pompously attends.
>
> Ha!
> Electricity poles—defunct.
> Water tap—broken.

Children—too lean and short for their age, and with oversized heads from which vivid eyes shine, like the guilty conscience of the government of India.

Yes, a typical Indian village paradise, Mr. Jiabao. (*Tiger*, 19–20)

Balram casts aside the smoke and mirrors of official data deployed by the Indian neoliberal state to reveal an "other" India—home to the disenfranchised millions who live without infrastructural support and who are only bystanders in the nation's march into the Asian Century.[36] Readers who are familiar with literary and filmic tropes of postcolonial modernism in twentieth-century India will recognize what Adiga is doing with the village of Laxmangarh. The allusion to a "typical Indian village paradise" reminds us that a modernist aesthetic celebrated the city as the space of modern citizenship while preserving the rural as a geographical metaphor for cultural ethics. To grasp what *White Tiger* does with this geographical divide, we might find it useful to turn briefly to an example of what is being parodied in the novel. Here is Vinay Lal's description of the rural as modernist aesthetic in a review of Bimal Roy's classic socialist-realist film *Do bigha zamin* (1953):

> The contrast of the village and the city is as old as literature itself, and it would not be too much to say that each has had its advocates. The village furnishes a "moral economy" which anchors lives and customs; but the village is also incapable of providing sustenance in conditions of modernity, and its inhabitants are bred in an atmosphere of ignorance, open to exploitation and oppression. Yet Bimal Roy is equally candid in his representation of the brutality of city life, of the callousness, anonymity, and instrumentality that appear to mark most human relationships in the urban setting. Not all that strangely, almost the only occupants of the city who display any humanity are recent migrants from the village.[37]

The migrant to the city in the 1950s film is already a displacement of the socialist state's avowed caretaking role that has not extended to the rural (or preserved the small and the beautiful); the village will perish under the influence of the city. In Adiga's novel, if the same message resonates, it does this not by invoking sentimentality about a vanishing rural but by extending neoliberal values into that space of potential nostalgia. In the film, *Do bigha zamin*, Roy is "unequivocally clear that the morality of the oppressed [the migrant Sambhu] is superior to the morality of the oppressor." Lal describes how, in a touching scene from the film, Sambhu loses the patronage of the family whose two children he ferried to school on his hand rickshaw but forgoes another customer to take the two little girls to school without payment. The message is clear: one cannot put a price on every human activity, nor ought human relationships be subjected to the "laws of commodities."[38]

In Adiga's novel we get Balram, the rural migrant turned entrepreneur with a vengeance, rising up in a world where nothing and no one can escape the law of the commodity, his rags-to-riches story made possible by murdering and robbing his former employer. Meanwhile, Balram's father, also a rickshaw driver (the figure of rural ethics), is consumed by hard labor, feudal oppression, and his own rapacious family—a form of cannibalism figured allegorically as the endemic violence that accompanies supralevels of rural exploitation. Neoliberal political legitimacy, like that of the economic formations that preceded it, is based on narratives of "fading memory and blunted sensibility" that erase the historical violence of capitalism in the villages.[39]

The image of Laxmangarh is ripe with the kind of signifying power that Benjamin invokes with allegory's double structure—operating synchronically within language (what I have been calling wordplay) and diachronically within history as a past to which one turns for inspiration rather than out of nostalgia.[40] Here, the representational process of allegory is constituted by an internal difference: between an old meaning that is lost and a new one that replaces it, between a past historical ruin that is almost forgotten and its reappearance in memory as a transformative image for the future. Unlike ancient or early modern allegories, whose mode was a gateway to a transcendental, often divine or didactic, meaning or whose ideal system was bent into a totality through highly organized interrelationships between images, emblems, and agents, modern and post-Romantic allegories have undoubtedly used a different tack.[41] In the works of many twentieth-century theorists and authors, starting with Benjamin, allegory is characterized by "a sense of loss and decay, a structure of feeling steeped in mourning."[42] Bainard Cowan has argued that in Benjamin's era, allegory had to go underground, "to emerge from time to time in a sporadic, terroristic campaign against the reigning version of secular reality."[43] In *White Tiger*, the task of framing constellations of allegorical images that signal such "campaigns" is handed over to its cynical narrator. It is he, rather than a revolutionary subject, who produces before the reader's eyes "a petrified landscape," a world that is "meaningful only in the stations of its decay."[44]

The village of Laxmangarh is, thus, not only a place from which the state seems to have withdrawn but also a continued site for resource appropriation. The urban-based virtual economy has not yet taken over the rural, but it has mobilized a residual "feudal" that is now effectively redone for the global (as a sort of local-in-the-global). The language of animality is pressed into service at this point for an allegory of the residual rural that survives hand in hand with new forms of capital. There are, we are told, four landowners in Laxmangarh who are nicknamed the Buffalo, the Stork, the Wild Boar, and the Raven. Together they extract tribute from the villagers in the shape of river tolls from boatmen, a share of catch from fishermen, bonded work from sharecroppers, grazing fees from goatherds, and licensing bribes from rickshaw pullers. The power lines of these feudal structures reach out into the Indian diaspora—from the rural to the secessionist globalizing class: "The four animals had sent their sons and daughters away, to Dhanbad or to Delhi" (*Tiger*, 25). Balram's employer, Ashok, we learn, is one of these returning sons, a banker who relinquishes his career in New York City to come home and start up something new in booming India. Through conversations Balram overhears in the car while working as the family chauffeur, we learn that the new family business is a form of poaching on the old socialist state—illegally exporting coal acquired from the government's nationalized mines in Dhanbad to China. Bribes sent to politicians in New Delhi to facilitate the export of coal thus complete the rural-urban-global circuit of capital (Laxmangarh-Dhanbad–New Delhi–China), as extraction from goatherds joins ecological devastation of the planet. The novel thus makes its own plot movements into a story of multinational capital at the anagogical level of the allegory, whereas the historical-literal level contributes to this level of the story with the account of old residual power structures that use the rural as a sort of interdiction of the global and the local, all without really touching the megacity of high-tech capital.

In the literal story of the Indian case we might therefore speak of Adiga's novel as representing both the crisis of the nationalist-socialist state of the 1950s and the emergence of the neoliberal globalizing state in the 1980s. The allegorizing of a past that is in ruins and being cannibalized by the present depends, as I have already mentioned, on a method that Benjamin indexed with the metaphor of the "constellation." In Benjamin's "Theses" essay as well as in the *Arcades Project*, this term is instrumental in defining the critical force of modernist allegory. The astronomical metaphor is, in fact, a radical perspective on history, one that interrupts the linear and progressive trajectory of its narrative. Just as a constellation is made up of some stars that are nearer and others farther away, historical events, too, can from the here and now appear to take on a significant configuration. The notion of history as a continuum—what Benjamin describes as "telling the sequence of events like the beads of a rosary"—is now transformed by a reconfiguration of past and present in a moment of startling juxtaposition.[45]

In allegory, the constellation can appear with a background-foreground distinction, as happens when sublime scenery is more than a backdrop for the emblematic and begins to resemble a moral landscape. In *White Tiger* an iconic shot of a seemingly sleepy village viewed from the vantage point of an old, ruined fort on a hill at first merely reminds the reader of the erstwhile princely and feudal lineages in the rural outpost, but, importantly, instead of a radical break with the past (where the fort might represent a vanished India), the novel removes it from the landscape and reworks the ruin as a trope of repetition and continuity. In an earlier reference in the novel, Balram describes the Black Fort as a reminder of India's colonization by foreigners, although now, he tells us, "the foreigners have long abandoned the Black Fort, and a tribe of monkeys occupy it" (*Tiger*, 22). Then, this image that repeats history, first as colonialism and then as postcolonial farce, is redone into a trope in a different story as Balram announces that the fort holds the clue to his disappearance as a murderer and his reemergence as a rich businessman: "I bet you they [the police] missed the most important clue of all, which was right in front of them: I am talking about the Black Fort, of course." The image of the fort thus connects, metonymically, the historical trauma of foreign conquest with Balram's own life story, folding one into the other as the novel keeps a national frame in place, even as the image is turned into a vehicle for *psychomachia*—an allegory about Balram's inner conflict at the moral-subjective level. For the reader, the psychological and the historical are now connected allegorically as parallel stories. Balram represents a historical emergence and overcoming of seemingly inescapable social realities, not only for himself as servant-slave but also for a "servant class"—a collectivity with which he constantly self-identifies. As a child Balram was frightened of the fort because his grandmother told him that an enormous lizard lived there. After that point he could watch the fearful beauty of the fort only from a distance, mindful that it held the key to his liberation: "*They remain slaves because they can't see what is beautiful in this world*" (40; emphasis mine).

One day, after his return to the village, Balram tries to climb the hill on which the fort stands and succeeds for the first time. We witness at that moment the death of the child-servant and Balram's rebirth as the White Tiger. Here is the scene:

> Putting my foot on the wall, I looked down on the village from there. My little Laxmangarh. I saw the temple tower, the market, the glistening line of sewage, the landlord's mansions—and my own house, with that dark little cloud outside— the water buffalo. It looked like the most beautiful sight on earth.

>I leaned out from the edge of the fort in the direction of my village—and then I did something too disgusting to describe to you.
>
>Well, actually, I *spat*. Again and Again. And then, whistling and humming, I went back down the hill.
>
>Eight months later, I slit Mr. Ashok's throat. (*Tiger*, 41–42)

In the last sentence, the anachronic deviation (of skipping eight months) makes an explicit connection between Balram's act of spitting upon this scene and the subsequent murder. It is hard to miss in the method of the employer's murder the pun on the market's self-undermining practice of cutthroat competition. Balram gets his venture capital from his murdered employer. The link between the spitting and the murder is drawn gradually in the paragraph through the paratactic accumulation of details that operate metonymically—with a succession of fragments—but these fragments are not a neutral piling up of facts about "my little Laxmangarh." Instead, they are now familiar allegorical emblems representing abstractions: the temple tower and market are already ominous symbols along with the sewage (environmental degradation), landlords' mansions (continuing feudal oppression), and a fattened buffalo (appropriation of labor power). From his vantage point, Balram sees a scene of continuing colonization of the rural.

The temporal split in the narrator's achronic perspective also juxtaposes two separate pasts (the time of the picnic and the time of the murder), thus analogizing the historical constellation of past events and the split consciousness of the subject, or "I," that constellates into an allegorical double vision. The allegorical significance is clear now—the village scene has already fulfilled its role and brought about Balram's transformation as the novel transposes the original temporal data into the figurative spatial simultaneity of Laxmangarh. Now a future where symptoms and narratives accumulate (in the way Benjamin's Angel of History signals the resurrection of the future from the ruins and destruction of the past) is not the story of Benjamin's messianic future or the story of a single murder but a portent of the collective political violence of liberated servants to come.

What is without question interrupted and critiqued, as I have argued here, when Balram walks away from the "most beautiful sight on earth," is the image of the rural rife in many literary and cinematic representations of Indian modernity, where the village is the custodian of idealized peasant virtues. As long as the critique of neoliberalism in India depends on holding onto the village as a site of essential values, we will miss the point of the novel. Adiga, it seems to me, wants to show the *as if*: What if this last bastion of imagined collectivity also falls to neoliberalism? What if even the poor villager is now in the pores of global capitalism? If we are witnessing neoliberalism's globalism, as Wendy Brown terms it, when economic reason permeates "all forms of life,"[46] the binary opposition between rural and urban values no longer holds. To me, the iconic symbol that works here is that of the buffalo. Anyone following the writing by proponents of microcredit and its so-called transformative power in the rural South will notice that among the common examples of "small capital" for poor people raising themselves out of poverty are the cell phone and the buffalo. This is economization from the ground up, or training the poor to become entrepreneurs. The buffalo is therefore a parodic allusion to microcredit: a fattened animal remains the hope of all members of the family, but it consumes calories that are diverted from hungry stomachs, and the entire family seems to be working for it rather than the other way around.

Because allegory in its contemporary forms moves across material boundaries (cyber, print, virtual), stylistic and generic categories, linguistic registers, and geographies (global-local), it enables a recognition of the multiplicity and heterogeneity of signs spun by new media as well as the continuing residual power of signs that are not yet completely in ruins (because uneven development also produces a cultural palimpsest of meanings). In Adiga's novel, it is still possible to talk about the materiality of production and the time of commodity markets that is not divorced from economic history—we can still see bonded labor, manual labor, tithes, land rent, wages, coal money, and even tech money, in Balram's "start-up." All of these activities, instruments, and products involve concrete and particular uses of time, their appearance and disappearance signaling changes in the mode of production as a whole. Balram's transformation, from a waged servant doing semifeudal work to the proprietor of a taxi service for call centers, is a sure sign of India's growing appetite for economic restructuring and a globalized economy. In the contact zone of the call center in Bangalore, we can already glimpse a new kind of economic time thrusting its way into the scene of urban work: the time of financial markets, which is measureless, empty, abstract, and proleptic. Here, historical time retreats even further under pressure from a future that becomes urgent. As the stock market condenses the time of the profit-taking today, a new rhythm of the "future" enters cultural productions like narrative fiction and comes to be deeply intertwined with the way we live our own individual lives and imagine our collective future. The intensification and urgency of this time frame, as happens during a financial crisis, is the focus of the next section.

The Future as Endless Supply

In an essay published in December 2001, Don DeLillo describes the attack on the World Trade Center as a defining moment that broke the hold of a powerful structure of temporality over American (and non-American) lives: "In the past decade the surge of capital markets has dominated discourse and shaped global consciousness. Multinational corporations have come to seem more vital and influential than governments. The dramatic climb of the Dow and the speed of the internet summoned us all to live permanently in the future, in the utopian glow of cyber-capital, because there is no memory there and this is where markets are uncontrolled and investment potential has no limit."[47] The global expansion of capital markets in the 1990s and the US public's access to them through various financial instruments created the ability to invest "anywhere" and nowhere in particular. For DeLillo, the catastrophic events of September 11 changed all that. If Americans had imagined the endless continuation of a decade of surging markets in which cybercapital and the internet made it possible for us all to "live permanently in the future," such a world ended on that day. Parts of the United States' world "crumbled" into the world of terror and a lived present of "danger and rage." The future no longer promised technological and economic utopia, only impending violence against America and American culture.

It is hard not to see in these historical events, as DeLillo characterizes them, conditions ripe for allegorical representations that resonate with Benjamin's theorization of the form as an experience—of the world as no longer permanent, as conveying a "sense of its transitoriness," an "intimation of mortality."[48] DeLillo's allegorical vision depicts the fate of the United States swinging from a plot previously determined by the promise of finance capital, to one where the nation becomes the object of atavistic terror. At the collective-political level, a new form of global conflict comes into view—a conflict over time. Whereas anti-globalization protests circa 2001 were trying to "decelerate the global momentum," slow things down, and "hold off the white-hot future," the terrorists of September 11, DeLillo argues, were trying to "bring back the past." The future that Americans had woven with the "great skeins of technology" has disintegrated and yielded to terror's "medieval expedience and the old slow furies of cut-throat religion." As a small group of men literally altered the skyline, "we have fallen back in time and space" says he, and it is their technology that marks these moments of regress: "The small, lethal devices, the remote-control detonators they fashion out of radios, or the larger technology they borrow from us, passenger jets that become manned missiles."

At one point in this remarkable essay, DeLillo makes a proleptic reference to the protagonist of his yet unpublished novel, *Cosmopolis* (2003), with this comparison: The terrorist is not "the self-watcher" or "the soft white dangling boy who shoots someone to keep from disappearing into himself" but rather, one whose narrow plot ends in a "vision of judgment and devastation." In this fraying context it is the terrorist who occupies (if this were cast as a Benjaminian messianic plot), the position of the revolutionary subject. Like the White Tiger, DeLillo's terrorist brings back the past with the allegorical emblems of religious apocalypse. However, the figure of the self-watching, soft, white dangling boy, whose taste for self-inflicted pain resembles that of *Cosmopolis*'s protagonist, Eric Packer, is no less allegorical. Unlike the violence of terror that looks to the past to destroy the structures of Western capitalism and neoliberalism, Eric Packer, the financial speculator, neither turns his face to the past nor does he live in the present. Instead, he is a dematerialized being, a prolifically active mind occupying an unfeeling shell of a body, a man with little memory of his past but whose relationship to the present takes the form of an obsessive attention to his own body as a compromising object that forces him back to a lived present. The hollowing out of the present (as concretely lived) makes this character into DeLillo's allegorical figuration, a personification of the temporal regime of finance capital that exhorts Americans to live permanently in the future, to place little value on the past, and to act without control and without limits.

At the literal or historical level, *Cosmopolis* seems deliberately sparse about plot and setting. The novel is set in New York City but it could be "anyplace," a cosmopolis that reminds one of the Weimar-era filmmaker Fritz Lang's silent allegory, *Metropolis* (1927)—a city of light with an underlying ugly darkness.[49] The novel's action is a series of disconnected episodes, each taking place along a drawn-out crosstown limousine ride interrupted by meetings with chorus-like figures who tell us something about the complex workings of financial markets. Although conventional norms about genre, action, and character have dissolved in this abstract setting, the novel keenly suggests that decentralization and abstraction are themselves the concern of the novel's collective level. Here, the existential or systemic reality of globalization (the world market) suggests that two years after DeLillo's essay declared the end of the world where Americans dwelled permanently in the future, a form of capital that raids our collective present has reconstituted itself even more powerfully than before.

DeLillo's *Cosmopolis* makes us wonder whether the novel represents a turning of the tide with regard to the allegorical form. Once associated with collective visions of third-world and premodern cultures, allegory seems to have found its fulfillment as a meaningful form of "American" counternarrative, as a better alternative to the unappetizing versions that have emerged in the wake of 9/11. These alternatives that "end in the rubble," as DeLillo characterizes them, include narratives that feed the desire for apocalyptic wars to end all wars or that elicit nostalgia for another Cold War. *Cosmopolis* seems to roll back these preferences by setting its actions in a recent past before 9/11. A complex interrelationship emerges between the literal-historical and the anagogical levels when the novel titles its opening section, "In the Year 2000: A Day in April." The month, year, and unspecified day do not have any immediately recognizable historical referents, but the setting in New York City foreshadows, for its readers today, the catastrophic events in the year to follow. The temporal reference also corroborates, in my view, Agamben's insight (discussed in the introduction to this book) that 9/11 forever changed the "first glimpse" of New York City's skyline for its future visitors. It is as if every novel that invokes New York City, irrespective of its own plot time, will retroactively register for the contemporary reader the shock of an event that is now more than two decades old. The paradoxical temporality of *Cosmopolis*, the "before" of its setting and the "after" of its reception, thus wonderfully illustrate the double movement of allegory between a literal-historical and an anagogical-collective level. From this critical perspective, *Cosmopolis* is a post-9/11 novel, the temporal effect of which is to make its reader poise in anticipation, as if on a threshold, feeling the precarity of the present and the catastrophe that awaits.

Cosmopolis constitutes the overall unity of its allegorical levels with several interlocking stories. At the literal-historical level, the unnamed day in April is chockful of unseen events unfolding in the background, while in the foreground, a sparser episodic plot follows the protagonist as he leaves his apartment to go for a haircut.[50] For Packer, a twenty-eight-year-old billionaire fund manager–cum-speculator, this day in April seems just like any other in the euphoria of a market boom, but as the day wears on, Packer, who has leveraged hundreds of millions of dollars, his entire personal fortune, on a bet that the Japanese yen will fall in the currency markets, becomes the allegory of the market itself. The novel tracks a single day in his life from morning till night—a plot time that is stretched to take him several hours to get from his apartment on the East Side to the shabby hairdresser's shop on the West Side, the part of the city where he spent his childhood years. As he gets into his stretch limousine outfitted with surveillance cameras and monitor screens that continuously feed him world news, stock prices, and currency values, the sound-proofed, bullet-proofed limo becomes a place of business, a place of physical gratification, and a slow-moving target for an assassin who has made a threat on Packer's life. As the limousine weaves its way at snail's pace through the streets of Manhattan, a Black Swan event is cascading by the minutes and seconds, as market fluctuations defy all the experts' expectations. Other events are going on around him, creating the traffic jams that slow his crosstown journey: streets closed for a presidential motorcade, a massive funeral procession for a celebrity musician, and an anti-globalization protest turned violent. If there is any literal reference for the year 2000, it is this: In the history of the stock market, that year marked the end of an eight-year boom that began in 1992, a boom still considered one of the most spectacular rises in the history of the Dow. The US economy grew nonstop for more than a hundred months, and the index climbed above 11,000 points to an all-time high.[51]

The allegorical elements of Packer's journey to the barbershop take on an "epic" dimension when chorus-like figures join him at various points along the route. There are brief stops to accommodate lunch with his wife, a sexual encounter with a mistress, and then meetings with a series of one-dimensional figures who present us with various aspects of the complex abstractions of the financial market. First on the scene is the "chief of technology," who assures Packer that their online trading accounts and the data associated with them have been secured against manipulators and hackers. Despite the confidence in the technological infrastructure, the chief philosophizes, "People eat and sleep in the shadow of what we do," but "do you get the feeling sometimes that you don't know what is going on?" (*Cosmopolis*, 14). The uncertainty intensifies when a nervous "currency analyst" climbs into the limousine to tell Packer that he cannot "chart" what is happening and cautions him that the firm may be "leveraging too rashly" and "speculating into the void" (21). Next in line is the "chief of finance," who goes on to confirm that Packer Capital's yen carry could crush them in hours, and the time had come to choose: it is not too late, he advises. Packer could ease off and "take a loss and come back stronger" (53).

But Packer is not listening. He has leveraged the yen too heavily to pull out. The so-called carry trade involves a trading strategy that borrows at a low interest rate and invests in an asset that provides a higher rate of return. A carry trade is typically based on borrowing in a low-interest rate currency and converting the borrowed amount into another currency. Generally, the proceeds would be deposited in the second currency if it offers a higher interest rate. The proceeds could then be deployed into assets such as stocks, commodities, bonds, or real estate that are denominated in the second currency. In *Cosmopolis*, Packer and his pack of experts misread the trend: the yen was expected to be a falling currency, but it does not behave that way. The stronger the yen becomes, the more money needed to pay back the loan. With every fractional rise in the yen, Packer's firm loses millions.

By now, all indications are that Packer, who proudly announces to his mistress that he is "losing money by the ton" by betting against the yen, is the quintessential example of the sort of allegorical character that Angus Fletcher describes earlier in this chapter: obsessed with only one idea, with an absolutely one-track mind and a life patterned according to absolutely rigid habits from which he never allows himself to vary. He seems driven by a hidden private force, not in control his own destiny but controlled by some foreign force that is "outside the sphere of his own ego."[52] It remains to the most loquacious figure, Packer's "chief of theory," to unlock the nature of Packer's intransigence. Packer's drive may seem like the trajectory of an Icarus-like hubris-driven hero or the odyssey of the fate-driven hero, but what we are witnessing is the personified temporality of the financial market that captures the present and converts it into a risk-calculated future. The hold of the future is hard to break, and like a gambler who will not listen to reason and holds on to the possibility of a good hand, Packer will not pull back.

Packer's "chief of theory," Vija Kinski, is unlike the other doomsayers in his employ. She is on his wavelength. When she begins to speak in the limousine, Packer sits and listens silently: "We want to think about the art of money-making." *Mutatis mutandis*, she adds, "Money has taken a turn. All wealth has become wealth for its own sake. Money has lost its narrative quality the way painting did once upon a time. Money is talking to itself" (*Cosmopolis*, 77). This is Postmodernism 101 for the reader who may be unfamiliar with the cultural theory that now surrounds the virtual, immaterial, free-floating, abstract, and self-referential tendencies of finance capital. In *Cosmopolis*, money as finance capital finds its analogon in abstract art: no longer needing material supports of paper, plastic, and metal, the value of real commodities and stocks, money has become like abstract art that can be meaningful without representing real things in the world out there. In a sense, money is like an aesthetic object. Just as abstract art can make color, lines, texture, and shapes into self-referential meaning, money can talk to itself. This is not all; capital markets have also radically transformed our relationship to time, especially the ways in which we imagine the future. Here is the chief of theory on this point: "But you know how shameless I am in the presence of anything that calls itself an idea. The idea is time. Living in the future. Look at those numbers running. Money makes time. It used to be the other way around. Clock time accelerated the rise of capitalism. People stopped thinking about eternity. They began to concentrate on hours, measurable hours, man-hours, using labor more efficiently" (79). Capital markets have displaced the time of labor that was the materialist basis of commodity value in an earlier stage of capitalism. Now, traded value exists independently of the cost of goods, the cost of labor, the time taken to produce both, and the productivity (or time-efficiency) of labor itself. Then, time was money. Now, money is time, more precisely a nonhuman time that is no longer humanly measured as "clock time" or "man-hours." As the chief of theory tells Packer, "It's cyber-capital that creates the future. What is a measurement called nanosecond?" Kinski's point is that as humans we cannot "know" or experience a nanosecond or for that matter, a zeptosecond or a yoctosecond. A market operating with the technological support of cyberspace is now the foreign force that is outside Packer's ego. "Time is a corporate asset now," the theory chief concludes. "It belongs to the free market system." Within this new regime of temporal capture, "the present is hard to find. It is being sucked out of the world to make way for the future of uncontrolled markets and huge investment potential." In such a scenario, no human intervention can correct the acceleration of time or even allow a so-called financial expert or speculator to see a pattern or trend well enough to confidently bet on the future. Self-correction is the financial market's way of talking to itself. When the future "becomes insistent," predicts the chief, "something will happen soon, maybe today," and bring things "back to normal" (79).

The chief of theory speaks objectively, and we sense this because the novel leaves her speech uncontested. The scandal unveiled here is confirmation by insiders like Kinski and Packer that the financial market is all "random phenomena," that mathematics and other disciplines cannot apprehend its "laws." One is dealing with a system that is "out of control" and whose "hysteria at high speeds" attests that it is not the pathological control of the state that is at stake. The "frenzy" is of our creation, but it is now driven by "thinking machines that we have no final control over." Finally, this pronouncement by Kinski: "It is simply how we live" (*Cosmopolis*, 85).

As she is speaking, Packer is watching the screens in his limousine, where beneath the moving "data strips, or tickers," there were "fixed digits marking the time in the major cities of the world." It is as though the clocks stand still and register nothing but the physical and geographical accessibility enabled by teletechnologies of speed, a speed that makes it hard to follow what passes before the human eye. If the speed is the point, the thrust, the future, then it is also clear that at that speed and scale, "data" is no longer information to be processed by the human mind. As he watches his screens, the way "data dissolves at one end of the series" and "takes shape at the other," Packer knows he is not witnessing the "flow of information," only "pure spectacle"—information that has become "sacred, ritually unreadable," just as the small monitors of the office, home, and car become "a kind of idolatry here, where crowds might gather in astonishment" (*Cosmopolis*, 80).

By means of this lengthy discourse by Packer's chief of theory, the novel strives to make something of the notion that we "live" this teletechnological frenzy without noticing it. To show life—lived as though it is in the time of the market—means that the narrative has to move beyond a literal-historical level, beyond the events playing out that day and Packer's journey across town. The narrative has to do more than provide the allegorical level where the journey of a man going downhill from riches to bankruptcy is also the story of the boom-bust cycles of an out-of-control financial market. To these two levels, *Cosmopolis* adds a subjective-moral level, where we are to imagine a lived present, an everyday life, a biography and lifespan for this young man whose limousine has become an extension of his apartment—a deterritorialized space locatable anywhere, cut off from the world around it, and yet also completely immersed in the interconnected globe by way of teletechnologies and data streams.

The unity between the moral-subjective and the allegorical, the everyday-subjective and the market, is constituted by two separate but related strands in the story: in one, we see Packer's scrupulous attention to everyday language, the primary tool of subjectivity, as it is prodded by his desire to cast aside words that have become obsolete—ruined shells of their original meaning. In the other strand, we encounter a Packer who is dematerializing into a cyber-like mind that lives in a permanent future, a future into which, obviously, his biological body cannot follow. As a constraint on the mind that wants to dwell in the future, Packer's body is a drag on this accelerating time. The body thus becomes the site of obsessive care and self-inflicted pain (what DeLillo's essay calls "self-watching"). In a manner not unlike that of Hamid's and Adiga's characters, Packer's tug-of-war with his own body develops the temporal perspective of the human being who in possessing a life span is also able to bookend a life and any possible experience of a lived present. The story of Packer's dysfunctional relationship to his present also links to and activates the political unconscious of the allegory's collective level—we cannot but think of the tragic dehumanization of everything human by the posthuman temporal regimes of the market. I will address each of these two strands in the novel and their constitution of temporality: first, as Packer's attempted change of linguistic sign-systems, and then, as the dysfunctionality of the present in Packer's biological-biographical life.

The novel's linguistic wordplay is initiated by Packer himself when he anxiously sloughs off words whose meanings seem out of date, as though they have outlived their time and are headed for obsolescence. Packer makes a note to himself about the "anachronistic quality" of the word "skyscraper." For him, no recent structure "ought to bear this word," as it belonged to the "olden soul of awe," a narrative that existed long before he was born (*Cosmopolis*, 9). In contrast, Packer is all admiration for the bank towers he sees along his route, because they are "abstract," "interchangeable," "designed to hasten the future" and exist in a time "beyond geography and touchable money and the people who stack and count it" (36). In a similar vein are telephones that he describes as "vestigial" and "degenerate structures"; the "handgun," the word itself "was lost in blowing mist"; the computer, "dying in their present form," the word itself "sounds backward and dumb" (19, 104). Even the devices Packer uses are already transient, their use values and exchange values dissolving in an unswerving path toward obsolescence. A moment after typing the above-mentioned note to himself, he observes, "The hand-held device itself was an object whose original culture had just about disappeared. He knew he'd have to junk it" (9). For Packer, most words and concepts of everyday language are "aged and overburdened by [their] own historical memory." They are "anti-futuristic" and "cumbrous" (54).

The casting aside of his "hand-held" device is not only an indication of his desire to remove the body as an unmovable anchor of the present; it is also a nod to planned obsolescence as capital's destructive overcoming of the past and the present for the future. Packer sees words as ruins of older meanings, and these examples suggest that allegory is also allegorizing, through the genre's penchant for resignifying ruination, a way to combat the becoming-abstract of technologies that no longer need to be attached prosthetically (materially) to human bodies. With regard to this, we note that a word like "asymmetrical" holds a particular fascination for Packer. It appears without comment at first, only to take on greater significance at the end of the novel. Packer is worried he has an "asymmetrical prostate," but we learn that he is fascinated with the notion of asymmetry because it is a "counterforce" to balance and calm. What is intriguing to him in a "cosmological register" is spooky and fearsome when applied to his own body (*Cosmopolis*, 52). As I will discuss later, the word comes back with allegorical force at another level, when we learn later that Packer's killer too has an asymmetrical prostate.

Another way by which the subjective level and the allegorical level of the market form a complex interrelationship is within the novel's representation of Packer's dysfunctional relationship to his lived present. As I noted earlier, the time of the present is limited to a few hours over the span of a day, but the novel deliberately eschews the sort of subjective expansion that characters perform when they dance with the past as memory. To live in a permanent future is to have no memory, and Packer appears in many respects to be a dematerialized self whose life is one of social isolation and solipsism. His desire to flee from the present is coupled with an adamant refusal to remember his past, the nail on which the human subject hangs the hat of self-consciousness. As a character, Packer lacks all the predications one expects from characters in realist fiction— rounded out with the fullness of biographical detail that comes from a narrating self that unifies its identity, puts it together, that is, from memories of the past. Thus, before long, Packer's name too begins to emit its own allegorical signal. The character is merely a container into which the owner of the proper name tries to pack the future, a process that ultimately becomes a form of temporal cannibalization when the future loops around to consume the present. A curious pattern begins to repeat in the novel—a disconcerting temporal reversal of present and future, the subject's act and its subsequent representation. In his limousine Packer watches himself on the screen below an installed spy cam, an activity that reveals his fascination with the simultaneous capture of himself as image. But as he rubs his thumb along his jaw, he realizes that "he'd just placed his thumb on his chinline, a second or two after he'd seen in on-screen" (*Cosmopolis*, 22).

As Packer oversteps his time, sees himself as an outcome in the future before he has even acted in the present, the novel enacts a subjective-moral personification of the temporal regimes of financial capital. In economic terms this temporal regime correlates with a future that has not yet happened—market "risk," or the unknowable future, that enters into the calculation of commodity prices at the present time. In a recent study of the language of finance capital, Richard Godden explains how "the pricing of risk becomes key to the costing of manufacture."[53] Packer's lived present is a parable about our complete alienation as stakeholders in an economic system where huge amounts of money can be leveraged and traded, no longer based on the present or anticipated supply and demand for goods or stocks but based on a future beyond a future, a realm of abstraction that lies beyond the commodity form. This hollowing out of the present is represented in Packer's everyday life as an inability to really know what he wants. On the one hand, yes, he wants a haircut, but we suspect that this is simply an alibi for the trip when we encounter the heterotopic role of the barbershop. It is the barber who rounds out Packer with a past, from whom we learn about the young Eric growing up gifted in a family of modest means. Packer, who feels the thrill of living only when he is surrounded by the virtual reality of numbers, charts, and images on a screen, has his hair cut by the only person who knows him from the past he would like to keep at bay. This anchoring in a dismissed time and the body may have as its analogon another experience Packer submits to every day—his daily prostate exam: "He felt the pain. . . . It was here in his body, the structure he wanted to dismiss in theory even when he was shaping it under the measured effect of barbells and weights. He wanted to judge it redundant and transferable" (*Cosmopolis*, 48). In the last meeting Packer has with his wife, before he encounters the assassin who is waiting for him in a ruined building, he realizes that he has no "present" to speak of. Packer knows what he wants when a thought crosses his mind, but not beyond that: "He could not imagine. But he never could. It made sense to him that his immediate and extended futures would be compressed into whatever events might constitute the next few hours, or minutes or less. These were the terms of life expectancy he'd ever recognized as real" (122). Packer's lack of imagination is the lack of a lived present; the inability to see his own mortality is an inability to see a future that may be somewhat indeterminate but also programmable in terms of a directed purpose or end.

This is where, it seems to me, *Cosmopolis* places its bet—on the temporal notion of "life expectancy" as a way of asserting human agency over a future. The fate of this character seems to tell us something about the *ends* of capital in every sense—as a foreseeable end in time and as a purpose or goal. When Packer's fortune evaporates at the end of the day, he leaves the barbershop and inexplicably moves toward a ruined tenement where his former employee, Richard Sheets, is waiting for him, gun in hand. The end of novel is surrealistic. Packer oversteps his present into the future, but on this occasion he sees his life end, his lifeless body displayed as an image on his watch, seconds before he is actually shot. We are led to ask how the ending of Packer's life links to the course of financial events that are also unfolding—the spectacular crash of a financial market that was at a euphoric high when the novel begins.

If *Cosmopolis*'s main takeaway is the ironic standpoint that even for its greatest beneficiaries (Packer and his pack) the financial market is unreadable, this can hardly be welcome news to the victims of neoliberalism for whom the question that really matters is where the struggle is to be and against whom it must be directed. As Packer's financial assets evaporate, his wife, Elise, asks him, "Where does it go when you lose it?" (*Cosmopolis*, 178). Can one bring down a system by killing its personifications? Or to put it in Marx's terms, can one "make the individual responsible for relations whose creature he remains?" The novel seems ambivalent about mass protest too. When Packer's limousine is stuck on the street in the middle of an anti-globalization protest, he sees a "shadow of transaction between the demonstrators and the state." The riots appear to him to be "a form of systemic hygiene, purging and lubricating," validating only "the market culture's innovative brilliance, its ability to shape itself to its own flexible ends, absorbing everything around it" (99). DeLillo does not challenge Packer's skepticism about the ultimate efficacy of such mass protests with another viewpoint. Perhaps there is a clue in another uncontested insight, this one from the assassin, Richard Sheets, conveyed to Packer a few minutes before his life ends: "You forgot something along the way. . . . The importance of the lopsided, the thing that's skewed a little. You were looking for balance, beautiful balance, equal parts, equal sides. I know this. I know you. But you should have been tracking the yen in its tics and quirks. The little quirk. The misshape" (200). This is the asymmetrical as the glitch in the system, the internal feedback loop that will bring it all crashing down from time to time. But we know that the machine of the financial market will start up again. What will not begin again is the lifetime that Eric Packer has expended. One gets the feeling that DeLillo pins his hope on the notion that the future is not limitless like the knowable past.

If Eric's desire to relinquish the concrete time of everyday life and to exist, like financial data, in a realm of pure abstraction is self-destructive, then DeLillo's response is to show that such desires to live outside one's time are a symptom that human perception and human ability can no longer keep up with the new quality of speed that information-intensive technologies have attained. In this accelerated time, what is nearly no time, individual life seems to lose its significance. Nowotny's observation about the irreducibility of the past and future is useful here. Whereas the past could extend to "genuine or false infinity," and conceptions of human history could be destroyed and replaced by a world history of humanity, a geologic history of the planet, or even a cosmic history of the universe, with regard to the future, this stretch is impossible because it cannot be denied or repressed that "the lifetime still remain[s] the measure of meaningful life expectancy."[54]

In Hamid's novel *Filthy Rich*, it is this infinitely open future that is put into lifetime proportions when "you" and "pretty girl" live out the remainder of their lives in modest circumstances, relishing the time they can spend in caring and sharing. It is as though the future's real possibilities open up only when they execute an "exit strategy," leaving behind the calculus of market time to discover and shape time for themselves before their bodies break down and their lifetimes end. In the case of Eric Packer, no such luck. Mirroring the manner in which present markets are run by an endless series of anticipations that depend not merely on multiple futures but in whatever occurs subsequent to those futures, Packer vanishes in a process that lies in a future after the future. He sees his death displayed on the mini-screen of his watch minutes before he dies, ironically fulfilling his desire to live outside the given limits, in a chip, on a disk, as data. This might be welcomed by some as an evolutionary step in the right direction for our nervous systems, but for DeLillo the final lesson is that the "master thrust of cyber-capital" will find yet another level at which to extend human experience for the accumulation of profits. Killing Eric Packer does not stop the system; the money he has lost simply goes elsewhere. However, the body is the glitch. Just as Eric's "pain interfered with his immortality" and makes him realize that the "things that made him who he was could hardly be identified much less converted to data" (*Cosmopolis*, 207), the allegories of Hamid, Adiga, and DeLillo pin their stakes on the revelation of what it means to be sundered from anything resembling what we imagine to be a "proper" human existence imagined through a lived present, memory, and an imagined future in which one still plays a part.

The upsetting of natural or "proper" balances is the state of things when the biological and the economic outpace each other with teletechnologies; however, such discontinuities and breakdowns also characterize the relation between the biosphere and the geosphere today. But our awareness of this more recent imbalance and its potential consequences also means that the time scales in which the horrible consequences of present and past actions are to be expected have reduced considerably. The pressure of this future (what Srinivas Aravamudan calls a catastrophism) now hangs over our present and shadows the planet with an impending doom that we have never been able to imagine for the financial system, which comes back like a phantom menace, with a boom after every bust. Is the time of financial risk similar to or different from the time of climate change? How do both "events," if we might call them that, challenge the task of representation undertaken by literary art forms like the novel? Is it possible to represent human longings in temporal regimes that dispose of the future as though they were the present? How do we know whether our desire to reduce ourselves by imagining nonhuman scales of time is not another chronostrategy driven by capital's appropriation of the resource of human time? These questions are the focus of the final chapter of this book.

CHAPTER FIVE

Assemblages
Ethico-aesthetic Compositions for the Future

This book began with a novel that pluralizes the monoculture of an affluent, white, US home by entangling and drawing into it the intimate story of a young Black woman whose memories, like her labor, have a painful history. What we call economic globalization today is only emergent in Kincaid's *Lucy*, but the spectral appearance of Atlantic slavery and colonialism make the crucial point that all universalisms, whether they are globe-girdling notions or well-intentioned embraces of racial difference, work on the basis of a timeless time that is antihistoricist. The rapidly growing discourse of the Anthropocene in the humanities today requires careful parsing for similar reasons. It can become a discourse of mastery or a route to plurality, and the road taken depends on whether fantasies of unity and wholeness, what Steve Mentz calls the "singularity of capital-A Anthropos," are replaced by an "agglomeration of partially overlapping and sometimes conflicting perspectives."[1] As an epoch, the Anthropocene is the paradoxical bearer of the stamp of the Anthropos—the "geologic worldmaker/destroyer of worlds"—making it the most anthropocentric of all the epochs that have preceded it in earth history.[2]

In this chapter, I read Barbara Kingsolver's *Flight Behavior* (2012) as a text that challenges a new geologic language of the earth and its mastery by pluralizing the Anthropocene. The novel is set in the economic periphery of Appalachian Tennessee. Just imagining Kingsolver's fictionalized region, with its fossil forests, as a place where "fuel is being extracted not from spatially but from temporally distant places"[3] and as a place that is being hollowed out by globalization, reveals the complex entanglements of ecology and economy. How can we think the time of human-centered history and economic activity with that of nonhuman evolutionary time? Could novels reveal the imaginative work that goes into the ethico-aesthetic agglomerations (compositions, assemblages) that are necessary to pluralize the Anthropocene? More importantly, how might the imperative to pluralize avoid the construction of assemblages that continue to replicate the timelessness of universal mastery or the insignificance of human temporalities within geologic timescales?

Calls for such plurality have not been directed only at the national, racial, and class-based monocultures of environmental writing but also toward an antihistoricist bias that seems uninterested in how the Anthropos came to be put together. Following the epistemological interventions of postcolonial critics like Aimé Césaire and Sylvia Wynter, the geographer Kathryn Yusoff has argued that the invasion of the "New World" produced "the first geologic subjects of the Anthropocene," and they were Indigenous and Black.[4] She points out that even if the Anthropocene is but "a blink in time in the deformation of the planet," its original claim is to "render a new quality of the human." Thus, the Anthropocene's origination account of geologic mastery is another "category mistake" that can be claimed as truth only if slavery and the rendering of subject as "inhuman object" is "discounted from the experience of the human." The subject of slavery was already an assemblage, Yusoff contends, "a coercive interpenetration between human and inhuman categories . . . that predates the 'new' imagined subject of the Anthropocene."[5]

The historical questions about race and colonialism that Yusoff brings up and that have gone unaddressed with regard to the new "imagined subject of the Anthropocene" are partly a result of the bracketing of human history, as an insignificant temporality within the climate crisis debate. The narrative of geologic mastery entails the straddling of two distinct kinds of temporality, but large amounts of nonhuman time that form the geologic epochs of earth history get priority over the shorter (seemingly insignificant) spans of world history that are based on human-centered time. This disjunction troubles historians like Dipesh Chakrabarty, who argues for the relevance of human scales of time by asserting, one, that the Anthropocene itself involves "a constant conceptual traffic between Earth history and world history," and, two, that we are passing through a "unique phase of human history" when, for the first time ever, we "consciously connect events that happen on vast, geological scales—such as changes to the whole climate system of the planet—with what we might do in the everyday lives of individuals, collectivities, institutions, and nations (such as burning fossil fuels)."[6]

But how do we connect the everyday lives of individuals to the whole climate system of the planet? What relationship does an individual life have to the collective "we" of the human in the Anthropocene? Questions of collectivity and questions of scale are themselves reducible to apprehensions of time and space. For instance, while there is general consensus among scholars that we are *in* the Anthropocene, there is less agreement about how this collective "we" is constituted or why collectivity can be presumed without accounting for the striations and hierarchies that have resulted from the historical processes that we use to "date" the epoch: the move from forest to agriculture, European colonization and expansion in the New World, the Industrial Revolution, or the testing of the atomic bomb.

The newness of the contemporary moment, the insistence that the Anthropogenic intersection of the subjective-epochal times is unprecedented, should not blinker us from seeing continuities amid calls for rupture. While our grappling with these massive geologic temporal scales may be new, subjective response to scales of time that are beyond human calculation is not. In a powerful essay on the temporal scales of climate change, Srinivas Aravamudan reminds us that we have been here before. For the Christian believer, the biblical apocalypse was determinate although only partially realized—it could come like a thief in the night. For Americans living through the height of the Cold War, nuclear catastrophe was indeterminate, but all indications were that it would be quick. The case of climate change is different from both these apocalypses in that global warming is determinate and inevitable but also a slow ongoing process that is not yet fully realized. The relatively recent emergence of popular climate consciousness has encouraged a discontinuity with other forms of catastrophic thinking and their narrative temporalities; however, an understanding of catastrophic time is especially relevant when we realize the cruel paradox the Anthropocene has placed upon us as human agents: we should be able to act, counteract, because we have more time, but we cannot.

The question of human agency, when posed as an emergency response needed to avert planetary catastrophe, has perhaps never been clearer as a mode of chronopolitics. Political questions of agency when linked to the task of decentering human mastery imply that we have to entertain more intelligent and sustainable arguments about "the vitality of (nonhuman) bodies." However, to be part of a human-nonhuman assemblage, we also have to forge relationships over time with the "force of things."[7] For Aravamudan, the question of human agency is complicated even further by the possibility that the chronopolitics of history and that of (catastrophic) climate change move in different directions: "Similar to anachronism that reimagines the past in terms of the present, catachronism re-characterizes the past and the present in terms of a future proclaimed as determinate but that is of course not yet fully realized. To that extent, catachronism cannot function without the operational assumptions of a theological grasp of time, whereby anticipation, belief, and application on the present are integrated as inexorably leading to a known and inevitable outcome."[8] Aravamudan's distinction between anachronism and "catachronism" (his neologism) is not simply a reorientation of temporal direction in the way we might swing from a backward-looking glance to a forward-looking one. Rather, it is the anticipatory relationship to the Anthropocene as a recharacterization of the "past *and* the present" in terms of a determined future that is not yet fully realized. This anticipatory structure is one that is likely to make many cultural critics uneasy. How do we reconcile the determinate status of what is presented as impending doom with the "anthropological function of critique, whose rhetorical appeal depends on the prediction of an open rather than determined future?"[9] The challenge for the critic is twofold: first, how do we imagine forms of agency that are multiple and distributed (rather than individual), given the powerlessness one feels at the scale of the Anthropocene and the impossibility of knowing for certain whether human knowledge and deliberated human action can make a difference. Second, how do we understand these nonhuman forms of agency without letting go of human historical consciousness, even as this distributed agency is directing us toward an imaginative dismantling of the world we have built and the rearranging of it in anticipation of a survivable future for all?

In what follows, I want to offer some modest responses to these questions by a literary-enabled conceptual performance of *assemblage*, a term that in recent years has provided an exciting model for the imagining of human-nonhuman distributed agency. Assemblage, a notion borrowed from Deleuze and Guattari, has received considerable traction in posthumanist debates; however, these important discussions have focused mostly on questions of ontology and materiality (what is an assemblage? what is it made of?). There has been little attempt to think about the temporality and historicity of assemblages and their past capacity for agency, both human and nonhuman. For instance, when Yusoff argues that "slavery weaponized the redistribution of energy around the globe through the flesh of black bodies," what she does is change the bodily integrity of the subject of slavery from human subject (the possessive individual who drives the Anthropocene) to "flesh." The enslaved person is now part of an assemblage of material (energy) where the connection between geology and life is recognized both in the manner of biological, chemical, and geomorphic scales and in the "intimate contours of geologic life as a force and power with subjective life."[10] Such an assemblage forces us to look at the past and imagine the consequences of that undeniable history in the present. Alexander Weheliye underscores the politico-ethical aspect of this distributed agency of the enslaved as inhuman material in his critique of modalities of the human that do not consider the constitutive role of race in European modernity. A "new" language of the earth cannot be resolved, he points out, by simply adopting modes of inclusion of marginalized subjects because the biocentric subject has not disarticulated itself from its twin: "racializing assemblages."[11]

My discussion of distributed agency in this chapter attempts to present human and nonhuman actants on a less vertical scale, without bracketing the "question of the human" (pace the vibrant materialism of Jane Bennett).[12] Instead, I ask how the rich analysis of subjectivity that literature enables, especially in narrative forms like the realist novel, can further new conditions of possibility for reimagining the boundaries of the very human who is thinking the posthuman. How might narrative experimentation with depictions of setting and the plots of time enable the imagining of assemblages as a *historicized* human-nonhuman multiplicity and as a style of political analysis that can better account for the contributions made by nonhuman actants? The assemblage, as I see it, is how we recharacterize an ecological and economic past, and the present, for the future.

Before I move on to my reading of Barbara Kingsolver's *Flight Behavior* and its compelling disarticulation of the biocentric subject into various historical and contemporary assemblages, I am going to make an exorbitant claim: the novel is quintessentially an Anthropogenic form because it has the ability to perform an existential temporality in our acts of reading. Narration allows us to think of multiple ways of thinking of space and time and to organize our thinking of space and time using different stories. What does not change, however, is that as readers we cannot but think and perform space as extension and time as sequence.[13] Despite these limitations, the literary text allows the imagination to flex into scales of time and space that are not human, to be in the tempos and rhythms of other beings, and to insert ourselves into everyday lives that are not ours or of "our" time.

The contemporary novels I have discussed in this book are especially versatile at the staging of multiple spatial and temporal scales in the same story, and they do so without the luxury of verifiability. That singular aspect, of fiction being untrue, of being unverifiable, is probably the best approximation of the Anthropogenic future as we have discussed it—a future proclaimed as determinate but not yet fully realized. As I discussed in chapter 4, while the past can extend infinitely into geologic and cosmic scales, the future cannot stretch without limit as long as the individual's biological life span remains the measure of a meaningful life. With regard to climate change, is it difficult to persuade people to care about an abstraction unless it pinches them at the pump, raises their utility bills, or, worse, destroys their homes? When a narrative form like the novel consciously (or unconsciously) connects events that happen on vast, geological scales, such as changes to the whole climate system of the planet, with what is going on in the everyday lives of individuals, collectivities, institutions, and nations, those connections provide important insights into the imagining of agency and responsibility, individual and collective, when facing a far-off abstraction like species' demise.

Bringing the impact of climate change into the foreground, decentering the perspective of the human agent, and imagining assemblages that include humans with nonhumans—these are the central themes of the novel *Flight Behavior*. The cardinal event of the story is posed as a question that the novel must answer: "Why a major portion of the monarch population that has overwintered in Mexico since God set it loose there . . . would instead aggregate in the southern Appalachians for the first time in recorded history, on the farm of the family Turnbow."[14] There are other story lines that run parallel to the main one about the flight of lost butterflies, and they take turns in the foreground. I begin with a critical discussion of environmental writing that has depended on spatial, or topographical, differentiations rather than the topological aspects of an assemblage that incorporate subjective apprehensions of time.[15] Here, my point is to show how the "setting" of the novel, such as a sheep farm in rural Tennessee, can be transformed into a different kind of subjective experience by the use of narrative *description*. Descriptions abound in realist novels, but they are not always passive fillers between events. In Kingsolver's novel they signal the emergence of a narrative clearing where we sense multiple ways of thinking of time, ranging from the seasonal and the everyday to the biological and the planetary, as they intersect in the perceptual field of the subject. The novel's primary focalizer for these descriptions is Dellarobia Turnbow, a young white woman who considers her life on a struggling family farm a stifling routine she cannot escape.

The discussion of description as a literary object brings me to the next section about its conceptual correlate, the assemblage, as an alternative mode of encountering the nonhuman world. The stakes involved in putting this concept to work in discussions of globality are several, but I take up one key instance in the contrast between assemblages and a kind of structural analysis of the part-whole relationship that we call the economic world-system. When Kingsolver represents contemporary capitalist globalization in the novel, Appalachia is a staging ground for the flight of manufacturing capital from the United States. But the notion of assemblage gives us another way of imagining the part-whole relationship and forms of agency that exceed the limits of human-centered globalization. A subsequent section discusses what I call the novel's "planetary encounter"—Dellarobia's first sight of the monarch butterflies—as a sort of delayed decoding or temporal pacing within the narration that allows us to "see" a specialized assemblage form in the text and sense its facility for operating at multiple temporal and spatial scales. Here, I also point to the formal examples provided by the novel itself—one, the progressive expansion of scale signaled by the chapter titles as a way to read Dellarobia's entry into bigger and higher orders of assemblages, and two, the ways words in a language provide the ability of replication within assemblages as they shape a range of discourses: from the most intimate beliefs of persons to the content of public conversations and media coverage, from historically transmitted oral traditions of communities to scientific papers published on observable natural phenomena. The reception of the novel *Flight Behavior*, its publication, and its "migration" into higher-order assemblages that were not planned in advance by the author herself is another instance of this kind of replication.

The final two sections of this chapter discuss the key lessons that a distributed idea of agency teaches us. I look at the Turnbow farm as it becomes a scientific assemblage and the way the lives of the humans enmeshed in it are transformed by this multiplicity. A young African American scientist, Ovid Byron (modeled after Barack Obama, the novel hints), and his catalytic role in transforming the family farm into a specialized assemblage (a scientific lab) is Kingsolver's response to Yusoff's critique of "white geology." There are exotic outsiders in this white American heartland, but their necessary incorporation into the main story line reminds us that social realist fiction cannot mask its exclusions by resorting to abstract categories of the human. The descendants of Atlantic slavery and the descendants of conquest of Indigenous peoples in Meso-America enter Appalachia as scientists and seasonal workers. Kingsolver traces the color line, albeit in broad strokes, into the class and gender divide of the mainstream United States represented by the young protagonist, Dellarobia. In so doing, the novel reinscribes colonialism and slavery into the subjective lives of those inhabiting the extractive economies of a contemporary moment. In the final section of the chapter, I ask what the agency of assemblages, especially given assemblages' dependence on nonlinear temporal experiences, implies for future outcomes. Does it imply that we should, following Helga Nowotny's lead, embrace a politics of uncertainty as the way forward in the Anthropocene? Here, I look at the figuration of home in *Flight Behavior* as a multiscalar composition that embraces an uncertain future, a future in which the present can be analogized like the relationship between home as a place of belonging and the homes we make away from this original home that can also be a radical form of unbelonging. In the temporality of the future, the present like that home is temporary for everyone. This, as I see it, is the novel's most pointed move as an ethico-aesthetic composition: the loss of Dellarobia's home in a flash flood brings her family to the shared condition suffered by others in the novel, like the butterflies and the family of climate refugees from Mexico. The loss of home, however, is imagined as an opportunity to recompose the present for the future.

Narrative Description and Time Lapse

In a recent work that tries to understand why contemporary culture finds it so hard to deal with climate change, Amitav Ghosh is disappointed that most serious writers of fiction continue to ignore this urgent subject. These writers, according to Ghosh, are no doubt part of a "broader imaginative and cultural failure," but it doesn't help at all that climate change presents "peculiar forms of resistance" to fiction.[16] Ghosh diagnoses the writers' problem by drawing on Franco Moretti's division of narrative episodes into two broad classes called "turning points" (cardinal events) and "fillers."[17] The problem of making what once seemed a far-off problem (like weather) into a daily event involves an imaginative spatiotemporal reversal of what, till now, has been a defining feature of the modern realist novel—its exceptional ability to make the fillers more significant than the turning points. The cardinal or "unheard-of" event, which was central to forms like the epic and other premodern narrative forms, is relocated by the novel to the background while "the everyday moves into the foreground."[18] Ghosh argues that serious writers find it impossible to move out of this foreground-background arrangement (that any serious consideration of the climate change will need) because they cannot deal with the underlying problem of probability: because modern novels focus on the everyday and the familiar, writers are invested in certainty rather than in improbability. Caught in the grip of these conventions, it is not surprising to Ghosh that novel writers resist incorporating the sudden, unexpected, and unheard-of weather phenomena that are harbingers of climate change. By implication, when smaller-scale weather-related phenomena do appear in fiction of our time, they come bearing a temporality that is appropriate for the fillers—weather is part of the story but only as an isolated or gradual (climate) change that is easily assimilated into quotidian life.

The spatializing of narrative elements like cardinal events and fillers into background and foreground disguises, it seems to me, a key element of novelistic representation that Ghosh records simply as "certainty" versus "improbability"—the irreducible dependence of the novel on a narrator, on subjective experience, the everyday and the lived present as the bases for thinking about the future. If we want to draw human experience into a future that is beyond human scales, the ecological imagination of the novel will have to attend to the experience of temporality and not just the spatial arrangements of landscape or setting, as Ghosh does predominantly. To be fair, this is a hard habit to break because descriptions of place have played a key role in environmental aesthetics.

In a novel, before there is "planet" there is "place." The making of a setting involves taming the world we know, and these conventions serve to make readers "enter" this world and become "emplaced" within them.[19] Natural bodies like a river, a hill, or a rainstorm are experienced up close as part of a landscape, thus disconnecting the setting from the massive spatial continuity of the planet. The setting becomes a "self-contained ecosystem" and banishes to the background the greater landscape of the "inconceivably large forces" that are in reality pressing upon us.[20] The framing of environmental struggle as one conjoined with "place" is a crucial element in post-Romanticist environmentalist writing to date. Ursula Heise has charted how US ecocriticism and environmentalist writing have consistently emphasized place and the local as the bases of individual and communal identity and idealized these natural landscapes as the "sites of connections to nature that modern society is perceived to have undone."[21] Heise is critical of US environmentalisms' "excessive investment" in the local and of the sluggishness of ecocritics in coming to terms with the central tenet of contemporary globalization: that the "increasing connectedness of societies around the globe entails the emergence of new forms of culture that are no longer anchored in place."[22] For Heise, environmental justice demands new scales, precisely those premised not on ties to local places but on "ties to territories and systems that are understood to encompass the planet as a whole."[23] Heise therefore questions whether "localism" is a necessary element in environmental thinking given that "place" is not a stable transcendent referent but, rather, an outcome of particular national traditions of thought and rhetoric.[24] Other critics of environmental aesthetics, like Timothy Morton, have tried to resignify the experience of place not as one of fullness but of emptiness. This means dealing with place as part abstraction, not as a concrete thing or field or world out *there*. Where Romantic ecology separated nature, or an aesthetic of place, from industry and noise and dirt, the world of getting and spending, Morton asks whether we might not instead combine the idea of a place with the "thinking generated by critical consumerism." Instead of a critical discourse of the *country* and a critical discourse of the *city*, Morton advocates, echoing David Harvey, an ecology that must "engage with urbanization" to have critical relevance in the twenty-first century.[25] Neither Heise nor Morton, in the two instances cited above, attempts to do more than reverse the idealisms of Romantics when discussing setting. There may be other ways to encounter the planet at the subjective level where, instead of a world "out there," the viewer becomes part of what they are seeing, part of an assemblage rather than a disconnected subject that faces and is "emplaced" in "nature."

In *Flight Behavior*, Kingsolver seems acutely aware of the need to represent her Appalachian setting without exoticism. There are descriptions of place that emphasize the alienated out-there-ness but even these are radically transformed, after Dellarobia's planetary encounter, into descriptions that are more like assemblages than landscapes. In my reading of the novel, I am interested in how "descriptions," as such, require a form of subjective emplacement but also timing. Although descriptions often seem to be only marginally important in narratives, they are, as the narratology theorist Mieke Bal explains, privileged sites of focalization where an inserted textual fragment attributes features to objects and draws the reader's attention to the persons or objects holding the interest of a narrator. Thus, descriptions are not only accounts of those things but also about the passage of a certain stretch of time.[26] When descriptions show us something that is happening, they add elements of narration or motivation to them. Looking at something takes time, and a description motivated by looking is incorporated into the narrative "time lapse."[27] The question, "Who looks?" requires our attention to the external factors that create the conditions for this lapse of time. Is it a walk? Is it a break in the action?

It is Dellarobia who is given the responsibility of description in the novel, and it is through her gaze that the Turnbow farm, the setting of the novel's events, first comes into view for the reader:

> The sheep in the field below, the Turnbow family land, the white frame house she had not slept outside for a single night in ten-plus years of marriage: that was

pretty much it. The widescreen version of her life since age seventeen. Not including the brief hospital excursions, childbirth-related. Apparently, today was the day she walked out of the picture. Distinguishing herself from the luckless sheep that stood down there in the mud surrounded by the deep stiletto holes of their footprints, enduring life's bad deals. They'd worn their heavy wool through the muggy summer, and now that the winter was almost here, they would be shorn. Life was one long proposition they never saw coming. Their pasture looked drowned. In the next field over, the orchard painstakingly planted by the neighbors last year was now dying under the rain. From here it all looked fixed and strange, even her house, probably due to the angle. She only looked out those windows, never into them, given the company she kept with people who rolled plastic trucks on the floor. Certainly she never climbed up here to check out the domestic arrangement. The condition of the roof was not encouraging. (*Flight*, 3)

The ecomimesis in this passage signals that the setting is constructed. The dead giveaway is the medial distance the text establishes between Dellarobia, who is looking down from the hilltop, and *what* she sees. Unlike an aestheticized view of the rural as landscape, what we get, instead, is an ironizing of the scene as *cinematic*, framed through different camera angles. The gaze is an alienated perspective that subsequently invokes a separation of self from nature: "From here it all looked fixed and strange." Dellarobia is like a fixed rather than moving camera, as the sheep from whom she has "distinguished herself," the field, the land, and the house are emplaced in the picture, the "wide-screen version of her life," from which she has just walked out. The separation between the scene and the subject is not a given; it is constructed by this framing. As Dellarobia resumes her walk up the hill, she becomes the locus of mobility, and the setting becomes a passing blur. Meanwhile, this picture holds her captive in an enclosure of domesticity. It makes the home not into a place of belonging but one where there is uprooting-in-place. She had "only looked out those windows, never into them." The anthropomorphic references to the sheep with their stiletto footprints reinforce through pathetic fallacy her own mute existence on the farm. There is action and temporality in this world of objects, but it is difficult to see unless we hold Dellarobia still like a fixed camera. There is the biographical span of a young woman's life marked by a marriage at the age of seventeen, the reference to childbirth as an "excursion" that is differentiated from but also linked, by a subsequent reference, to the reproductive rhythm of the animals and their seasonally driven lives: "Life was one long proposition they never saw coming." But the real crisis, of climate change, which is to become the focus of much of the novel, is ambient at this point, emerging only in the reference to a "drowned" pasture and a "dying" orchard in the next field over; both instances where the reader surmises that something unexpected has already happened—a moment of local recognition without the comprehension of something at the scale of climate change. Then Dellarobia's gaze goes back and pauses anticlimactically at the condition of the roofs of houses. The overall effect the passage delivers is one where nature is deromanticized by the injection of conceits of labor, technology, dilapidation, and death. The word "disaster" arrives only a few pages later, but here, too, climatic change is framed as a subjective and affective response to the washing away of "well-made plans": "There is no use blaming the rain and mud, these are only elements. The disaster is the failed expectation" (9).

As Dellarobia turns away from this view and marches uphill, this filler-description will be replaced by the novel's key turning point—an encounter with a spectacular anomaly that scuttles her own plan for an extramarital tryst in a cabin on the hilltop. But it is in the moment of description, in the time-lapse of Dellarobia's fixed gaze, that the world displays the heterotemporalities that humans experience within it and objects become things. The former denotes how something appears to a subject—as a name, identity, a template—while the latter signals the object looking back and the subject experiencing the object as uncanny.[28] While we do not see the distributed agency of the various elements that make up the agglomeration, the novel hints that this landscape is not to be idealized and that the home at the center of it is temporary, a place from which Dellarobia wants to move on—it is not a site of her belonging or her "proper self." Here, in this scene, is already a compositional reaching toward, what Deleuze has called in the context of filmic montage, "the assemblage [*agencement*] of movement-images as constituting an indirect image of time."[29]

At the rhetorical level, too, the novel's landscape descriptions eschew the auratic and unmediated beauty of nature, insisting instead on its reproducibility and historicity. When focalized through Dellarobia, the landscape becomes a site of the kind of ecological crosshatching that Morton calls "critical consumerism." Mundane objects of everyday life and unnatural elements enter into Dellarobia's impressions: "this mess of dirty white sky like a lousy drywall job"; a tree like "the corpse of the fallen monster"; "the view out across the valley . . . unreal, like a sci-fi movie"; "trunks and boughs were speckled and scaly like trees covered with corn flakes" (*Flight*, 2, 3, 5, 13). When Dellarobia sees what she believes to be glowing trees, she tries to imagine that what she is seeing is auratic and real, as far as possible from a commodified thing: "This was not just another fake thing in her life's cheap chain of events, leading up to this day of sneaking around in someone else's thrown-away boots. Here that ended" (15). But the novel's persistent point is that this "beautiful thing" we are witnessing, a flight of monarchs on a Tennessee hillside, is in fact a terrible thing—the possible extinction of a species. The aestheticization of nature only serves to disguise this future.

Flight Behavior thus eschews an ecocriticism that reifies the local, "nature," or home as bulwarks against the ravages of economic globalization. Although Dellarobia's privileged gaze shows that she is already an ecological subject in the making, as a poor, white, Appalachian woman without ready access to economic, cultural, or racial privileges, she is somewhat decentered from biocentric "Man." When one approaches the question of climate change from the rural back roads of Appalachia rather than from a spewing industrial town or a smog-overhung global city, the price that some groups may pay for the environmentally conscious policies of others is brought to the fore. Kingsolver's fictional rural has the expected but sparse references to drug addiction, mining jobs, unemployment, and discount and secondhand-goods stores, and behind the scenes there is the familiar story we have come to expect from the rural US South: economic and social devastation resulting from job losses in the local agricultural and coal-mining industries. The characters in Kingsolver's novel feel excluded from the nation, from the electoral "blue belt," and from the electronic world of the network. Still reeling from the diminishing dependency on fossil-burning resources and the closing of manufacturing units, their lives are already transformed by the overseas flight of US manufacturing capital. There is no ignoring the irony in Kingsolver's staging of an ecologically critical event (the interrupted life cycle of migrating monarch butterflies) in an Appalachian hamlet that is devastated by the short-term economic impact of reduced dependence on fossil fuels.[30] The novel's use of setting seems to reflect the view that if globalization sweeps away the ground under one's feet and undermines a coherent "sense of place," then a way to resist this encroachment would *not* be to preserve a corner of the world (or one's culture, one's subjectivity) from the indifferent calculations of mobile capital. The choice of a hill in rural Tennessee as the place to put down the butterflies does not prevent the location from entering into a web of global relationships. But while it is important to see how the novel makes these global economic connections, it is also important to note that the novel puts a totally different emphasis on the part-whole relationship, other than the local-global structuring of labor and capital in the world-system that is, when it shifts its attention to the butterfly event. What is at work here needs a careful unpacking of what Deleuze and Guattari, and others following them, call an assemblage.

Assemblage

The concept of *agencement* (translated into English as "assemblage") plays a central role in Gilles Deleuze and Félix Guattari's *A Thousand Plateaus*. In a set of conversations (with Claire Parnet) published before that work, Deleuze provides one of the clearest articulations of the term: "What is an assemblage? It is a multiplicity which is made up of many heterogeneous terms and which establishes liaisons, relations between them, across ages, sexes, and reigns—different natures. Thus the assemblage's only unity is that of co-functioning: it is a symbiosis, a 'sympathy.' It is never filiations which are important, but alliances, alloys; these are not successions, lines of descent, but contagions, epidemics, the wind."[31] "Multiplicity" invokes a philosophy of materiality that contends with other important theories of materiality, such as Marx's, and places more emphasis on the contributions of nonhuman forces. In Marx, it is human labor that animates discussions of objects in *Capital*, but for the materialists who want to counter what Jane Bennett calls the "narcissism of humans in charge of the world," the focus is on the nonhuman forces that operate in "nature," in the human body, and in human artifacts.[32] To think of collectives in terms of multiplicity is to imply that their "unity" has a radical heterogeneity that removes it from the control of any one group or power structure. It means not deciding beforehand who or what will be part of such a collective. Most importantly, the assemblage's unity does not come from a single cause but is determined by its cofunctioning, a cofunctioning that makes its agency into a distributed force emerging from the alliance and the set of relations that exist between its terms and elements.

The French word for assemblage, *agencement*, means "a construction, arrangement, or layout" and comes from the verb *agencer* (to construct, to piece together, and so on). The English word "assemblage," as it is used, puts more emphasis on the joining or union of two things. In his discussion of the term's translation, Thomas Nail makes the point that a layout or an arrangement (implied in the French usage) is quite different from a unity or a simple coming together (implied in the English usage).[33] Conflating the two meanings leads to a tendency to think of assemblage as a mixture of heterogeneous elements working in unity without deriving the unity from its functioning or the acts of recombination by its elements, or actants, moving from one assemblage to another. The notion of recombination or replication is important because it makes assemblages quite different from the flattened visualization of a network (and ironically, somewhat closer to the epidemic clusters of capitalism that Fredric Jameson offers us in chapter 3).

Manuel DeLanda makes a significant contribution to assemblage theory by bringing in temporality for the discussion of scale. In most of these instances, when he discusses the assemblage's capacity for "variable replication," "time-lags," and "temporal overlaps," DeLanda's analogy is that of language: the way language allows us to read a longer "life span" by the "transmission of semantic information across generations," even as it allows us to access the language use in specialized assemblages of varying scales.[34] Putting this analogy to work in the way DeLanda suggests it is to propose that just as "words" are the building blocks of bigger and bigger chunks of utterances and different kinds of discourses (personal to public to national-constitutional), any one assemblage is capable of operating at multiple spatial scales simultaneously. As he states, "Language shapes the intimate beliefs of a persons, the public content of conversations, the oral traditions of small communities, and the written constitutions of large organizations and entire governments." And just as "linguistic replicators" operating at one scale can move to another, human or nonhuman elements of an assemblage can "replicate" vertically by becoming part of higher (more abstract) assemblages or move horizontally into other assemblages and in so doing introduce "alien routines, procedures, rituals which layer, rather than preserve, the identity of social assemblages."[35]

These replications suggest agency, but what kind of agency? Deleuze and Guattari refer to the assemblage's "abstract machine"—that which actually supports the conjunction or combination, "the hidden principle which makes visible what is seen."[36] This element is important because, as I have argued in chapter 3, the use of networks as flattened ontologies and surface readings does not answer the question, "What brings the elements together on a plane?" What are the conditions of possibility for the unity, its combination, and the relations between the elements? If, as *Flight Behavior*'s descriptions focalized through Dellarobia suggest, assemblages have concrete elements (to be described), what really matters is not their essence but what they can do together as a unit when the human too is emplaced within it. In other words, distributed agency. DeLanda does not necessarily emphasize this agential function, but the assemblage as developed by Deleuze and Guattari is unavoidably political because it implies a form of collective action in which the directing force does not come from top down but is an immanent action of "coadaptation" and "reciprocity."[37]

For the Anthropocene, this means thinking about agency differently given the scale of change, the force exerted by nonhuman agents, and the uncertainty that envelops phenomena like climate change whose future trajectory we cannot predict with any accuracy. Consider where we are now: if species extinction is inevitable, then the pessimistic future that awaits us requires no action from us. The pitiful and impossible scale of human agency (although, paradoxically, the Anthropocene makes humanity into the driving force) will not make a dent. But what if the pessimism is driven partly by our inability to think of agency beyond the boundaries of a Cartesian subject? Or is it because we do not believe we can act unless we can predict the exact outcomes? Assemblages offer us other ways of thinking about agency—not embodied in personhood but as a composition of human, nonhuman, and material elements—so that humans may share this agency while also attending to how we as a species are in this world with others. Being "with" is an ethical relationship that can transform the way we relate to planetary life and the materials of the planet that we have come to view as our "resources." Along these lines Diana Coole calls for a more distributionist notion of agency in hopes that theories of action and responsibility will draw from "across the human nonhuman divide" and look to "a spectrum of agentic capacities."[38]

I have spent a considerable part of this section describing the specificity of the concept-metaphor of the assemblage, but I want to end the discussion by distinguishing the concept from another part-whole relationship that has become crucial to our understanding of globalization: the economic structure of the world-system. This is not to imply that the assemblage cannot accommodate a critique of economic reason; rather, it is to insist on the exercise of keeping the assemblage's nonhuman agential aspects in view before seeking to find economic interpretations of the phenomenon. But part-whole analogies between the economic system and the assemblage are also inescapable. For instance, in *Vibrant Matter*, Jane Bennett seeks to flesh out a materialism that is not Marxist materialism by way of the assemblage. She is looking for a way to grasp the complex and gigantic "whole" of the planet while characterizing the relationality of its parts, yet she finds herself thinking about globalization: "At the end of the twentieth century, the arena in which stuff happens . . . seemed to many people to have expanded dramatically. Globalization had occurred and the earth itself had become a space of events. The parts of this giant whole were both intimately interconnected and highly conflictual." For Bennett, "assemblage" is the "term of choice" for describing a "kind of relation that exists between the parts of a volatile but somehow functioning whole."[39] My inclination is somewhat different. It is to make the case that an assemblage is a new kind of part-whole relationship and that its insights allow us to advance ways of addressing the tension between the temporal and spatial scales of human-centered globalization (the world economy) and the nonhuman temporal scales of the Anthropocene. In this regard, assemblage thinking enables *Flight Behavior* to take a crucial step toward addressing the "capitalism or climate change" dilemma.

The everyday life in the foreground of *Flight Behavior* is resolutely connected to the economic world, and it is hard not to think of the Turnbow family farm as a site where the planetary damage of climate change intersects with the global spread of agro-capitalism. In a chapter aptly titled "Global Exchange," Dellarobia and her husband, Cub, go shopping for Christmas gifts at the local Dollar Store (*Flight*, 157). As the young couple begin their slow waltz through the discount store's aisles, Kingsolver brilliantly secures what ecocriticism often fails to see in the nexus between consumerism and environmentalism. The structural irony is the Dollar Store's transformation of "nature" into objects like a set of green plastic binoculars that urges users to "explore, discover, get close to nature, all for $1.50," or horribly made plush raccoons or even kitsch objects like the knitted potholder shaped like a monarch butterfly that Dellarobia decides to buy (167, 175). The store contains enough plastic baubles, we are told, "to cover a hayfield." The sheer volume of stuff, whose quality is meant to ensure shorter and shorter cycles of consumption, calls desperately for demystification but as such still hides the vitality of plastic as a thing that has a time scale of its own. Plastic is also a hyperobject in a planetary assemblage. In that assemblage it separates itself from the assemblage of the commodity form and lives on long after the days of its human consumption are over. This is what I mean when I say that the assemblage and capitalism may not "see" the same thing. The novel, however, is not about to miss the chance of demystifying the commodity.

To Cub's initial suggestion that they do all their Christmas shopping at the Dollar Store, Dellarobia responded with sarcasm, "Great. . . . Family heirlooms made by slave children in China" (*Flight*, 157). Her unconscious use of a phrase that her mother often "spat out like a curse" brings back this memory: "That drab army of orphans she could still see in her mind's eye. She used to picture them . . . resentful of happy homes everywhere, undercutting her father's handmade furniture business and her mother's work as a seamstress. Eventually those brats even shut down the knitwear factory where her mother had stooped from business suits to underwear, in the last decade of her employable life. In hindsight, Dellarobia could fathom her mother's drinking" (158). This is globalization in Appalachia, but the hidden processes of economic restructuring are read by its first world victims as the machinations of resentful Chinese (enslaved-child) workers. Now, walking through the store, Dellarobia realizes that the makers of these plastic goods weren't probably the enslaved children that her mother cursed but, rather, "armies of factory workers making this slapdash stuff, underpaid people cranking out things for underpaid people to buy and use up, living their lives mostly to cancel each other out. A worldwide entrapment of bottom feeders" (159). This image is a vivid conjuration of capitalist relations as the structured connection between the poor people who produce these cheap plastic goods in one part of the world and the newly impoverished consumers, like Dellarobia and Cub, who have no option but to buy the very things that cost them their jobs. The metaphor of "bottom feeders" renders the globe into an oceanic mass, where the flows of goods and commodities reveal the mutual entrapment of China and Appalachia as "intimately interconnected and highly conflictual" parts of a whole. By connecting poverty in the United States to poverty in the manufacturing centers of Asia and the worldwide economy of cheap plastics that can "cover a hayfield," Kingsolver's global perspective challenges those of ecologists like David Abram, for whom ecological consciousness (the "sensuous world") is always a localized experience: "In contrast to the apparently unlimited, global character of the technologically mediated world, the sensuous world—the world of our direct, unmediated interactions—is always local."[40] This structuring of Appalachia and China as mutual feedback loops in the capitalist world-system is the sort of relationship that the quest for "networks" often uncovers, although networks would hardly be able to show the subjective experience of historical memory of this economic restructuring in Dellarobia's family over two generations. The novel doesn't gesture toward consumer agency in the world-system, but we notice that the couple quarrels and leaves the store without buying anything (except the knitted monarch-shaped potholder). What stays with us is Dellarobia's bitter observation that "she suddenly felt so allergic to Chinese plastic she couldn't breathe," as she heads out to the parking lot for a "seventy-five-cent smoke." These are the novel's subtle nudges that lead us away from a reading of economic structure and world-system to social assemblages in which, as Bennett puts it, we see the material agency of nonhuman forces and things (like plastic and nicotine) on and in the human body.[41]

When everyday life is shaped into assemblage-like forms instead of economic structure, the scene is suddenly replete with a wide variety of actants, and people seem to be engaged in "an intricate dance with nonhumans."[42] Here is a passage where mundane details of the everyday are observed in a frame like a van Gogh with "still life of muddy boots" in the foreground. The resulting "picture" creates an alterity in human intention by using the objects that surround the subject:

> The minute [Ovid Byron] hiked out of sight, her [Dellarobia's] impulse was to run to Hester's and get on the computer. She'd never thought to Google her own name. She lit a cigarette instead, and confronted the sight of her back porch with its still life of muddy boots, cardboard boxes, and a miniature Big Wheels bike lying on its side, looking comatose. Cub would be leaving for work in ten minutes, Cordie would want breakfast. Dellarobia exercised the only option generally available to her in times of personal upheaval. She walked to the side of the house where she couldn't be seen out of a window, and dialed Dovey. (*Flight*, 106)

Dellarobia's "family" is described here as a social assemblage that includes not just people but also a shared computer, an internet connection, a browser (Google), the cigarette that delivers the nicotine and provides her with hidden breaks from the family, and the cell phone that allows her access to a social network beyond her family. Although it is true that nothing about this picture allows us to ascribe a cause-effect relationship between Dellarobia's intention and her actions, what it does provide is an idea of human agency that is affect, more than intentionality or pure consciousness. The novel's teasing out and provisioning details allow us to imagine material "things" that also have an agentic force on her life in the human-centered assemblage we call a family.

What does it mean to think human agency over multiple and incommensurable scales at once? Given the centrality of agency to modern conceptions of politics, an embodied and rational subject persists as political actor despite various poststructuralist, psychoanalytic, and postmodernist challenges to presupposing such a subject's grounding in responsibility, autonomy, rationality, and freedom. Perhaps the difficulty in reimagining agency in ways that respond to the technocapitalist and ecological relations of the contemporary world, where the ontopological forms of identity are increasingly displaced and unsettled, is part of the reason that global aspirations of environmentalist politics seem pessimistic. Where does one start? In *Flight Behavior* Kingsolver begins Dellarobia's story with an encounter that gains significance only when it is understood and recognized as the sign of forces that we have taken for granted. Dellarobia's encounter with climate change is, at first, a message that cannot be interpreted with any certainty. But this is not unexpected, for, after all, "systemic risks," Nowotny tells us in a compelling book on the subject, are "barely visible and emit only weak signals." They build up slowly, through gradual processes that go unnoticed until they suddenly burst into the foreground.[43] It is as though the novel is saying that a planetary encounter is not about the spectacular or the awesome. It may involve something along the lines of an aesthetic attentiveness, an experience that involves not the mastery of knowledge but the act of not-knowing. Becoming a human-nonhuman assemblage means not absorbing everything else into human knowledge or standing apart detached and free from the part-whole relationship that binds everything. Indeed, we may have to think of the self in the way Kingsolver conceives of Dellarobia, as an impure human-nonhuman assemblage.

Planetary Encounters in the Lived Present

What I am calling the planetary encounter is catalyzed when the novel moves the environment from the background, from the distancing picture of failed human endeavor on land (dying orchard, drowning pasture), till it appears closer in view and exists around the subject in an ambient way and everything loses focus for a moment. Then it emerges, out of view of the subject, not squarely in the center of the frame, an object rising up toward Dellarobia's superficial knowledge: "Something in motion caught her eye and yanked her glance upward. How did it happen, that attention could be wrenched like that by some small movement? It was practically nothing, a fleck of orange wobbling above the trees. It crossed overhead and drifted to the left, where the hill dropped steeply from the trail. She made a face, thinking of redheaded ghosts" (*Flight*, 11). The scene depends on what Ian Watt has called "delayed decoding": the interjection of something else into the middle of a scene so that the reader is forced to hold off understanding till the writer is ready to deliver.[44] Without her glasses, it takes some doing for Dellarobia to get "a bead on the thing," but there it still was, "drifting in blank air above the folded terrain: an orange butterfly on a rainy day. Its out-of-place brashness made her think of the wacked-out sequences in children's books" (11). The anomaly of the butterfly is at first, simply, its *being there* on a rainy day. Delayed decoding withholds the significance of the butterfly's presence on the hilltop. Even the aggregation of the butterfly into a mass that explodes onto the page is couched in mystery. As Dellarobia rounded the open side of the slope, she "slammed on her brakes; here something was wrong." The trees above her were draped with "brownish clumps," "bristly things" like "cornflakes" (13). Then sunlight falls on the slope, and Dellarobia stands still, seeing but without comprehension: "The forest blazed with its own internal flame. 'Jesus,' she said. . . . Brightness of a new intensity moved up the valley in a rippling wave, like the disturbed surface of a lake. Every bough glowed with an orange blaze.... Trees turned to fire, a burning bush" (14). Where an entomologist may have been prepared for this sight after spotting the first orange butterfly, Dellarobia cannot know what she sees. For her the encounter is verbalized in part by the language of the sublime and in part by the language of religious rapture.

It is only several pages later, when Dellarobia brings her husband and in-laws up the hill to witness the sight, that the novel finally decodes what "it" is: "Golden darts filled the whole of the air, swirling like leaves in a massive storm. Wings. The darts underfoot also were wings. Butterflies. How had she failed to see them?" (*Flight*, 52). As Dellarobia and the Turnbows stand in the middle of the field, they become "human-boulders in the butterfly-filled current." Dellarobia's body feels the shock: "She felt her breathing rupture again into laughter or sobbing in her chest, sharp, vocal exhalations she couldn't contain. The sounds coming out of her veered toward craziness." Hester, her mother-in-law says, "Lord Almighty, the girl is receiving grace" (57). Here, the planetary encounter is strange but also strangely familiar in the way Aravamudan describes it—there is something theological about the sublime and something messianic about the ecological end times we call the Anthropocene. The perception of an emergency in the midst of the familiar and mundane suggests that the planet is all around us, but to "enter" the planet one crosses a frontier. Till then we are boulders in its stream, not part of the flow.

The Appalachian Tennessee of the novel is a place of massive deforestation, pasturage, agriculture, fossil fuel extraction, meth addiction, cheap Chinese goods, shopping malls, and ecological toxification. The attribution of uncanniness means that the butterfly, like the rural in the novel, is not totally strange but already an assemblage of collective meanings that bring into play human, nonhuman, and material things. The butterfly itself is part of a linguistic assemblage that establishes historical continuities as well as synchronously lived or shared presents. As the local church's congregation ponders the meaning of this miraculous event, the Turnbow family finds itself questioning the wisdom of logging trees on the mountain where the congregation now believes a divine revelation has taken place in "our Lord's abundant garden" (72). The butterfly's name designates not a single thing but several histories. When the orange butterflies are first named in the novel, it is not by their scientific name, *Danaus plexippus*, but rather by a popular nickname that Hester Turnbow, Dellarobia's mother-in-law, gives them—"King Billies." Later in the book we learn the etymology. King Billy's provenance is in colonial history, apparently named by white settlers in North America after the colors associated with William of

Orange (coregent with Mary after the Glorious Revolution of 1688 and the hero of Protestant England for his victory over the Roman Catholic James II).[45] The name most familiar to English-language speakers, "monarch," first appears in a novel untranslated from Spanish: *mariposas monarcas*, but its origin is relayed again when a little girl, Josefina Delgado, who goes to school with Dellarobia's son, brings her parents, migrant workers, to see the butterflies on the Turnbow farm. They say, "The *monarcas* are from Michoacan, and we are from Michoacan" (98). Dellarobia herself remembers hearing the name "monarch" on a television show, *Animal Planet*. The novel's textual play with partial knowledge, intuition, and information from multiple sources is a reminder that ecological knowledge does not necessarily come from the outside but that it, too, emerges in manifold ways. God's "abundant garden" is one of those ways, as is an immigrant family's association of it with their former home. The butterflies are strangers that have already dwelled among us, and the multiplicity of their meaning is evidence of coexistence and of recognition.

This linguistic play on the name of the monarch suggests that the novel too is an assemblage that operates at multiple spatial and temporal scales simultaneously. To use Manuel DeLanda's example, just like "genes are active within cells, but at another level govern the functioning of organs, and influence the behavior of entire organisms," language too shapes "the intimate beliefs of persons, the public content of conversation, the oral tradition of small communities, the written constitutions of large organizations," and so on.[46] But these oral traditions, one originating from the Anglo-Saxon conquest of North America and the other from the Spanish conquest of the New World create a racialized assemblage in the present day, carrying with it the temporal "genes" transmitted from the days of European colonialism. The linguistic assemblage itself operates at a larger scale as a continental history in which the story of Indigenous Meso-America has also appeared. Similarly, Kingsolver's choice of Ovid Byron, the entomologist-lepidopterologist, as the lead scientist investigating the monarch phenomenon in the novel is almost as exotic as the other "nonnatives" (the butterflies, the Mexican migrants) in a predominantly white town. Byron's home in New Mexico ("the state, not the country," as he says to Dellarobia) and his St. Thomas island upbringing are hardly accidental. Both places signal the historical continuity between the colonization of Indigenous land in the United States and the use of islands populated by Atlantic slavery for US nuclear testing in the twentieth century. Both nuclear power and plantation agriculture, we are reminded, played catalyzing roles in Anthropogenic acceleration.

The historical sedimentations of assemblages need some careful unpacking;

what is more obvious is assemblage's ability to operate at spatially larger scales. When the rural Tennessee of the novel is shown to be anything but a closed-off, demographically homogeneous biosphere, this resolve to render boundaries porous is mirrored in the novel's reference to scale variance in its chapter titles, which perform a consecutively sequenced act of zooming out. The titles of the first eight chapters perform a series of expansions: "The Measure of a Man," "Family Territory," "Congregational Space," "Talk of a Town," "National Proportions," "Span of a Continent," "Global Exchange," and "Circumference of the Earth." Within these titles Dellarobia's space expands outward even if she has never left the town of Featherstone (another name tag for a human-nonhuman assemblage). Dellarobia never moves, but her assemblages get bigger and bigger, all dependent on the scale at which they operate: in chapter 1, we have a married couple, then family, church, town, nation, continent, globe, and finally planet. Also present in the chapter titles are terms associated with measurement (measure, territory, space, proportion, span, circumference, and exchange)."[47] By placing the narrator, or Dellarobia, in the center of the frame, the novel, like a film, can create the impression of a panoptic mastery that domesticates these scales for the reader. This is not a nested doll or story-within-a-story narrative. While there is no escaping the relationship between the magnification of the social entities imagined at various scales and the narrator who is the one imagining them, in another sense, the figuration of the planet is resolutely posthumanist. After all, can we not imagine the planet going on even after all humans have ceased to exist? Consider what happens when Kingsolver reaches the planetary scale in chapter 8, which is titled "Circumference of the Earth." Instead of beginning a smooth journey back to the solitary Dellarobia climbing the hill in chapter 1, what we get instead is a descending order of scale variance where collectivities show functional interdependencies rather than simply expanding space around the human subject. Here are the titles of the five remaining chapters: "Continental Ecosystem," "Natural State," "Community Dynamics," "Kinship Systems," and "Mating Strategies." These titles conjure up territorialized social "assemblages" that involve causal interactions as well as reasons and motives.[48] We cannot get to these assemblages by moving in a reverse zoom back to the starting point of the novel; rather, they complicate what had earlier have been mapped as a series of expanding circles on a linear spatial scale from smallest to largest. The static geographical place ("continent") now becomes, in this new iteration, a charged material cluster of an "ecosystem." Nature engenders a "state," towns become "community dynamics," family is imagined as "kinship systems," and heterosexual coupling is changed to species reproduction ("mating strategies"). Each of the novel's five closing chapters thus injects an analytical abstraction into what had been intimately familiar or mappable space and thus transforms the earlier collectivities into agential terms that are even less human centered in their envisioning.

Assemblages, by definition, go beyond the level of the "individual" or that of "society"—an obvious form of micro- and macro-reductionism that hinders social analysis—rather, assemblages are capable of looking at social entities in their multiple scales. This is because the components or parts that make up an assemblage are not defined by the "roles" they play in one assemblage (i.e., a relation of interiority); rather, like the novelistic character Dellarobia, who can be unplugged from one assemblage and put into another without losing herself (maintained by the linguistic coding of her proper name), components can exist variously in assemblages that are complex and nonlinear and formed or affected by the populations of lower-level assemblages: family-church-town-nation-continent-globe-earth-ecosystem. Ontologically, any one of these entities, like the family or the town, irrespective of its operative scale, is an individual singularity, the whole of which is always larger than its parts.[49] I began this chapter by posing the question whether assemblages have a distinct history of formation and whether this "history" exceeds the temporal scales of human-centered collectives. It seems to me that more than the spatial scale, it is the possibility of longer temporal scales in assemblages that makes their agency different from that of human-centered collectives. Imagining agency over longer durations that exceed the finite life spans of any of its parts is a different way of imagining the human part with the human-nonhuman whole, and consequently it allows for theories of action and responsibility that crosses this divide.

Temporal Scales and the Agency of Assemblages

It goes without saying that when we think of a biological species, we imagine it enduring for much longer than the organisms that compose it. Perhaps the same can be said for families or even nations, those human-centered assemblages for which individuals often sacrifice their lives and imagine persisting long after their own demise. Yet the family, as a smaller assemblage, cannot survive if its members do not reproduce and replenish their numbers. Similarly, just as the speed at which the parts must replicate or replace themselves plays its part in the endurance of an assemblage, change also happens in assemblages at varying speeds. Does it take longer for change to happen in organizations than in families, in towns than in nations, in nations than in the world? Can such calculations melt into air when the nonhuman agent is a highly contagious and deadly virus? The COVID-19 pandemic was an assemblage in which human-engineered boundaries and time lines proved useless against a virus that coded or unified the part-whole relations at a global scale. Any hope of long-term survival lay not in barricading ourselves against it but by gradually exposing ourselves to it to establish herd immunity or by introducing it in some weakened form into our bodies as a vaccine.[50]

In *Flight Behavior* the most compelling example of an assemblage is the scientific lab. The lab is not simply "in" a barn on the Turnbow farm. The farm opens outwardly, materially, spatiotemporally, and aesthetically into an assemblage of a higher order. This lab is also no longer grounded in the sterile buildings of a university. It moves in the lifeworld of the farm and the forest in which the monarchs have congregated and in so doing also becomes part of the human-animal assemblage we call the planet. The arrival of the lab at the farm deterritorializes not only the rural space but also the language of science and everyday language, theory and intuition, the practices of the educated elite and habits of citizens. The lab also represents a medial site between the micro and the macro levels of climate change. Dellarobia's part-time job as an assistant in Ovid Byron's lab moves her into a new assemblage. Even though she still lives at "home," this home has moved outward. It makes it possible for her to escape her daily routine, to displace herself from the central subject positions she sees for herself: poor, poorly educated, unhappy wife and tired mother. The words "butterfly lab" make little sense to Dellarobia initially, but the phrase begins to assemble a remarkable list of parts that reveal the whole of this remarkable territorial assemblage: there are the graduate students from a university; Byron's grant funding from the government; the trailer, their living quarters, that is plugged into the farm's energy grid; and an office housed in the farm's barn. Also included are the various instruments for measuring, weighing, centrifuging, and recording and the labor that Dellarobia contributes. Hospitality, the novel makes clear, is women's (unpaid) work: repaired zippers, clean laundry, dilly beans, and home-cooked meals. The "butterfly money," that Dellarobia earns as a lab worker now begins to transform her and Cub's home in major ways: it pays for their mortgage and purchases gifts for the family. The connections are endless, but this shagginess is how the novel demonstrates that the lab has various agentic functions that we fail to notice if we concentrate only on each person's contribution to the scientific work. Assemblages are about complexity. We are in the presence of indirect, nonlinear relationships between the interactive parts and dimensions of the whole, feedback loops, and indirect cause-effect relations.

As an assemblage, the lab also includes the objects of its study, the monarchs, but the humans, too, are affected by their object of study. At the study site in the forest, Byron and his assistants set up a simple tarp tent with a plywood table and folding chair. Standing there silently, looking out at the forest in what the novel describes as their "house without walls," Dellarobia and Ovid begin to sense "the concentrated atmosphere of their aloneness." The forest surrounding the lab and the farm is not a garden or idealized landscape. It suddenly appears to have no center. It expands the farm into the whole of earth. In this shared moment, the expert and the novice find a common language in which they have a new sense of their part-whole relationship:

> "An animal is the sum of its behaviors," he said finally. "Its community dynamics. Not just the physical body."
>
> "What makes a monarch a monarch is what it does, you're saying."
>
> He stood looking out at the forest, arms crossed. Not exactly facing her, but not turned away. "Interactions with other monarchs, habitat, the migration, everything. The population functions as a whole being. You could look at it that way."
>
> She did, often. This butterfly forest was a great, quiet, breathing beast. Monarchs covered the trunks like orange fish scales. Sometimes the wings all moved slowly in unison. Once while she and Ovid were working in the middle of all that, he had asked her what was the use of saving a world that had no soul left in it. Continents without butterflies, seas without coral reefs, he meant. What if all human effort amounted basically to saving a place for ourselves to park? He had confessed these were not scientific thoughts." (*Flight*, 317)

"What makes a monarch is what a monarch does" is nice way to sum up the agency of the assemblage. We can think this way only by doing away with the notion of human-centered agency that depends on the "physical body" (the embodiment that grounds human autonomy, self-referentiality, and causality).

Like the monarchs, we, too, as Anthropos have functioned as a sum of our behaviors, and we have impacted the earth as a "whole being" across history and across space. Here, in what might be called a cross-species moment, it is the butterflies' assemblage that comes into view: a complex set of "interactions with other monarchs, habitats, the migration, everything." As Dellarobia contemplates the butterflies, the forest around her also transforms into a larger living body of which the butterflies themselves are parts, their wings moving in unison, covering the trees like "orange fish scales" on an even larger being, a larger assemblage in which it is the combined effort of the monarch population, bracing itself and using the tree's warmth, that enables it to survive the cold and avoid its own possible collective demise.

Yet such collective mobilization has elements of uncertainly. There are other agents working against this collective. We cannot see them with the naked eye; they are visible only under a microscope: "[Dellarobia] fiddled with the focus, and it jumped up in 3-D: a strange collage of ridged, transparent ovals that overlapped slightly like roof shingles. These were the scales that covered a butterfly's wings, [Ovid Byron] said, magnified times three hundred. Nestled among the scales she saw smaller, darker shapes like water beetles, and these, he told her, were the parasites. OE for short" (*Flight*, 243). The novel plays with the focus to show us the scale variances of assemblages and the differences in their agentic capacities at these varying scales. In the higher-level assemblage, the butterflies' wings are scales of a living forest. In the passage quoted above, the butterflies themselves have scales, and on those scales are parasites that exist in relation to the whole butterfly in the same way the butterfly related to the forest.

These different levels make it difficult to attribute a single cause or to trace causality in a linear direction. Are these microscopic parasites the cause of the butterflies' diversion to Tennessee instead of Mexico? Is the parasite sapping the butterfly's strength and preventing a longer migration? Ovid does not know, but he tells Dellarobia that they could be looking at a correlation rather than at a cause: correlations between rising average temperatures, increasing parasite infestations, and abnormal butterfly migrations. Dellarobia is disappointed because while, for Ovid, the task of science is to "measure and count" without jumping to conclusions, for her it is to "explain" the "deep and terrible trouble [that] had sent the monarchs to the wrong address" (*Flight*, 244, 245). Assemblages give us a "what" and "how," but the question of "why" is harder to answer. It is to Kingsolver's credit that scientific practice in the novel is a rumination on coming to terms with uncertainty, where outcomes arise from unexpected quarters or from causes that even Byron's precise calculations and instruments cannot predict. Here the scale variance suggests that the fate of the butterfly (or its life cycle) can just as much be determined by the dynamics of the parasites on its wing as it can by the combined effort of the monarch population bracing itself and using the tree warmth to survive the cold. The parasite becomes part of one assemblage as a microbe, but its role changes as the monarch becomes part of a higher-level assemblage: different scales, different causes, different cascades of effects.

The novel's plotting of two lifecycles, the human and the nonhuman, in a contrapuntal way is its embrace of what Nowotny has called the "cunning of uncertainty."[51] Uncertainty can be a powerful incentive for human action; the scientific lab with its earnest quester-researchers is a sign of that striving toward what Jacques Derrida has called a "trajection": not a purposiveness that is goal oriented but rather a messianicity that is waiting for someone or something.[52] It is a different way of thinking about our temporal relationship to the future. The Dellarobia we meet in the early pages of the novel tries to imagine another world from the one that she had not left in years. The Turnbow farm as an assemblage of families, animals, equipment, the lab, activists, tourists, trees, banks, churches, and butterflies—in which each actant is enmeshed in a relationship with the others—makes us less uncertain about outcomes, but it is to grant that everyone is in suspense about a future that is on its way. The disadvantage arises from the great challenge of climate change itself—our inability to grasp the complexity of the interactions between the natural forces and the changes wrought by human behavior. Perhaps the point is that we are like the parasites on the wings of the butterfly. We do our thing even if we cannot know in advance how that will affect the scale at which the butterfly-forest assemblage functions.

Kingsolver chronicles various cascading effects on the human scale to show outcomes that could not have been foretold in advance: the money provided by tourists, butterfly watchers, and researchers allows the Turnbow family to save their farm: pay off equipment and farm loans, keep the farmhouse, continue to support God's beautiful creation, and cancel a contract to log the trees on the farm. This "cascade" will for a time stall the deforestation and mudslides that probably resulted from an earlier, more economically "rational" decision—to log the trees on which the butterflies have set down, to save the farm.[53] Thinking about the novel's everyday events as taking place in the shadow of its cardinal event, as cascade effects, suggests that distributed agency is a distribution of connections not just across space but also across time. The novel provides its own examples of such temporal paradoxes: in the short term, bad weather (the micro-level effects of climate change) brings work, income, and benefits to some people living in the areas of its impact. At another scale, and in the longer term, we suspect that this cascade foretells dire situations to come, for everyone in Dellarobia's neck of the woods and on the planet as a whole.

Assemblages that go beyond the level of the individual or human society challenge us to account for entities at all scales as "contributors." As DeLanda has pointed out, the ecosystem is also an assemblage with the contributions of many: there is the *material role* performed by the soil, sunlight, trees, and animals; the *expressive role* by the forms, colors, and habits of the components; and the *territorializing role* by factors or processes in which the component is involved such as food chains, adaptive traits, conducive climate, and other elements that maintain the components and their relationships and thus the identity and durability of the assemblage. Besides the contributory roles, there is the *deterritorializing role* played by climate change, invasion by exotic species, evolutionary mutation, and anthropogenic forces, including the economic, that recombine or replace various components and roles within the assemblage, leading to its dissipation or reformulation.[54] An important temporal aspect of a social assemblage is what DeLanda calls its "relative endurance." We are born in a "world of previously existing institutions," and we die leaving behind many of those same institutions. Friendship networks may not outlive our friends, but "large spatial extensions" correlate with "long temporal durations."[55] Consider how such a perspective about contributors would change discussions of so-called sustainability in climate-change debates. If we thought of the world's resources not as objects that should be used more efficiently so we can consume them for a longer time but instead as contributors or "workers" who also produce energy through their "labor," then global capital could be held accountable for its overconsumption of energy and its usage of common resources as "rent," rather than allowing it to shift seamlessly from one form to the other (from fossil to solar to wind and so on). Finally, the distributive agentic capacity of assemblages exacts a price; it also "unsettles a host of inherited concepts, including cause, time, culture, nature, event, life, kinship—and also responsibility."[56] One of the most important ways in which responsibility is displaced is by disentangling it from territoriality. If one does not "belong" to a place but is only situated in it temporarily, then unbelonging or temporariness rather than permanence can be the basis of a non-ontopologically derived identity—deterritorialized nomad. The suspension of home-as-location is the beginning of a more radical basis of hospitality. As Gayatri Spivak puts it, "The planet is in the species of alterity, belonging to another system; and yet we inhabit it, on loan."[57] To think of humanity, then, as a "planetary accident," one of many, whose residence on earth is never permanent but always temporary in both a historical as well as an evolutionary sense, tells us that as planetary creatures we are all resident aliens.

Living with the Uncertain Future

In a recent book on ecological aesthetics, Matthew Fuller and Olga Goriunova look at various figurations of home, including this compelling conceptualization of home as an assemblage: a "set of shifting multiscalar compositions spreading across various registers, as they change consistency and reassemble."[58] Their critical aim, as I understand it, is to establish a way to "look for oneself" without subscribing to the sort of solipsistic self-absorption that refuses to encompass other people or sociopolitical identity. They also want to constitute the world as territory to which one moves away, and where one plants oneself elsewhere, without falling into colonialism, nationalism, or fascism—fantasies that fill in the "unfillable void" of home imagined solely as a "grounding point" of origin, identity, and belonging.[59] What I find especially provocative about their notion of home as a site of ethico-aesthetic considerations is the formulation, following Deleuze, that "home is first of all the making of territory by an animal." Something (like Deleuze's example of birdsong) can start a home and organize space around a center. Yet this center carries with it "forces of the earth, the natal." The natal is both place and time of birth—but it is earthly time and cosmic time that establishes this "origin." Such a figuration of home is, say Fuller and Goriunova, "a foundation that can become creative, not acting as a force pulling us down into the void—the black hole of ancestors, death, and closure—but opening up into the universe, linking the earth vector into cosmic forces at many scales."[60]

At the end of the novel, Dellarobia's immediate future is up for grabs, but there is little question that the monarchs have brought about a profound sort of deterritorialization. To put it in terms that Deleuze and Guattari give us, like the monarchs, she too imagines migration as exceeding capacities of any possible assemblage, entering another plane:[61] "Dellarobia was floored to think of these fragile creatures owning the span of a continent, from Canada to Mexico, moving back and forth across the wide face of a land. Each one was so little and sure to die, yet they constituted a force, like an ocean tide. . . . If these butterflies were refugees of a horrible misfortune, there could be no beauty in them" (*Flight*, 143). Learning to tell the difference among different forms of nonunified, multilayered, or diasporic subjectivity is a key ethical and methodological issue. The refugee cannot be a metaphor for the deterritorialized "home" of the ecological subject, but thinking of the butterflies as refugees allows Dellarobia to link the Mexican "home" of the monarchs with that of migrant families seeking work in her town. Her son Preston's schoolmate Josefina and her family are Mexicans in Appalachia, undocumented like the monarchs, refugees of horrible misfortunes. Their flight behavior is a mode of survival that brings them to new homes. Here, home overwrites the nation-state with the ecosystem. Immigration policies that stop people at the southern border are contrasted to the flight behavior of the monarchs across the continent. "Canada to Mexico" also evokes the

North American Free Trade Agreement, the conveyor of global capital across the continent. The novel challenges us to think of the ecosystem as a model of survival in which even humans are caught. Are the monarchs Mexican, American, or Canadian? Kingsolver provocatively displaces this opposition (between migrating continental insects and bounded national citizens) by inscribing the planet itself as a space of motion, where migrations by human as well as nonhuman agents abound, driven by instincts as well as by push-pull factors. Assemblages do not stop at national borders. The big-scale versions of assemblages, like ecosystems, remind us the planet (unlike the globe) has no borders; its weather systems, life cycles, and geological patterns cannot be contained. We may know the circuits and tracks shaped by histories of migration, settlement, and colonialism, but there are other migrations from one home to another of species of every kind, and of humans too, that span more time and space than our current knowledge of the nonhuman and material migrations can access.

For Dellarobia, everyday interaction with the insects is the start of her imaginative retraining. If it is Ovid Byron who describes the butterflies as a "complicated system," it is Dellarobia who imagines it in the novel: "His 'complicated system' began to take shape in her mind, a thing she could faintly picture. Not just an orange passage across a continent as she'd imagined it before, not like marbles rolling from one end of a box to the other and back. This was a living flow, like a pulse through veins, with the cells bursting and renewing themselves as they went" (*Flight*, 146). Here "living flow" is not shorthand for the movement of capital and goods (as it gets used in accounts of globalization); rather, it is a planetary vision that substitutes for human (scientific) knowledge an awesome force running without human inputs. Here flow is a normal borderlessness that frames an ethics of hospitality for all fellow living beings (to whom the planet is loaned) and for taking care of common resources, while also recognizing the right of those (the First People of hospitality) who have not moved for a long, long time and now face displacement by human and nonhuman forces. In *Flight Behavior* the unavoidable contrast is between the monarchs, on the one hand, whose circuitous life cycles depend on transcontinental travel without a point of origin in either and whose flight behavior is set by an internal clock in their antennae that helps them navigate based on the horizontal movements of the sun.[62] On the other hand are the humans, like Dellarobia, who cannot move. When Dellarobia weeps at the end of the novel, she realizes that it is for the years and years of "fantasies of flight where there was no flight" (419). After the lab packs up and leaves, she moves too—to the town of Cleary to attend community college, her admission secured in part by a glowing recommendation letter sent in by Ovid Byron. We learn that she wants to become a veterinarian or even a scientist.

The closing paragraphs of the novel come back to a vision of collective agency of a force, instead of the individual decisions that will change the life of one character. As the snow melts on the bare hills behind the farm, a flash flood lifts Dellarobia's house off the foundations. Alone at the time but safe on the same hilltop where she had stood months ago, she watches the house "departing as gently as an ocean liner," "floating on the buoyant command of the air sealed carefully inside." The words that come to her at this juncture are from the book of Job: "'Man is born into trouble as the sparks fly upward' ... made for a world unraveling into fire and flood" (*Flight*, 432). Yet in the middle of this maelstrom, she notices that the surviving monarch butterflies are on the move too, "not just a few, but throngs, an airborne zootic force flying out in formation, as if to war." They fly ahead in the same direction, down the mountain, "like the flood itself occurring on other levels." To Dellarobia's astonishment, many—maybe a million—have survived, as though the "shards of a wrecked generation had rested alive like a heartbeat in trees, snow-covered, charged with resistance." She imagines that they will "gather on other fields and risk other odds, probably no better or worse than hers" (433). This blasted landscape that ends the novel allows us to explore, through Dellarobia's vision, the shared homelessness of the human and the animal in their collective existence. In the novel, floods wash away the "homes" of the butterflies, those of the immigrant workers from Mexico, and finally, Dellarobia and Cub's home in Tennessee. In this shared space, a space of ethical action and common cause, there is also a new kind of temporality—one that involves survival and action despite the "risk" and "odds" of the outcome. This is the distributed agency of the assemblage: the capacity to act is no longer localized in a human body or in a collectivity that is produced only by human (or by butterfly) efforts. It is a form of agency that survives over longer periods and spaces.

Giving meaning to the random event, as an assemblage, draws it into a medial level, between what is invisible (abstract) and what is too familiar (concrete). In so doing, we use uncertainty in a creative way that opens our eyes to the "contingency behind, within, and between the many things" that are intertwined in complex ways.[63] Our range of understanding cannot predict the consequences of our actions in a world whose complexity is mostly invisible to us. However, as Nowotny points out, if there is not hope, there is at least the "cunning of uncertainty," an "interactive collusion," ready to guide us in unexpected ways.[64] This is the final lesson of Kingsolver's novel—that the future always enters the present when we try to make sense of what seems senseless or capricious. When Dellarobia asks Ovid Byron whether he is the sort of person who can "watch an extinction," the scientist asks her by way of a response what she would do if someone she loved were dying. Dellarobia's answer is what we would expect, but the novel startles us when it pitches that personal question as a response to climate change: "You do everything you can. . . . And then, I guess, everything you can't. You keep doing, so your heart won't stop" (*Flight*, 320). The temporality of uncertainty is something we embrace in our everyday lives—after all, we are all living and dying at the same time. In its focus on climate change as a large-scale process that has become more systematically and historically encompassing, the novel seeks out more narrative, conceptual, and metaphorical tools that will resist the shrinking of our imaginations but also lets us contemplate the worlding of a future that can emerge in the wake of the impossibility of predicting how exactly change will happen.

Coda

What might the novelist and journalist Will Self mean when he asserts, in an essay on the future of literary fiction, "The literary novel as an art work and a narrative art form central to our culture is indeed dying before our eyes"?[1] One thing is for sure: he is not saying that narrative prose fiction tout court is on its way out because, as he points out, some kinds of prose fiction, namely "the kidult boywizardsroman" and the "soft sadomasochistic porn fantasy," are clearly in "rude good health." Neither does he think that digital media's dissemination of e-formatted fiction widely and cheaply through handheld devices is indisputable evidence of the novel's impending demise. What Self laments instead is the decline of the "serious novel," a category that he leaves largely undefined, for the essay provides no examples of it, at least not after 1939. For Self, the disappearance of the so-called serious novel has to do with the manner in which our way of knowing has changed with new information technology: "Digital media is not simply destructive of the codex, but of the Gutenberg mind itself." The novel form, opines Self, emerged in a world without the distractions of telecommunications and thus cannot survive for long in an environment permeated by this technology. He has come to realize, he says, "that the kind of psyche implicit in the production and consumption of serious novels (which are what, after all, serious artists produce), depends on a medium that has inbuilt privacy."[2]

Although it is tempting to agree with Self and maintain the poignancy of the novel's entry into the countercurrent of an era that is more preoccupied with the "sharing of trivia," is it possible to take at face value his earlier claim that the novel as a serious art form declined in the post–World War II era? Even if one were to go along with Self's historical benchmark (Joyce's *Finnegan's Wake*), his history seems curiously oblivious to the worldwide dissemination of this art form in the era of its zombification. Taken up by generations of postcolonial authors writing in English and the vernacular, from Asia, Africa, and the Caribbean in the second half of the twentieth century, "serious" novels were pressed into service to represent newly invented national traditions. Today, the novel as an object text has multiplied in audiovisual and digital formats and remains an utterly democratic genre that is accessible to modestly educated readers and writers. Its inherited embodiment of the codex format also lives on in digital technologies (here think "pages," "folders," "files," and "documents"). And regarding Self's point about the rewiring of our "Guttenberg mind," I wonder whether it is that easy to change the human sensory platform. Instead, are we not simply settling for interfacial or prosthetic arrangements with these new technologies?

The point on which I agree wholeheartedly with Self is the suggestion that the novel's dogged survival might have something to do with its narrative affordances: "The capability words have when arranged sequentially to both mimic the free flow of human thought and investigate the physical expressions and interactions of thinking subjects; the way they may be shaped into a believable simulacrum of either the commonsensical world, or any number of invented ones; and the capability of the extended prose form itself, which, unlike any other art form, is able to enact self-analysis, to describe other aesthetic modes and even mimic them."[3] I have addressed these and other affordances of the novel in various chapters, and I would like to return in these closing pages to two aspects that underscore the novel's importance as a tool for the imaginative practice of critical globality: the capacity to offer us a ready-at-hand simulacrum and the ability to be a site of self-analysis. These critical functions summon another meaning of "text," a meaning that is different from (but not unrelated to) the one that has been central to Self's discussion. Here the distinction is between the text as "an object of knowledge at the intersection between paleography and philology" and the "*text* as paradigm."[4]

In his influential essay "From Work to Text," Roland Barthes asserts this difference as the one that exists between "work" (or the text as an object that is tangible and can be "held in the hand") and the paradigmatic text that is a "methodological field" because it can be held only in language, demonstrated through a reading, and exist in the movement of discourse.[5] While Self is more preoccupied with the disappearance of serious novels as objects of consumption, he provides an opening for the paradigmatic text when he laments the amnesiac effect of media forms that make almost all the music produced over time instantly available: "The web and the internet have created a permanent Now, eliminating our sense of musical eras." Self is stating what is already obvious to many cultural critics working in the contemporary era of digital reproduction: the new information technology makes it harder to think the present historically.

This book's central point has been to reflect upon the implications of a curious feature we encounter in a wide range of novels that represent the world of contemporary globalization: they seem hitched to what Self calls "a permanent Now" because of the imperative to represent globality as laterally expanded space; however, such a desire is often at odds with the novel's formal tendency toward linearity and representation of various levels of temporality. Robert T. Tally's analogy between "dialectical thinking" and a "fundamental situatedness" that affects how we make sense of the world through narrative art is useful here because it depends on a similar contradictory structure—the simulacrum is in play not only when the world appears in the work but also when through the execution of a reading, the text offers us an experience of the discontinuities and contradictions of "real life."[6] Dialectical thinking, says Tally, is a thinking that "tries to get at the multiple temporal frames of reference—our own biological span, a historical epoch, a geological age, and so forth—in which both the subject who interprets and the object to be interpreted are also situated." Novels, by showing us the changeability of the situation and allowing "certain things to be possible and others not," enact through the simulacrum how the subject is conditioned and how its situatedness is "implacably historical (and geographic)."[7] By focusing on narratological elements and rhetorical figures, I make the additional point that even when the novel seeks to displace historical determinations so that it can show a fake or ironized contemporary (like those represented in the novels by Kunzru, Adiga, and DeLillo), such representations are inevitably challenged by resonances that are audible (and describable) within the experience of literary language and aesthetic form—in the unconsciousness of literary expression itself. When the literariness of literature is the focus of our attention, all novels are serious; all novels are complex epistemological fields that offer us what Gayatri Spivak calls figurations of "ethical situations" with the "quite other" with whom we may be unprepared to coexist consciously. The novel as a play of figures can give us something along the lines of an "imaginative access to the experience."[8]

Such imaginative access is now readily available in the academic discipline of literary studies. The universal use of English has made it impossible for the US reader (and whatever one imagines to be contemporary "American" literature) to be party to the privileged myopia of the old imperial centers where one was not prepared to know about radically different conditions of existence, other places, and other lives. Following Jameson, I invoke the global of critical globality as that "unpresent invisible framework [that] conditions our personal and political ideologies; just as the status of the nation in the world system unconsciously orients the conscious concerns of its citizens and writers or artists."[9] Even if a global novel departs from the conventions of social realism, it still represents in a refracted way the conditionality of the world in which the work emerges, and it is this present absence of a totality that the novel tries to grasp (as a vision of collectivity) even if it succeeds in showing us only a part of this collectivity, an abstracted version of it, or even a version that is grasped through stereotypes and cliches.

The challenge of conceptualizing the unconceptualizable (and often unnamable) collectivity of planetary life that has been unified by the world market may be phrased another way: one wants to read *in* the expanded narrative space of the synchronic the temporalities and cultural times of the diachronic. In other words, how does one talk about globalization not only in terms of allegories of space but also in terms of allegories of time? The common complaint that the global novel lacks nuance, detail, and complexity misses the important function of abstraction, which too is a fiction in that it strips ideas of their particular traits in order to make a norm or a template. What Rosa Braidotti says about an abstraction like the "human" may also be applicable to a historical construct like the "global." It is "neither an ideal, nor an objective statistical average or middle ground" but rather "spells out a systematized standard of recognizably—of Sameness—by which all others can be assessed, regulated and allotted to a designated social location."[10] Therefore, the notion of globality does not necessarily curtail the capaciousness of social realism such as individualized characters, cultural difference, or geographical specificity. The point is that all these differences can be transposed into general equivalents in narratives that try to capture the sense of borderlessness effected by technological, ecological, and economic forces that expand individual perception; or by the present-absent globe that presses on a small corner of the world and connects one location to another topologically rather than topographically; or by individual characters who cognitively map the global by way of migration and uprooting in place. I have argued that, unlike the expanded worlds of other (archaic or early modern) historical junctures, the fiction of contemporary globalization is mostly preoccupied with economic, technological, and more recently, environmental visions. These are often represented through the flattened spatializing strategies that are exemplary of the infamous "scapes" of cultural flows and circulations that were taken up by the early cultural theorists of globalization in the 1990s: ethnoscapes, technoscapes, ideoscapes, financescapes, and mediascapes.[11] Although I too focus on the novel's play with concepts and metaphors, I attend to the abstractions that we use to grasp the newness of globality and the conditions of their emergence from a historical juncture that has made it possible for us to think the abstractions. The only way to historicize these keywords, it seems to me, is to look at the push and pull of logic and rhetoric in our reading of a literary text.

How is the play of figures related to the abstractions of globality? The five central keywords organizing the chapters of this book are "concept metaphors." Such a designation draws our attention to the indispensable role of metaphors in the constitution of new knowledge and to the possibility that concepts function as metaphors in the initial stages of their deployment. My choice of these five concepts is historically justified because they are especially valuable heuristics for reading globality when forms of a fake contemporary (like Self's "permanent Now" or Castells's "timeless present") have made forms of mediation between the subject and the truth of its experience almost imperceptible. It was Stuart Hall who alerted us to the mediation that cultural and literary texts can do when we encounter our own status as subjects (meaning also that we become objects in the weave of the text): "The terms through which men [sic] 'make sense' of their world, experience their 'objective' situation as a subjective situation, and come to consciousness of who and what they are, are not in their keeping and will not, consequently, transparently reflect their situation."[12] It is key therefore that in an age when virtual and teletechnologies prevent us from "seeing" the objective situation in a transparent way, we interrogate how these concepts themselves are mediations by which certain things are possible and others not. For example, we have seen in chapter 4 that the "market" signals a form of mediation by which one kind of relation (the social) is made to appear as another kind of relation (individual). In Don DeLillo's *Cosmopolis* the market becomes a metaphor for the unconceptualizable level of an economic system in which international currency trading takes place. Here the calculations of hedge fund managers are no longer the result of human analysis (or exchanges) but undertaken by computer programs. By operating as a metaphor, "the market" allows the translation of one level of reality into another in a way that make the algorithmic nature of financial risk seemingly transparent and comprehensible to those of us who can only use old knowledge to understand the new realities.

Like "markets," this book's companion concept metaphors—specters, attachments, networks, and assemblages—taken together, underscore the point that there is no effective reading or even an effective politics that does not accept translation as a common quandary. The act of reading a novel is an analogy of such politics when we use concepts as general equivalents or bridges in the analysis of texts but proceed without fully deciding in advance what precisely these concepts mean. My own readings of the novels thus cannot do without these terms; however, I have striven to let the terms emerge within the field of the text where they are contested, their translatability is challenged, and they confront the limits of their own epistemological horizons. Judith Butler makes this point cogently when she states why Walter Benjamin's standpoint on mediation is so different from Theodor Adorno's. Whereas Adorno maintained that it was possible to relate specific cultural traits to the total social process by means of social theory, for Benjamin (whose prose abounds with metaphorical expressions) "social reality is riven . . . by the absence of such mediation." The ineffability of this social totality (for Benjamin, the commodity economy) is then figured, says Butler, " relentlessly, through metaphors in which the relation of substitution between terms does not really culminate in a mediation between them, in which, rather, a disjunction and irretraversibility is restaged again and again."[13] The social theory of critical globality, it seems to me, must work metaphorically when we lack concepts that can adequately mediate the relation between the individual, the technological network, and capitalism (as in chapter 3) or between the individual, the Anthropos, and climate change (as in chapter 5). In these discussions, the conceptual is subjected to the metaphorical or figural dimension of networks and assemblages, respectively, that find their rhetorical partners in literary expression by way of figures like parataxis and the narrative modality of description.

Finally, there is in the act of reading, an optimism about imaginative training that sustains critics and teachers like me. A few years ago Dorothy Hale noted that a renewed "pursuit of ethics" had surprisingly unified critics as different as Spivak, Butler, Derek Attridge, and Martha Nussbaum. All generally agree, says

Hale, that "the ethical value of literature lies in the felt encounter with alterity that it brings to its reader."[14] I am inspired by this trend, if one may call it such, because it reveals the overly exaggerated claims of those calling for "surface" and "descriptive" readings in place of "interpretation" on the grounds that historical and dialectical readings are modes grounded in suspicion and paranoia, and thus serve only to impose ethico-political agendas that constrain and reduce the reader's experience of literary language. I hope this book has shown that rhetoricity or figurality of language does not depend on a critique of historicism (as it may have done for critics like Paul de Man). The historical situatedness of these novels move into the foreground when we ask why a story is told one way rather than another and what historical conditions might make such stories comprehensible to its readers. Similarly, the complexity of the abstracted space of critical globality emerges when we begin to notice at the stylistic level of the novel the dependence on certain syntactical and rhetorical elements that I capture variously through the workings of metalepsis, parataxis, palimpsest, allegory, and description.

The novels of critical globality use concepts of time against space and in so doing declare their optimism about political community at a time when the borderlessness of globalization has upended political subjectivity. They offer us opportunities to think the present historically at a time when historical thinking is neither popular nor understood to have much to do with ethics (except when serving as reminders of the oppressions inflicted on the ancestors of those living in the present). But reaching toward a past or future from an imagined present is not only activated by such desiring subjects of historical knowledge but also by the desiring subjects of ethics. Derrida eloquently asserts that there is no way to think ethics, justice, or politics without the "principle of some responsibility, beyond all living present, within that which disjoins the living present, before the ghosts of those who are not yet born or who are already dead."[15] The specters and attachments (of chapters 1 and 2) show us the bridging work of metaphors that bring individual memory into contact with a history that the novel represents as an antagonism with no resolution (and thus no responsibility). If literature's value is attested in the simulacrum of the world that we use to exercise our imaginations, then it is in this world (that feels unmediated by time) that the critic must strive to put aside the infinite and dizzying expansion of space for a reading of temporality as a difference from the present, as a noncontemporaneity of the present that is hard to grasp in an age when speed is king.

NOTES

Introduction • What Is the Contemporary?

1. Fukuyama, *The End of History*.
2. See Menand, "Francis Fukuyama Postpones the End of History." In a recent essay, Fukuyama points to the war in Ukraine, the unpopularity of China's pandemic response, and the student protests in Iran as evidence of "grievous weaknesses" at the core of authoritarian states. These events, he says, reveal that none of the "proffered alternatives" to liberal democracy are doing any better and that it is (still) premature to pronounce the "rise of strong states." Fukuyama hopes for a "comeback" of liberal democracy, but such a return, he concedes, is premised on the belief that people who have taken it for granted are now "willing to struggle for it." See Fukuyama, "More Proof That This Really Is the End of History."
3. I have noticed that colleagues who specialize in American literature and who are customarily attuned to national-historical frames for bookending the literature of the previous century with descriptors like the naturalist period (1910–1914), the modern period (1914–1939), or the beat generation (1944–1962), seem resigned to use such designations in curriculum planning without asserting a break of any kind for a "contemporary period."
4. Agamben, "What Is the Contemporary?," 44.
5. Ophir, "Concept II," *Political Concepts: A Critical Lexicon*, https://www.political concepts.org/concept-ii-adi-ophir/.
6. Bennett, *Formalism and Marxism*, 23.
7. Shklovsky, "The Novel as Parody," 170.
8. See Levitt, "The Globalization of Markets"; and Feder, "Theodore Levitt, 81, Who Coined the Term 'Globalization,' Is Dead."
9. I have borrowed this distinction between term and concept, and the discussion of the "what is" question, from Ophir's excellent critical elaboration in "Concept II."
10. Soja, *Postmetropolis*, 191.
11. Brooke, "Living in 'New Times,'" 28.
12. Harvey, *The Condition of Postmodernity*, 147, my emphasis.
13. Harvey, *The Condition of Postmodernity*, 183.
14. Rosa, "Social Acceleration," 23.
15. A list of important academic as well as mass-market titles of spatialized methodol-

ogies might include Appadurai's classic essay, "Disjuncture and Difference in the Global Cultural Economy"; and Thomas Friedman's popular paean to globalization, *The World Is Flat*.

16. See Berlant, *Cruel Optimism*.
17. See Vallette, "Larry Summers's War against the Earth."
18. Porter, "Struggling to Rise as Coal Declines."
19. Latour, *Down to Earth*, 2, 8–9.
20. Latour, *Down to Earth*, 9.
21. Latour, *Down to Earth*, 6–8, 14–15.
22. Latour, *Reassembling the Social*, 174, 183.
23. I have borrowed these terms from Jameson's discussion in *Allegory and Ideology*, 135.
24. Friedman, *The World Is Flat*.
25. For some of the ongoing research conducted by the Time and Globalization Working Project at McMaster University, see https://globalization.mcmaster.ca/research/time-and-globalization-working-project. The exploratory questions and projects are summarized in Huebener et al., "Exploring the Intersection of Time and Globalization."
26. For speculative finance and futurity, see Bahng, *Migrant Futures*. The differential speed of experiencing environmental degradation is the focus of Nixon's *Slow Violence and the Environmentalism of the Poor*.
27. For a discussion of this point, see Jameson, *Allegory and Ideology*, 137.
28. Castells, *Network Society*.
29. Tsing, *Friction*, 269.
30. Quoted in Rivera, "Ghostly Encounters," 122.
31. Huyssen, *Present Pasts*, 12, 17.
32. For a reading of de Man in ways that call for the literary as anti-literality and for the metaphorical, see Wang, "Disfiguring Monuments"; and Spivak, *Death of a Discipline*, 71–72.
33. Wang, "Disfiguring Monuments," 634.
34. The international dominance of the "global novel" has not been without its critics in the mainstream and academic press. In a review titled "The Dull New Global Novel," Tim Parks blames "rapidly accelerating globalization" and English's status as the "language of globalization" for the pressure writers feel to seek international audiences. Parks bemoans that the result of this marketing drive on European, African, Asian, and South American authors is the "tendency to remove obstacles to international comprehension." By offering works that require no "effort" on the part of the reader, use "simple English," and deploy highly visible tropes, these global novels, now devoid of "culture-specific clutter and linguistic virtuosity," have purportedly become "wearisome." Similarly, other reviewers have critiqued novels like Adiga's *The White Tiger* for its lack of "authenticity" and "cynical anthropology." See also Sanjay Subrahmanyam, "Another Booker Flop"; and Amitava Kumar, "On Adiga's *The White Tiger*."
35. Spivak, "Remembering Derrida," 18.
36. Jameson, *Allegory and Ideology*, 136–37.
37. Jameson, *Allegory and Ideology*, 136.
38. Jameson, *Allegory and Ideology*, 136.
39. Jameson, *Allegory and Ideology*, 136.

40. Derrida, *Specters of Marx*, 62, 4, xix.
41. Ophir, "Concept II."
42. Balibar, "Concept," *Political Concepts*, http://www.politicalconcepts.org/concept-etienne-balibar/.
43. Berlant, *Cruel Optimism*, 3.

Chapter 1 · Specters

1. Derrida and Stiegler, *Echographies*, 115–17.
2. Benjamin and Chang, "Jacques Derrida, the Last European," 144.
3. Rivera, "Ghostly Encounters," 120–21.
4. Quoted in Rivera, "Ghostly Encounters," 121; and Huyssen, *Present Pasts*, 17.
5. Spivak, "Extempore Response," 143; quoted in Rivera, "Ghostly Encounters," 122.
6. Shakespeare, *Hamlet, Prince of Denmark*, 1.1.54, in *Complete Works*, 1128. Quoted in Derrida, *Specters*, 176.
7. For the discussion of Derrida's use of this line and his refusal to emote the past, see Spivak, "Extempore Response," 141.
8. Spivak, "Extempore Response," 141.
9. I am using "emergent" in the way Raymond Williams uses it: to distinguish (from the residual and the dominant) new alternative or opposing cultural ideas and practices that are being created constantly in a society by groups and individuals. See chapter 8 of his *Marxism and Literature*. For a discussion of the genealogy of the term globalization, see James and Steger, "A Genealogy of 'Globalization.'"
10. Quoted in Blanco and Peeren, *Spectralities*, 92.
11. I have taken this cue from Anna Kornbluh's excellent reading of *Capital* along these lines and from Gayatri Spivak's reading of *Lucy*. See Kornbluh, "On Marx's Victorian Novel," 15; and Spivak, *Aesthetic Education*, 351–71.
12. The phrase is from Spivak, *Aesthetic Education*, 351. Katherine Sugg has noticed this elision as a refusal of multicultural identity talk: "The novel—like its protagonist—refuses to participate in now-familiar postcolonial plots of cultural reconnection and return." For Sugg, *Lucy* reads as a "pitched battle against the assumptions that shape many of the oppositional narratives of exile and displacement (most known through their cultural nationalist incarnations)." See "'I Would Rather Be Dead,'" 156.
13. For Derrida's use of this neologism, see *Specters*, 82.
14. See, for instance, Alison Shonkwiler's discussion of specters as abstract figurations of circulation and exchange in *The Financial Imaginary*, 18. Other notable examples are Derrida, *Specters of Marx*; and Vogl, *Specter of Capital*.
15. Kornbluh, "On Marx's Victorian Novel."
16. Spivak, "More Thoughts on Cultural Translation," 5.
17. Gramsci, *Prison Notebooks*, 324.
18. Kincaid, *Lucy*, 3. Further references to the novel will be cited parenthetically in the text.
19. Hardt and Negri, *Empire*, 290–94; Hardt and Negri, *Multitude*, 103–15; and Hochschild, *The Outsourced Self*, 146–56.
20. Enloe, *Bananas, Beaches and Bases*, 177.
21. Sassen, *Globalization and Its Discontents*, 190; my emphasis.
22. Beck, *What Is Globalization?*, 2.

23. Bloom, *A Map of Misreading*, 128.
24. Bloom, *A Map of Misreading*, 74.
25. Hollander, *The Figure of Echo*, 133–34.
26. Hollander, *The Figure of Echo*, 134.
27. Quintilian, *Institutes* 3.6.37–39. Quoted in Hollander, *The Figure of Echo*, 135.
28. Spivak, "Diasporas Old and New," 245.
29. Harvey, *The Condition of Postmodernity*, 117.
30. Quoted in Axel Honneth, *Reification*, 91. In his introduction to the published lectures by Honneth, Martin Jay asks, apropos of that notion, "Who is doing the forgetting? What is being forgotten? And will remembering suffice to produce change in actual social practices and institutions?" (3).
31. Kornbluh, "On Marx's Victorian Novel," 26.
32. Marx, *Capital*, 1:157.
33. Marx, *Capital*, 1:140–52.
34. Kornbluh, "On Marx's Victorian Novel," 27.
35. Kornbluh, "On Marx's Victorian Novel," 23.
36. Wordsworth, "I Wandered Lonely as a Cloud," 801.
37. On "trace," see Derrida, *Cinders*.
38. Referring to Marx's own use of literary devices in *Capital*, Anna Kornbluh says, "Capital effects this metaleptic rhythm in its narrative through its succession of paradoxes and through what it calls 'double results' and dual forms of appearance, and through its perpetual motion of lifting the veil, starting anew the analysis from a different point of view. It is, in other words, in the texture of the textual movement that we find a stunning engagement with the text's subject, a galvanized model of the metaleptic movement of capital itself." See "On Marx's Victorian Novel," 27.
39. Marx, *Capital*, 1:163.
40. Marx, *Capital*, 1:163.
41. Marx, *Capital*, 1:165.
42. Jameson, *The Geopolitical Aesthetic*, 51.
43. Althusser, *Lenin and Philosophy*, 236.
44. Hall, "Culture, the Media and 'the Ideological Effect,'" 320.
45. Jay, introduction to Honneth, *Reification*, 7.
46. Jay, introduction to Honneth, *Reification*, 7.
47. Gramsci, *Prison Notebooks*, 324.
48. Gramsci, *Prison Notebooks*, 322.
49. Said, *Orientalism*, 25.
50. Žižek, *For They Know Not What They Do*, 202.
51. Žižek, *For They Know Not What They Do*, 202.
52. Žižek, *For They Know Not What They Do*, 213. For a further elaboration of this point as an exposure of the highly contingent nature of modernity's origins, see Hawes, *The British Eighteenth Century and Global Critique*. The metaleptic projection can go either way—to the past or the future. Compare these two populist exhortations: Ronald Reagan's "America's best days are yet to come" and Donald Trump's "make America great again."
53. Žižek, *For They Know Not What They Do*, 214; Hawes, *The British Eighteenth Century and Global Critique*, xvii.

54. For a discussion of how Stuart Hall frames this unconsciousness as a "textual figure," see Spivak, *Aesthetic Education*, 352.

55. If there are political stakes in Mariah's desired consensus over the daffodils (the establishment of a collective subject, for instance), one way to understand them would be to look at the discourse of beauty in play. Terry Eagleton characterizes the aesthetic in Immanuel Kant as "pseudo-knowledge" because, although it provides an entryway into a desirable universalist ethics and critical judgment, it can also mystify the political. As Eagleton points out, "When, for Kant, we find ourselves concurring spontaneously in an aesthetic judgment, able to agree that a certain phenomenon is sublime or beautiful, we exercise a precious form of intersubjectivity, establishing ourselves as a community of feeling subjects linked by a quick sense of our shared capacities." It is part of Eagleton's argument that if "the aesthetic must bear the burden of human community, then political society, one might suspect, must leave a good deal to be desired. See Eagleton, *Ideology of the Aesthetic*, 75.

56. This is the process that Spivak describes as the "spectralization of the rural." See *Aesthetic Education*, 370.

57. Spivak, *Aesthetic Education*, 210–17. In *Lucy* we might think of Mariah's countryside as a rural setting where towns are ghostly reminders of the past, a wasteland inhabited only by the "left-behind," particularly children and the elderly, and increasingly cannibalized by the urban for development.

58. Hall, "Culture, the Media and 'the Ideological Effect,'" 325.

59. Hall, "Culture, the Media and 'the Ideological Effect,'" 370.

60. For this point about Lucy's lack of "growth" into something "real" see Spivak, *Aesthetic Education*, 357.

61. Spivak, *Aesthetic Education*, 360.

62. In an important volume of essays titled *Global Woman: Nannies, Maids, and Sex Workers in the New Economy*, Ehrenreich and Hochschild aim "to make the invisible visible again." The recursion implied in the use of the word "again" is interesting because a careful consideration of the introduction, from which I have extracted these quotes, suggests that they are not referring to labor that is repeating in a self-similar way or to events that directly cause earlier forms of labor to disappear. What they are pointing to is a strange paradox: as more and more domestic work in upper-middle-class families is outsourced to migrant women, such labor is no longer decked out as uniformed servants, the status symbols of yore; rather, a contemporary culture that militates against "acknowledging help or human interdependency" of any kind, and a gendered ideology that exhorts American career women to "do it all" has helped to keep this labor out of sight. In the recursive signaling of "again," we also understand that there is some continuity between the older servant class drawn from the racialized labor of US minorities and the racialized labor of women who have just arrived from poorer countries.

63. For paratactic construction as temporal arrangement, see Spivak, *Aesthetic Education*, 358.

Chapter 2 • Attachments

1. Sassen, *Losing Control?*, xix.

2. The notion of hyphenated spaces comes from Gayatri Spivak's discussion of Salman Rushdie's *Satanic Verses* in *Outside in the Teaching Machine*, 243.

3. Agamben, "What Is the Contemporary?," 42.

4. Glissant, "Creolization," 88.

5. See Sassen, *Losing Control?*; and Brown, *Walled States*, 22.

6. Brown, *Walled States*, 24.

7. For the story of the social contract as a story of possessive individualism, see MacPherson, *Political Theory of Possessive Individualism*. For the novel as biography of the nation, the classic discussions are those in Anderson's *Imagined Communities* and Jameson's "Third-World Literature in the Era of Multinational Capitalism." Armstrong's *Desire and Domestic Fiction* describes how the novelistic form was pressed into service for English middle-class female individualism.

8. Hamilton, *The Examination* 7 (January 7, 1802) and *The Examination* 8 (January 12, 1802), *Founders Online*, National Archives, https://founders.archives.gov/documents/Hamilton/01-25-02-0282. (Original source: Hamilton, *Papers*, 25:495–97.) A series of eighteen articles entitled "The Examination" and signed by "Lucius Crassus" appeared in the *New York Evening Post* during the winter of 1801 to 1802 and were intended to refute the points raised by Thomas Jefferson in his first annual message to Congress on December 8, 1801.

9. Hamilton is not for abolishing white European immigration altogether (only Europeans were eligible for citizenship in 1802); rather, he seeks to maintain without the possibility of repealing (as Jefferson was proposing) the increased restrictions on foreigners instituted by President John Adams's Alien and Sedition Acts of 1798. These controversial acts were aimed at the quick deportations of and restrictions on foreigners in the wake of growing anti-French sentiment as the United States prepared to go to war with France. Perhaps it was the worry that Jefferson would scrap the waiting period in its entirety that ultimately led Hamilton to propose a compromise: a "reasonable term" of five years rather than the existing fourteen-year waiting period that would enable aliens to "get rid of foreign and acquire American attachments; to learn the principles and imbibe the spirit of our government." See Hamilton, *The Examination* 8.

10. Guha, "The Migrant's Time," 156.

11. Guha, "The Migrant's Time," 156.

12. Glissant, "Creolization," 83–84.

13. Glissant, "Creolization," 83.

14. Glissant, "Creolization," 89.

15. Butler, *Precarious Life*, 32.

16. Cole, *Open City*, 156. Further references to the novel will be cited parenthetically in the text as *City*.

17. Najafi, Serlin, and Berlant, "Broken Circuit."

18. For the distinction between "palimpsestic" and "palimpsestuous," see Dillon, "Reinscribing De Quincey's Palimpsest," 245.

19. For a detailed treatment of the novel's contrapuntal elements as described, see Neumann and Kappel, "Music and Latency in Teju Cole's *Open City*," 32–33.

20. Derrida, *The Politics of Friendship*, 32.

21. Spivak, *Harlem*, 11.

22. For "fugues," see Vermeulen, "Flights of Memory," 40–45.

23. Agamben, "What Is the Contemporary?," 51.

24. Freud, "A Note upon the 'Mystic Writing Pad,'" 228.

25. Dillon, "Reinscribing De Quincey's Palimpsest," 251–52.

26. Derrida, *Spectres of Marx*, xix.
27. Dillon, "Reinscribing De Quincey's Palimpsest," 249.
28. Foucault, "Nietzsche, Genealogy and History," 76.
29. Foucault, "Nietzsche, Genealogy and History," 76.
30. Najafi, Serlin, and Berlant, "Broken Circuit."
31. Massumi, *The Politics of Affect*, 61, 60.
32. Butler, *Precarious Life*, 30.
33. Freud, "Mourning and Melancholia," 243.
34. Freud, "Mourning and Melancholia," 243.
35. Freud, "Mourning and Melancholia," 244.
36. Freud, "The Ego and the Id," 29.
37. For this point, see Spivak, *Outside in the Teaching Machine*, 243.
38. Butler, *Precarious Life*, 30.
39. Butler, *Precarious Life*, 26.
40. Vermeulen, "Flights of Memory," 40.
41. Freud, "Mourning and Melancholia," 244.
42. According to the psychologist Silvan Tomkins, the shame experienced by the child when the object of desire, for example, the mother, does not reciprocate and breaks the circuit of attachment leads to an emotional disorientation in which the child internalizes disconnection. Cultural theorists like Berlant and Eve Sedgwick have adopted the notion of the "broken circuit" as a way of examining how specific social relations could shame members of marginalized groups—as shamed subjects. But forms of emotional disconnection may not necessarily lead to self-loathing. See Najafi, Serlin, and Berlant, "Broken Circuit"; and Sedgwick, *Touching Feeling*, 93–122.
43. Klein, "Mourning and Its Relation to Manic-Depressive States," 125–26.
44. Klein, "Mourning and Its Relation to Manic-Depressive States," 143–44.
45. For useful distinctions that can be made about memory's affective actions in the present, see Massumi, *The Politics of Affect*, 59–62.
46. Massumi, *The Politics of Affect*, 61–62.
47. Open secrets leave narrative traces that tell us something is being withheld (as opposed to simply omitted without a trace). Most secrets are "open secrets." As Miller points out, if a story gives a secret some importance, the narrative must hint occasionally that something is being withheld even if it chooses when to disclose it. See Miller, *The Novel and the Police*, 192–220.
48. Abraham and Torok, "Mourning and Melancholia," 125.
49. Butler, *Gender Trouble*, 68.
50. Butler, *Gender Trouble*, 71.
51. Butler, *Dispossession*, 2.
52. Butler, *Precarious Life*, 22.
53. Butler, *Gender Trouble*, 69, 68.
54. Berlant, *Cruel Optimism*, 26.
55. Robbins and Horta, *Cosmopolitanisms*, 1–2.
56. Gandhi, "Utonal Life," 77.
57. Gandhi, "Utonal Life," 78.
58. This is also a theme that runs through J. M. Coetzee's fiction, most notably *Disgrace*, in which an ethically compromised Afrikaner character confronts his own white

male privilege while coming to terms with the sexual violence his daughter suffers at the hands of those who have been victimized by apartheid.

Chapter 3 · Networks

1. Tsing, *Friction*, 5–6.
2. Zhou and Coleman, "Accelerated Contagion," 285.
3. Fox, Shin, and Emamdjomeh, "How Epidemics like Covid-19 End."
4. Zhou and Coleman, "Accelerated Contagion," 289.
5. Zhou and Coleman, "Accelerated Contagion," 289.
6. Levine, *Forms*, 113–14.
7. Zhou and Coleman, "Accelerated Contagion," 290.
8. Fletcher, *The Topological Imagination*, 18.
9. See Webster, "For Homeless in New Orleans"; Davenport, Gregg, and Timberg, "Working from Home Reveals Another Fault Line"; and Roy, "The Pandemic Is a Portal."
10. Beacock, "Germany Gets It."
11. Bordwell, "Lessons from BABEL," www.davidbordwell.net/blog/2006/11/27/lessons-from-babel/.
12. Jameson, "Culture and Finance Capital," 260.
13. Jameson, "Culture and Finance Capital," 285.
14. Friedman, *The World Is Flat*, 8
15. For a gloss on the digital and internet novel, see, respectively, Irr, *Toward the Geopolitical Novel*, 58–65; and Gupta, *Globalization and Literature*, 54. Gupta discusses Geoff Ryman's *253*, an unusual example of a novel that appeared in print and as a website, not only thematizing the internet but becoming part of it.
16. The phrase is from Arvidsson and Colleoni, "Value in Informational Capitalism."
17. Anderson, *Imagined Communities*, 22–31.
18. See the possibilities posed by Roy in "The Pandemic Is a Portal."
19. Kunzru, *Transmission*, 3. Further references to the novel will be cited parenthetically in the text.
20. The philosopher Michel Serres provides a useful way to differentiate what he calls the "science of nearness and rifts" (topology) and the "science of stable and well-defined distances," (metrical geometry): "If you take a handkerchief and spread it out in order to iron it, you can see in it certain fixed distances and proximities. If you sketch a circle in one area, you can mark out nearby points and measure far-off distances. Then take the same handkerchief and crumple it, by putting it in your pocket. Two distant points suddenly are close, even superimposed. If, further, you tear it in certain places, two points that were close can become very distant." Serres with Latour, *Conversations on Science*, 60. I am grateful to Cary Wolfe for this reference.
21. For this point about the technological sublime, see Spivak, "Remembering Derrida," 18.
22. Pattern recognition is a branch of machine learning that focuses on the recognition of patterns and regularities in data, although it is in some cases considered to be nearly synonymous with machine learning.
23. Perelman, "Parataxis and Narrative," 316. Perelman's essay is partly a response to Fredric Jameson's reading of his poem "China," in *Postmodernism*, 28–29.
24. Castells, *Network Society*, 1:1.

25. Castells, *Network Society*, 13.
26. Castells, *Network Society*, 18.
27. Castells, *Network Society*, 477; my emphasis.
28. Jonathan Joseph, "The Problem with Networks Theory," 128.
29. Jonathan Joseph, "The Problem with Networks Theory," 128.
30. Castells, *Network Society*, 1:18.
31. Spivak, "Remembering Derrida," 18.
32. Castells, *Network Society*, 1:464.
33. Castells, *Network Society*, 1:464.
34. Castells, *Network Society*, 1:21.
35. I have derived this formulation of an inconsistency in globalization theory from Spivak's critique of Castells in "Remembering Derrida," 17–18.
36. Jameson, *Postmodernism*, 38.
37. Arvidsson and Colleoni, "Value in Informational Capitalism," 141.
38. "Hari Kunzru on Networks, the Novel, and the Politics of the Author," interview by Max Haiven, *Public Books*, October 2, 2013, www.publicbooks.org/hari-kunzru-on-networks-the-noveland-the-politics-of-the-author/.
39. Kunzru, keynote lecture delivered at the Literary Consultancy Conference, London, "Writing in a Digital Age," June 8, 2012, quoted in Haiven, "Hari Kunzru on Networks." Brackets in the original.
40. Kunzru, quoted in Haiven, "Hari Kunzru on Networks."
41. For a description of media affordances and their manifestation as narrative metalepsis, see Kukkonen, "Metalepsis in Popular Culture," 1–21.
42. Serres, *Angels*, 57.
43. Aneesh, *Virtual Migration*, 62.
44. Even where there is a public outcry about subcontracted labor taking over American jobs, this labor pool is mostly invisible, given their shaky status as temporary workers. For a recent example, see Preston, "Lawsuits Claim Disney Colluded to Replace U.S. Workers with Immigrants."
45. Crang, "Between Places," 569. See also Creswell, *On the Move*, for a modern history of the concept of mobility.
46. Castells, *Informational City*, 126–71.
47. Jameson, *Postmodernism*, 37–38.
48. Pratt, "Virgin of Zapopan," 278.
49. Pratt, "Virgin of Zapopan," 277.
50. Pratt, "Virgin of Zapopan," 277.
51. Wark, *Virtual Geography*, xii.
52. Jameson, "Culture and Finance Capital," 248.
53. Jameson, "Culture and Finance Capital," 248–49.
54. Jameson, "Culture and Finance Capital," 251.
55. Jameson, "Culture and Finance Capital," 249.
56. Roy, "The Pandemic Is a Portal."

Chapter 4 · Markets

1. For an illuminating discussion of the idea that such simultaneity is feigned or illusory, see Nowotny, *Time*, 26–27.

2. Martin, *The Financialization of Daily Life*, 3.

3. This description of markets is from Lee and LiPuma, "Cultures of Circulation," 197–98. The market, standing in as a general term for the "economy," or an interconnected system of production, exchange, and consumption driven by its own laws, now includes, as we have seen, not only currencies but also highly complex and abstract instruments like derivatives that derive their value from hedging, leveraging, and securitizing the value of other assets like stocks, commodities, and currencies.

4. Vogl, *Specter of Capital*, 69.

5. Vogl, *Specter of Capital*, 123.

6. Taylor, "Modern Social Imaginaries," 92.

7. Nowotny, *Time*, 51.

8. Quilligan, *Language of Allegory*, 28.

9. Jameson, *Allegory and Ideology*, 34.

10. Jameson, *Allegory and Ideology*, xvii.

11. Jameson, *Allegory and Ideology*, 19.

12. Brown, *Undoing the Demos*, 31.

13. Brown, *Undoing the Demos*, 33.

14. Adiga, *The White Tiger*, 6. Further references to the novel will be cited parenthetically in the text as *Tiger*.

15. Benjamin, *Charles Baudelaire*, 100.

16. DeLillo, *Cosmopolis*, 5. Further references to the work will be cited parenthetically in the text.

17. Li, "The Untimely in Globalization's Time," 257.

18. Jameson, "Third World Literature."

19. Jameson, *Allegory and Ideology*, xix.

20. Fletcher, *Allegory*, 39.

21. Hamid, *How to Get Filthy Rich in Rising Asia*. Further references to the novel will be cited parenthetically in the text as *Rich*.

22. Çalişkan and Callon, "Economization, Part 1," 373.

23. Benjamin, *Origin of German Tragic Drama*, 178.

24. Cowan, "Benjamin's Theory of Allegory," 116.

25. Jameson, *Allegory and Ideology*, 6.

26. Marx, *Capital*, 1:93.

27. Kornbluh, "On Marx's Victorian Novel, 23.

28. The targeted use of microcredit to capture the poorest of the poor is this principle at work in the real world. The state can retreat from its caretaking role and leave everyone to take on debt from private actors. The Nobel Prize–winning economist Mohammed Yunus, for instance, created a much-lauded microcredit institution, the Grameen Bank, to turn poor Bangladeshi women into entrepreneurs.

29. Brown, *Undoing the Demos*, 10.

30. Harvey, *Brief History of Neoliberalism*, 2.

31. Çalişkan and Callon, "Economization, Part 1," 373.

32. See Betty Joseph, "Neoliberalism and Allegory."

33. Latour, "On Some of the Affects of Capitalism" (lecture given at the AIME Workshop, Danish Royal Academy of Science, February 26, 2014), www.bruno-latour.fr/node/552.

34. Schumpeter, *Capitalism, Socialism, and Democracy*, 87.

35. *Wired*, "China, India: Rule Global Tech," October 4, 2005.

36. The talk about nutritional standards and benchmarks for development connects urban governance strategies of making the poor vanish through beautification projects and making poverty vanish through economic and social indicators devised by the World Bank and adopted in UN development projects. See Roy, *Capitalism*, 1–3; and Patnaik, "Neoliberalism and Rural Poverty in India," 3132–50.

37. Lal, "Do Bigha Zamin."

38. Lal, "Do Bigha Zamin."

39. Eagleton, "Capitalism and Form," 119.

40. Benjamin, *Origin of German Tragic Drama*, 178.

41. See Owens, "The Allegorical Impulse."

42. Tambling, *Allegory*, 152–73.

43. Cowan, "Benjamin's Theory of Allegory," 120.

44. Benjamin, *Origin of German Tragic Drama*, 166.

45. Benjamin, "Theses on the Philosophy of History," 263.

46. Brown, *Undoing the Demos*, 21.

47. DeLillo, "In the Ruins of the Future." All subsequent references in the text are to this version.

48. Cowan, "Benjamin's Theory of Allegory," 110.

49. As Gunning discusses in *The Films of Fritz Lang*, it is well known that Lang used New York City as the model for his metropolis (13). In turn, DeLillo himself has acknowledged the influence of Lang's film on his earlier novel *Underworld* (1997). See DePietro, *Conversations with Don DeLillo*, 164.

50. Other critics have noticed the allegorical nature of *Cosmopolis*. For Gupta in *Globalization and Literature*, the character of Eric Packer "appears to represent free market capitalism" (14). For Vogl in *Specter of Capital*, the novel is "an allegory of modern finance capitalism" that invokes both historical ideas and contemporary economic theories (2). Shonkwiler's reading of the novel in *Financial Imaginary* is more specific about the historical conjuncture—she sees the convergence between a "neoliberal fantasy of technology" and the "seductions of 'transpoliticized' capital" (76). These are excellent readings, and I have drawn on all of them, but their discussions of allegory are mostly thematic and do not analyze the form's temporal and figurative complexities.

51. These specifics are from Vogl, *Specter of Capital*, 1.

52. Fletcher, *Allegory*, 39.

53. Godden, "Language, Labor, and Finance Capital," 413. The notion that financial markets now trade in the future as a commodity is exemplified in the complex instrument called a derivative. When a firm can predict the volatility of prices, it incorporates that risk into the pricing of the commodity in the future, or it can leverage this risk by buying a sort of insurance, or derivative, that will pay out a settlement if there are losses. A derivative is thus a product that takes its value from something else. It is an instrument for translating volatility into security insofar as it assesses the cost of risk, for a price. The game-changing aspect of the financial economy is that the derivatives themselves can be delinked from any real tracking of the cost fluctuations in the actual commodity that generated this whole chain of transactions and become a commodity in itself—it is no longer tied only to the actors in the originally transacting firms, the seller that had agreed

to sell *x* product at *y* price and the buyer that agreed to buy. The firm that sold the derivative can now offer them as a bet to other market players, who might buy such an option or future on a corporate share, amounting to a bet on an anticipated price that may be sold and sold again before the deadline on which the two firms actually execute their transaction.

54. Nowotny, *Time*, 46.

Chapter 5 · Assemblages

1. Mentz, *Break Up the Anthropocene*, 1–2.
2. Yusoff, *Black Anthropocenes*, 25.
3. Fuller and Goriunova, *Bleak Joys*, 152.
4. Yusoff, *Black Anthropocenes*, 57.
5. Yusoff, *Black Anthropocenes*, 56–57.
6. Chakrabarty, "Anthropocene Time," 124. See also related discussions in Chakrabarty, "Climate and Capital"; "The Climate of History"; and "Postcolonial Studies and the Challenge of Climate Change."
7. For a key discussion of the vitality and force of things, see Jane Bennett, *Vibrant Matter*, viii.
8. Aravamudan, "The Catachronism of Climate Change," 8.
9. Aravamudan, "The Catachronism of Climate Change," 9.
10. Yusoff, *Black Anthropocenes*, 14.
11. Weheliye, *Habeas Viscus*, 8.
12. Jane Bennett, *Vibrant Matter*, ix.
13. For this point, see Spivak, "Remembering Derrida," 18.
14. Kingsolver, *Flight Behavior*, 122. Further references to the novel will be cited parenthetically in the text as *Flight*.
15. For the distinction between the topological and topographical, see chapter 3.
16. Ghosh, *The Great Derangement*, 7–9.
17. Ghosh, *The Great Derangement*, 17; Moretti, "Serious Century," 367.
18. Moretti, "Serious Century," 372.
19. Ghosh, *The Great Derangement*, 59.
20. Ghosh, *The Great Derangement*, 61.
21. Heise, *Sense of Place and Sense of Planet*, 9.
22. Heise, *Sense of Place and Sense of Planet*, 10.
23. Heise, *Sense of Place and Sense of Planet*, 10.
24. Heise, *Sense of Place and Sense of Planet*, 9. This is apparent in recent electoral debates in the United States where the reclaiming of (national) space from the corroding effects of global trade have also provoked xenophobic rhetoric of closing borders, building walls, preserving heartland values and small-town USA, bringing back jobs, owning guns, and—even at the subjective level—protecting a right to politically incorrect speech. The irony, of course, is that the economic and market promotion of national interest has now put many environmental protections under the axe. Heise is not unaware of the role that local ties can play in environmental struggles (the revolutionary movement in the Chiapas or the struggles of forest dwellers against big dams and mining companies are good examples).
25. Morton, *Ecology without Nature*, 169.

26. Bal, *Narratology*, 36.
27. Bal, *Narratology*, 37.
28. Mitchell, *What Do Pictures Want?*, 156–57.
29. Deleuze, *Cinema 1*, 30.
30. These contradictory crosscurrents show how global trade policies and environmental policies may sometimes offset each other, as when old industries of nonrenewables, like coal, already facing competition from new national (US) and *greener* resources like natural gas, have to export globally and depend on the boom-bust cycles of a Chinese economy. See Rapier, "Don't Blame Renewable Energy." For trends in coal, see US Energy Information Administration, *Annual Coal Reports*, www.eia.gov/coal/annual/.
31. Deleuze and Parnet, *Dialogues*, 69.
32. Jane Bennett, *Vibrant Matter*, xvi.
33. Nail, "What Is an Assemblage?," 22.
34. DeLanda, *New Philosophy*, 43–45.
35. DeLanda, *New Philosophy*, 45.
36. Deleuze and Guattari, *A Thousand Plateaus*, 265. Quoted in Nail, "What Is an Assemblage?," 25.
37. Nail, "What Is an Assemblage?," 24–26. I find it interesting that the work of post-1968 French intellectuals like Deleuze, Guattari, and Michel Foucault show some uncanny crosshatchings. Whereas power is what is increasingly distributed in the work of Michel Foucault, in the work of the former pair, it is agency that is distributed. While it is popular to talk of assemblages as though they are only nomadic and indefinite in shape (DeLanda, Latour), the assemblages of Deleuze and Guattari range in size and complexity. There is "home," an assemblage of concrete elements coded by territory, but also complex assemblages with strata and vertical divisions coded by the state and even systemic assemblages like feudalism and capitalism.
38. Coole, "Rethinking Agency."
39. Jane Bennett, "Agency of Assemblages," 445; and *Vibrant Matter*, 23.
40. Quoted in Morton, *Ecology without Nature*, 128.
41. See Morton, *Hyperobjects*.
42. Jane Bennett, "Agency of Assemblages," 454.
43. Nowotny, *The Cunning of Uncertainty*, 140.
44 Watt, *Conrad in the Nineteenth Century*, 169.
45. Kingsolver, *Flight*, 392. For origins of the nickname, see Burke, *Varieties of Cultural History*, 51.
46. DeLanda, *New Philosophy*, 45.
47. Woods, "Scale Critique for the Anthropocene," 135, 137.
48. For a description of "mechanisms" within social assemblages, see Delanda, *New Philosophy*, 18–19.
49. DeLanda, *New Philosophy*, 40.
50. The pandemic has also shown us that spatial scales do have temporal consequences. One effective response to the pandemic involved analysis of the projected time lapse between spikes in New York, New Jersey, and Connecticut. Studying such a model led the governor of New York State, Andrew Cuomo, to put aside the practice of competing for high-cost and scant medical equipment (like ventilators) and move toward a collective use of resources by the three states. This meant directing them toward the hot spots that

peaked first and then moving them to those that came later. This emphasis on temporal rather than spatial unity resembles the sort of agentic possibilities that, I think, might emerge in the assemblage as an "open-ended collective." It involves thinking of the human and nonhuman in feedback loops, in temporal cycles and time lags, rather than by way of the flattened ontology of everyone distributed equally on a level playing field.

51. Nowotny, *The Cunning of Uncertainty*.
52. Derrida, "Marx and Sons," 248, quoted in Jane Bennett, *Vibrant Matter*, 32.
53. A distributive notion of agency, instead of focusing on a single effect, pays attention to a linked series of them: "An unstable cascade spills out from every 'single' act." Here, rather than deny intentionality per se to the "moral subject," one should loosen the sole connection between the action and predictable outcomes and invite oneself to think instead about "the power to make a difference." See Jane Bennett, "Agency of Assemblages," 457.
54. DeLanda, *New Philosophy*, 12–13.
55. DeLanda, *New Philosophy*, 43.
56. Jane Bennett, "Agency of Assemblages," 452.
57. Spivak, *Death of a Discipline*, 72.
58. Fuller and Goriunova, *Bleak Joys*, 124.
59. Fuller and Goriunova, *Bleak Joys*, 123, 144.
60. Fuller and Goriunova, *Bleak Joys*, 130.
61. Deleuze and Guattari, *A Thousand Plateaus*, 326.
62. For the research that established this aspect of monarch migrations, see Taylor et al., "Timing, Pace, and Success of the Monarch Migration."
63. Nowotny, *The Cunning of Uncertainty*, 171.
64. Nowotny, *The Cunning of Uncertainty*, 171.

Coda

1. Self, "The Novel Is Dead."
2. Self, "The Novel Is Dead."
3. Self, "The Novel Is Dead."
4. I am using a distinction that John Mowitt provides in "What Is a Text Today" (1217).
5. Roland Barthes, "From Work to Text," 156–57.
6. For an elaboration of this point see Spivak, "Ethics and Politics," 18.
7. Tally, "On Always Historicizing," 543.
8. Spivak, *Aesthetic Education*, 352.
9. Jameson, "Criticism and Categories," 565.
10. Braidotti, *The Posthuman*, 26.
11. Arjun Appadurai, "Disjuncture and Difference in the Global Cultural Economy," 296–99.
12. Hall, "Culture, the Media and 'the Ideological Effect,'" 320.
13. Butler, "Values of Difficulty," 213.
14. Hale, "Aesthetics and the New Ethics," 899.
15. Derrida, *Specters of Marx*, xix.

Abraham, Nicolas, and Maria Torok. "Mourning and Melancholia: Introjection versus Incorporation." In *The Shell and the Kernel*, trans. Nicholas T. Rand, 125–38. Chicago: University of Chicago Press, 1994.
Adiga, Aravind. *The White Tiger*. New Delhi: HarperCollins, 2008.
Agamben, Giorgio. "What Is the Contemporary?" In *What Is an Apparatus? and Other Essays*, trans. David Kishik and Stefan Pedatella, 39–54. Stanford, CA: Stanford University Press, 2009.
Althusser, Louis. *Lenin and Philosophy and Other Essays*. Translated by Ben Brewster. New York: Monthly Review Press, 1971.
Anderson, Benedict. *Imagined Communities: Reflections on the Origin and Spread of Nationalism*. London: Verso, 1983.
———. *The Spectre of Comparisons: Nationalism, Southeast Asia and the World*. London: Verso, 2000.
Andrews, Edmund L. "Greenspan Concedes Error on Regulation." *New York Times*, October 23, 2008.
Aneesh, A. *Virtual Migration: The Programming of Globalization*. Durham, NC: Duke University Press, 2006.
Appadurai, Arjun. "Disjuncture and Difference in the Global Cultural Economy." *Theory, Culture & Society* 7, nos. 2/3 (June 1990).
Aravamudan, Srinivas. "The Catachronism of Climate Change." *Diacritics* 41, no. 3 (2013): 6–30.
Aren, Katherine. "*Stadtwollen*: Benjamin's *Arcades Project* and the Problem of Method." *PMLA* 122, no. 1 (2007): 43–60.
Armstrong, Nancy. *Desire and Domestic Fiction: A Political History of the Novel*. New York: Oxford University Press, 1987
Arrighi, Giovanni. *The Long Twentieth Century*. London: Verso, 1994.
Arvidsson, Adam, and Elanor Colleoni. "Value in Informational Capitalism and on the Internet." *Information Society: An International Journal* 28, no. 3 (2012): 135–50. http://dx.doi.org/10.1080/01972243.2012.669449.
Bahng, Aimee. *Migrant Futures: Decolonizing Speculation in Financial Times*. Durham, NC: Duke University Press, 2017.

Bal, Mieke. *Narratology: Introduction to the Theory of Narrative.* Toronto: University of Toronto Press, 1997.
Barthes, Roland. "From Work to Text." In *Image-Music-Text.* Translated by Stephen Heath, 155–64. London: Fontana Press, 1977.
Beacock, Ian. "Germany Gets It." *New Republic*, April 1, 2020. https://newrepublic.com/article/157112/germany-gets-coronavirus.
Beck, Ulrich. *What Is Globalization?* Cambridge: Polity Press, 2000.
Benjamin, Ross, and Heesok Chang. "Jacques Derrida, the Last European." *SubStance* 35, no. 2 (2006): 140–71. www.jstor.org/stable/4152890.
Benjamin, Walter. *The Arcades Project.* Translated by Howard Eiland and Kevin McLaughlin. Cambridge, MA: Harvard University Press, 1999.
———. *Charles Baudelaire: A Lyric Poet in the Era of High Capitalism.* Translated by Harry Zohn. London: Verso Books, 1997.
———. *The Origin of German Tragic Drama.* Translated by John Osborne. London: Verso, 1977.
———. "Theses on the Philosophy of History." In *Illuminations*, edited by Hannah Arendt, translated by Harry Zohn, 253–64. New York: Schocken Books, 1969.
Bennett, Jane. "The Agency of Assemblages and the North American Blackout." *Public Culture* 17, no. 3 (2005): 445–65.
———. *Vibrant Matter: A Political Ecology of Things.* Durham, NC: Duke University Press, 2010.
Bennett, Tony. *Formalism and Marxism.* London: Routledge, 1989.
Berlant, Lauren. *Cruel Optimism.* Durham, NC: Duke University Press, 2011.
Blanco, Maria del Pilar, and Esther Peeren, eds. *The Spectralities Reader: Ghosts and Haunting in Contemporary Cultural Theory.* London: Bloomsbury, 2013.
Bloom, Harold. *A Map of Misreading.* Oxford: Oxford University Press, 2003.
Braidotti, Rosa. *The Posthuman.* Cambridge: Polity Press, 2013.
Brooke, Stephen. "Living in 'New Times': Historicizing 1980s Britain." *History Compass* 12, no. 1 (2014): 20–32. https://doi.org/10.1111/hic3.12126.
Brown, Wendy. *Undoing the Demos: Neoliberalism's Stealth Revolution.* New York: Zone Books, 2015.
———. *Walled States, Waning Sovereignty.* New York: Zone Books, 2014.
Burke, Peter. *Varieties of Cultural History.* Ithaca, NY: Cornell University Press, 1997.
Butler, Judith. *Dispossession: The Performative in the Political.* Cambridge: Polity Press, 2013.
———. *Gender Trouble: Feminism and the Subversion of Identity.* New York: Routledge, 1990.
———. *Precarious Life: The Powers of Mourning and Violence.* London: Verso, 2004.
———. "Values of Difficulty." In *Just Being Difficult: Academic Writing in the Public Arena.* Edited by Jonathan Culler and Kevin Lamb, 199–215. Stanford, CA: Stanford University Press, 2003.
Çalışkan, Koray, and Michel Callon. "Economization, Part 1: Shifting Attention from the Economy towards Processes of Economization, Economy and Society." *Economy and Society* 38, no. 3 (2009): 369–98. www.tandfonline.com/doi/abs/10.1080/03085140903020580.

Castells, Manuel. *The Informational City: Information Technology, Economic Restructuring, and the Urban-Regional Process.* Oxford: Basil Blackwell, 1989.
———. *The Rise of the Network Society.* 2nd ed. Oxford: Blackwell, 2000.
Chakrabarty, Dipesh. "Anthropocene Time." *History and Theory* 57, no. 1 (2018): 5–32. https://doi.org/10.1111/hith.12044.
———. "Climate and Capital: On Conjoined Histories." *Critical Inquiry* 45, no. 1 (Autumn 2014): 1–23.
———. "The Climate of History: Four Theses." *Critical Inquiry* 35, no. 2 (Winter 2009): 197–222.
———. "Postcolonial Studies and the Challenge of Climate Change." *New Literary History* 43, no. 1 (Winter 2012): 1–18.
Coetzee, J. M. *Disgrace.* New York: Viking Penguin, 1999.
Cole, Teju. *Open City.* New York: Random House, 2012.
Connif, Richard. "Tracking the Causes of Sharp Decline of the Monarch Butterfly." Interview with Orley Taylor, *Yale Environment 360*, April 1, 2013. https://e360.yale.edu/features/tracking_the_causes_of_sharp_decline_of_the_monarch_butterfly.
Coole, Diana. "Rethinking Agency: A Phenomenological Approach to Embodiment and Agentic Capacities." *Political Studies* 53, no. 1 (2005): 124–42.
Cowan, Bainard. "Walter Benjamin's Theory of Allegory." *New German Critique*, no. 22 (1981): 109–22. https://doi.org/10.2307/487866.
Crang, Michael. "Between Places: Producing Hubs, Flows, and Networks." *Environment and Planning* 34 (2002): 569–74.
Creswell, Tim. *On the Move: Mobility in the Modern Western World.* New York: Routledge, 2006.
Davenport, Christian, Aaron Gregg, and Craig Timberg. "Working from Home Reveals Another Fault Line in America's Racial and Educational Divide." *Washington Post*, March 22, 2020. www.washingtonpost.com/business/2020/03/22/working-home-reveals-another-fault-line-americas-racial-educational-divide/.
Defoe, Daniel. *Robinson Crusoe.* Edited by Michael Shinagel. New York: W. W. Norton, 1994.
DeLanda, Manuel. *A New Philosophy of Society: Assemblage Theory and Social Complexity.* London: Continuum Books, 2006.
Deleuze, Gilles. *Cinema 1: The Movement-Image.* Translated by Hugh Tomlinson and Barbara Habberjam. Minneapolis: University of Minnesota Press, 1986.
Deleuze, Gilles, and Felix Guattari. *A Thousand Plateaus.* Translated by Brian Massumi. Minneapolis: University of Minnesota Press, 1987.
Deleuze, Gilles, and Claire Parnet. *Dialogues.* Translated by Hugh Tomlinson and Barbara Habberjam. New York: Columbia University Press, 1987.
DeLillo, Don. *Cosmopolis.* New York: Scribner, 2003.
———. "In the Ruins of the Future." *Guardian*, Books, December 22, 2001. www.theguardian.com/books/2001/dec/22/fiction.dondelillo.
de Man, Paul. "The Rhetoric of Blindness: Jacques Derrida's Reading of Rosseau." In *Blindness and Insight: Essays in the Rhetoric of Contemporary Criticism*, 102–41. Minneapolis: University of Minnesota Press, 1983.
DePietro, Thomas, ed. *Conversations with Don DeLillo.* Jackson: University Press of Mississippi, 2005.

Derrida, Jacques. *Cinders*. Translated by Ned Lukacher. Minneapolis: University of Minnesota Press, 2014.

———. "Marx and Sons." In *Ghostly Demarcations: A Symposium on Jacques Derrida's Specters of Marx*, ed. Michael Sprinker, 213–69. London: Verso, 1999.

———. *The Politics of Friendship*. Translated by George Collins. London: Verso, 1997.

———. *Specters of Marx: The State of the Debt, the Work of Mourning, & the New International*. Translated by Peggy Kamuf. New York: Routledge, 1994.

Derrida, Jacques, and Anne Dufourmantelle. *Of Hospitality*. Translated by Rachel Bowlby. Stanford, CA: Stanford University Press, 2000.

Derrida, Jacques, and Bernard Stiegler. *Echographies of Television*. Translated by Jennifer Bajorek. Cambridge: Polity Press, 2002.

Dillon, Sarah. "Reinscribing De Quincey's Palimpsest: The Significance of the Palimpsest in Contemporary Literary and Cultural Studies." *Textual Practice* 19, no. 3 (January 1, 2005): 243–63.

Eagleton, Terry. "Capitalism and Form." *New Left Review* 14 (March–April 2002): 119–31.

———. *Ideology of the Aesthetic*. Oxford: Basil Blackwell, 1990.

Ehrenreich, Barbara, and Arlie Russell Hochschild. *Global Woman: Nannies, Maids, and Sex Workers in the New Economy*. New York: Henry Holt, 2002.

Enloe, Cynthia. *Bananas, Beaches and Bases: Making Feminist Sense of International Politics*. Berkeley: University of California Press, 1990.

Feder, Barnaby J. "Theodore Levitt, 81, Who Coined the Term 'Globalization,' Is Dead." *New York Times*, July 6, 2000. www.nytimes.com/2006/07/06/business/06levitt.html.

Fletcher, Angus. *Allegory: The Theory of a Symbolic Mode*. Princeton, NJ: Princeton University Press, 2012.

———. *The Topological Imagination: Spheres, Edges, and Islands* (Cambridge, MA: Harvard University Press, 2016.

Foucault, Michel. "Nietzsche, Genealogy and History." In *The Foucault Reader*, edited by Paul Rabinow, 76–100. New York: Pantheon, 1984.

Fox, Joe, Youjin Shin, and Armand Emamdjomeh. "How Epidemics like Covid-19 End (and How to End Them Faster)." *Washington Post*, February 19, 2020. www.washingtonpost.com/graphics/2020/health/coronavirus-how-epidemics-spread-and-end/.

Freud, Sigmund. "The Ego and the Id." In *The Standard Edition of the Complete Psychological Works*, translated and edited by James Strachey, 19:13–64. London: Hogarth Press, 1961.

———. "Mourning and Melancholia." In *The Standard Edition of the Complete Psychological Works*, translated and edited by James Strachey, 19:243–58. London: Hogarth Press, 1961.

———. "A Note upon the 'Mystic Writing Pad.'" In *The Standard Edition of the Complete Psychological Works*, translated and edited by James Strachey, 19:227–32. London: Hogarth Press, 1961.

Friedman, Thomas L. *The World Is Flat: A Brief History of the Twenty-First Century*. New York: Picador/Farrar, Straus and Giroux, 2007.

Fukuyama, Francis. *The End of History and the Last Man*. New York: Free Press, 1992, 2006.

———. "More Proof That This Really Is the End of History." *Atlantic*. October 17, 2022.

www.theatlantic.com/ideas/archive/2022/10/francis-fukuyama-still-end-history
/671761/.
Fuller, Matthew, and Olga Goriunova. *Bleak Joys: Aesthetics of Ecology and Impossibility*. Minneapolis: University of Minnesota Press, 2019.
Gandhi, Leela. "Utonal Life: A Genealogy for Global Ethics." In *Cosmopolitanisms*, edited by Bruce Robbins and Paulo Lemos Horta, 65–90. New York: New York University Press, 2017.
Ghosh, Amitav. *The Great Derangement: Climate Change and the Unthinkable*. Chicago: University of Chicago Press, 2016.
Glissant, Edouard. "Creolization in the Making of the Americas." *Caribbean Quarterly* 54, nos. 1/2 (2008): 81–89.
Godden, Richard. "Labor, Language, and Finance Capital." *PMLA* 126, no. 2 (2011): 412–21.
Gramsci, Antonio. *Selections from the Prison Notebooks*. Translated and edited by Quentin Hoare and Geoffrey Howell Smith. New York: International, 1971.
Grossman, Jonathan. *Charles Dickens's Networks: Public Transport and the Novel*. Oxford: Oxford University Press, 2012.
Guha, Ranajit. "The Migrant's Time." *Postcolonial Studies* 1, no. 2 (July 1, 1998): 155–60.
Gunning, Tom. *The Films of Fritz Lang: Allegories of Vision and Modernity*. London: British Film Institute, 2000.
Gupta, Suman. *Globalization and Literature*. Cambridge: Polity, 2009.
Haiven, Max. "Hari Kunzru on Networks, the Novel, and the Politics of the Author" (interview). *Public Books*. October 2, 2013. www.publicbooks.org/hari-kunzru-on-networks-the-noveland-the-politics-of-the-author/.
Hale, Dorothy J. "Aesthetics and the New Ethics: Theorizing the Novel in the Twenty-First Century." *PMLA* 124, no. 3 (May, 2009): 896–905.
Hall, Stuart. "Culture, the Media and 'the Ideological Effect.'" In *Mass Communication and Society*, edited by James Curran, Michael Gurevitch and Janet Woollacott, 315–48. London: Edward Arnold, 1977.
Hamid, Mohsin. *How to Get Filthy Rich in Rising Asia*. New York: Riverhead Books, 2013.
Hamilton, Alexander. *The Papers of Alexander Hamilton*. Vol. 25. *July 1800–April 1802*. Edited by Harold C. Syrett. New York: Columbia University Press, 1977.
Hardt, Michael, and Antonio Negri. *Empire*. Cambridge, MA: Harvard University Press, 2001.
———. *Multitude: War and Democracy in the Age of Empire*. New York: Penguin Books, 2005.
Harvey, David. *A Brief History of Neoliberalism*. Oxford: Oxford University Press, 2005.
———. *The Condition of Postmodernity*. Oxford: Blackwell, 1990.
———. "Marxism, Metaphors, and Ecological Politics." *Monthly Review* 49, no. 11 (April 1998). https://monthlyreview.org/1998/03/01/marxism-metaphors-and-ecological-politics/.
Hawes, Clement. *The British Eighteenth Century and Global Critique*. New York: Palgrave Macmillan, 2005.
Heise, Ursula. *Sense of Place and Sense of Planet: The Environmental Imagination of the Global*. Oxford: Oxford University Press, 2008.

Hochschild, Arlie Russell. *The Outsourced Self: Intimate Life in Market Times*. New York: Henry Holt, 2012.

———. *Strangers in Their Own Land: Anger and Mourning on the American Right*. New York: New Press, 2016.

Hollander, John. *The Figure of Echo: A Mode of Allusion in Milton and After*. Berkeley: University of California Press, 1981.

Honneth, Axel. *Reification: A New Look at an Old Idea*. Oxford: Oxford University Press, 2008.

Huebener, Paul, Susie O'Brien, Tony Porter, Liam Stockdale, and Yanqiu Rachel Zhou. "Exploring the Intersection of Time and Globalization." *Globalizations* 13, no. 3 (May 3, 2016): 243–55. https://doi.org/10.1080/14747731.2015.1057046.

Huyssen, Andreas. *Present Pasts: Urban Palimpsests and the Politics of Memory*. Stanford, CA: Stanford University Press, 2003.

Inden, Ronald. "The Campaign That Lost Its Sheen." Interview by Prasun Sonwalkar. *Hindu*, October 3, 2004.

Irr, Caren. *Toward the Geopolitical Novel: U.S. Fiction in the Twenty-First Century*. New York: Columbia University Press, 2013.

James, Paul, and Manfred Steger. "A Genealogy of 'Globalization': The Career of a Concept." *Globalizations* 11, no. 4 (2014): 413–34.

Jameson, Fredric. *Allegory and Ideology*. London: Verso, 2019.

———. "Criticism and Categories." *PMLA* 137, no. 3 (2022): 563–67.

———. "Culture and Finance Capital." *Critical Inquiry* 24, no. 1 (Autumn 1997): 246–65.

———. "Future City." *New Left Review* 21 (2003): 65–79.

———. *The Geopolitical Aesthetic: Cinema and Space in the World System*. Bloomington: Indiana University Press, 1992.

———. *Postmodernism, or the Cultural Logic of Late Capitalism*. Durham, NC: Duke University Press, 1991.

———. "Third-World Literature in the Era of Multinational Capitalism." *Social Text* 15 (Autumn 1986): 65–88.

Jay, Martin. Introduction to *Reification: A New Look at an Old Idea*, edited by Axel Honneth, 3–16. Oxford: Oxford University Press, 2008.

Joseph, Betty. "Neoliberalism and Allegory." *Cultural Critique* 82 (2012): 68–94.

Joseph, Jonathan. "The Problem with Networks Theory." *Labor History* 51, no. 1 (February 2010): 127–44.

Kincaid, Jamaica. *Lucy*. New York: Farrar, Straus and Giroux, 1990.

Kingsolver, Barbara. *Flight Behavior*. New York: Harper Collins, 2012.

Klein, Melanie. "Mourning and Its Relation to Manic-Depressive States." *International Journal of Psychoanalysis* 21 (1940): 125–53.

Kornbluh, Anna. "On Marx's Victorian Novel." *Mediations: Journal of the Marxist Literary Group* 25, no. 1 (Fall 2010): 15–38.

Kukkonen, Karin. "Metalepsis in Popular Culture: An Introduction." In *Metalepsis in Popular Culture*, edited by Karin Kukkonen and Sonja Klimek, 1–21. Berlin: Walter de Gruyter, 2011.

Kumar, Amitav. "Bad News: Authenticity and the South Asian Political Novel." *Boston Review* (November/December 2008). http://bostonreview.net/BR33.6/kumar.php.

———. "On Adiga's The White Tiger." *Hindu*, November 2, 2008. www.hindu.com/lr/2008/11/02/stories/2008110250010100.htm.

Kunzru, Hari. *Transmission*. New York: Dutton, 2004.

Lal, Vinay. "Do Bigha Zamin." *MANAS: India and Its Neighbors*. 2008. http://southasia.ucla.edu/culture/cinema/films/do-bigha-zameen/.

Latour, Bruno. *Down to Earth: Politics in the New Climatic Regime*. Translated by Catherine Porter. Cambridge: Polity Press, 2018.

———. *Reassembling the Social: An Introduction to Actor-Network-Theory*. Oxford: Oxford University Press, 2007.

Lee, Benjamin, and Edward LiPuma. "Cultures of Circulation: The Imaginations of Modernity." *Public Culture* 14, no. 1 (2002): 191–213.

Leonard, Philip. "'A Revolution in Code'? Hari Kunzru's Transmission and the Cultural Politics of Hacking." *Textual Practice* 28, no. 2 (2014): 267–87.

Levine, Caroline. *Forms: Whole, Rhythm, Hierarchy, Network*. Princeton, NJ: Princeton University Press, 2017.

———. "Narrative Networks: Bleak House and the Affordances of Form." *Novel: A Forum on Fiction* 42, no. 3 (2009): 517–23.

Levitt, Theodore. "The Globalization of Markets." *Harvard Business Review*, May 1, 1983. https://hbr.org/1983/05/the-globalization-of-markets.

Li, Victor. "The Untimely in Globalization's Time: Don DeLillo's *Cosmopolis*." *Globalizations* 13, no. 3 (2016): 256–69.

Macpherson, C. B. *The Political Theory of Possessive Individualism: Hobbes to Locke*. Oxford: Oxford University Press, 1962, 2011.

Martin, Randy. *The Financialization of Daily Life*. Philadelphia: Temple University Press, 2003.

Marx, Karl. *Capital: A Critique of Political Economy*. Vol. 1. Translated by Ben Fowkes. New York: Vintage, 1977.

Marx, Karl, and Friedrich Engels. *The Manifesto of the Communist Party*. Accessed May 4, 2017. http://marx.eserver.org/1848-communist.manifesto/.

Massumi, Brian. *The Politics of Affect*. Cambridge: Polity Press, 2015.

Menand, Louis. "Francis Fukuyama Postpones the End of History." *New Yorker*, August 27, 2018. www.newyorker.com/magazine/2018/09/03/francis-fukuyama-postpones-the-end-of-history.

Mentz, Steve. *Break Up the Anthropocene*. Minneapolis: University of Minnesota Press, 2019.

Miller, D. A. *The Novel and the Police*. Berkeley: University of California Press, 1988.

Minden, Michael, and Holger Bachmann, eds. *Fritz Lang's Metropolis: Cinematic Visions of Technology and Fear*. Rochester, NY: Camden House, 2002.

Mitchell, W. J. T. *What Do Pictures Want? The Lives and Loves of Images*. Chicago: University of Chicago Press, 2005.

Moore, Jason W. "The Rise of Cheap Nature." In *Anthropocene or Capitalocene: Nature, History and the Crisis of Capitalism*, edited by Jason W. Moore, 78–115. Oakland, CA: PM Press, 2016.

Moretti, Franco. "Serious Century." In *The Novel*, edited by Franco Moretti, 1:364–400. Princeton, NJ: Princeton University Press, 2006.

Morton, Timothy. *Ecology without Nature: Rethinking Environmental Aesthetics*. Cambridge, MA: Harvard University Press, 2009.

———. *Hyperobjects: Philosophy and Ecology after the End of the World*. Minneapolis: University of Minnesota Press, 2013.

Mowitt, John. "What Is a Text Today?" *PMLA* 117, no. 5 (2002): 1217–21.

Nail, Thomas. "What Is an Assemblage?" *SubStance* 46, no. 1 (2017): 21–37.

Najafi, Sina, David Serlin, and Lauren Berlant. "The Broken Circuit: An Interview with Lauren Berlant." *Cabinet* 31 (2008). http://cabinetmagazine.org/issues/31/najafi_serlin.php.

Neumann, Birgit, and Yvonne Kappel. "Music and Latency in Teju Cole's *Open City*: Presences of the Past." *ARIEL* 50, no. 1 (2019): 31–62.

Nixon, Rob. *Slow Violence and the Environmentalism of the Poor*. Cambridge, MA: Harvard University Press, 2011.

Nowotny, Helga. *The Cunning of Uncertainty*. Cambridge: Polity Press, 2017.

———. *Time: The Modern and Postmodern Experience*. Cambridge: Polity Press, 1994.

Owens, Craig. "The Allegorical Impulse: Toward a Theory of Postmodernism." *October* 12 (1980): 67–86.

Palumbo-Liu, David. *The Deliverance of Others: Reading Literature in a Global Age*. Durham, NC: Duke University Press, 2012.

Parks, Tim. "The Dull New Global Novel." *New York Review of Books* (blog), February 9, 2010. www.nybooks.com/daily/2010/02/09/the-dull-new-global-novel/.

Patnaik, Utsa. "Neoliberalism and Rural Poverty in India." *Economic and Political Weekly* 42, no. 30 (July 28–August 3, 2007): 3132–50.

Perelman, Bob. "Parataxis and Narrative: The New Sentence in Theory and Practice." *American Literature* 65, no. 2 (June 1993): 313–24.

Porter, Eduardo. "Can a Coal Town Reinvent Itself?" *New York Times*, December 6, 2019. www.nytimes.com/2019/12/06/business/economy/coal-future-virginia.html.

———. "Struggling to Rise as Coal Declines." *New York Times*, December 13, 2019.

Pratt, Mary Louise. "Why the Virgin of Zapopan Went to Los Angeles." In *Images of Power: Iconography, Culture and State in Latin America*, edited by Jens Andermann and William Rowe, 271–90. New York: Berghahn, 2004.

Preston, Julia. "Lawsuits Claim Disney Colluded to Replace U.S. Workers with Immigrants." *New York Times*, January 25, 2016.

Quilligan, Maureen. *The Language of Allegory: Defining the Genre*. Ithaca, NY: Cornell University Press, 1979.

Quintilian. *Institutio oratoria*. Edited by Harold Edgeworth Butler. 1922. http://www.perseus.tufts.edu/hopper/text?doc=Quint.%20Inst.%209.2&lang=original.

Rapier, Robert. "Don't Blame Renewable Energy for Dying U.S. Coal Industry." *Forbes*, March 18, 2016. www.forbes.com/sites/rrapier/2016/03/18/whats-killing-the-coal-industry/#59d87d7b5281.

Rivera, Mayra. "Ghostly Encounters: Spirits, Memory, and the Holy Ghost." In *Planetary Loves: Spivak, Postcoloniality and Theology*, edited by Stephen D. Moore and Mayra Rivera, 119–35. New York: Fordham University Press: 2010.

Robbins, Bruce, and Paulo Lemos Horta. *Cosmopolitanisms*. New York: New York University Press, 2017.

Rosa, Hartmut. "Social Acceleration: Ethical and Political Consequences of a Desynchronized High-Speed Society." *Constellations*, 10, no. 1 (2003): 3–33.

Roy, Arundhati. *Capitalism: A Ghost Story*. Chicago: Haymarket Books, 2014.
———. "The Pandemic Is a Portal." *Financial Times*, April 3, 2020. www.ft.com/content/10d8f5e8-74eb-11ea-95fe-fcd274e920ca.
Said, Edward. *Orientalism*. New York: Vintage, 1979.
Sassen, Saskia. *Globalization and Its Discontents: Essays in the New Mobility of People and Money*. New York: New Press, 1999.
———. *Losing Control? Sovereignty in an Age of Globalization*. New York: Columbia University Press, 2015.
Schumpeter, Joseph Alois. *Capitalism, Socialism, and Democracy*. Allen and Unwin, 1976.
Sedgwick, Eve. *Touching Feeling: Affect, Pedagogy, Performativity*. Durham, NC: Duke University Press, 2003.
Self, Will. "The Novel Is Dead (This Time It's for Real)." Culture, *Guardian*, May 2, 2014. www.theguardian.com/books/2014/may/02/will-self-novel-dead-literary-fiction.
Serres, Michel. *Angels: A Modern Myth*. Translated by Francis Cowper. Paris-New York: Flammarion, 1995.
Serres, Michel, and Bruno Latour. *Conversations on Science, Culture, and Time*. Ann Arbor: University of Michigan Press, 1995.
Shakespeare, William. *Complete Works*. New York: Collier, 1925.
Shonkwiler, Alison. *The Financial Imaginary: Economic Mystification and the Limits of Realist Fiction*. Minneapolis: University of Minnesota Press, 2017.
Shklovsky, Victor. "The Novel as Parody: Sterne's *Tristram Shandy*." In *Theory of Prose*. Translated by Benjamin Sher, 147–70. Illinois: Dalkey Archive Press, 1991.
Smith, Adam. *The Wealth of Nations*. New York: Random House, 2003.
Soja, Edward. *Postmetropolis: Critical Studies of Cities and Regions*. Boston: Wiley, 2000.
Spivak, Gayatri Chakravorty. *An Aesthetic Education in the Era of Globalization*. Cambridge, MA: Harvard University Press, 2012.
———. *A Critique of Postcolonial Reason: Toward a History of the Vanishing Present*. Cambridge, MA: Harvard University Press, 1999.
———. *Death of a Discipline*. New York: Columbia University Press, 2003.
———. "Diasporas Old and New: Women in the Transnational World." *Textual Practice* 10, no. 2 (1996): 245–69.
———. "Ethics and Politics in Tagore, Coetzee, and the Certain Scenes of Teaching." *Diacritics* 32, nos. 3/4 (2002): 17–31.
———. "Extempore Response to Susan Abraham, Tat-siong Benny Liew, and Mayra Rivera." In *Planetary Loves: Spivak, Postcoloniality, and Theology*, edited by Stephen D. Moore and Mayra Rivera, 136–48. New York: Fordham University Press, 2010.
———. "Ghostwriting." *Diacritics* 25, no. 2 (Summer 1995): 64–84.
———. *Harlem*. Calcutta: Seagull Books, 2013.
———. "More Thoughts on Cultural Translation," *Transversal* 4 (2008). https://transversal.at/transversal/0608/spivak/en.
———. *Other Asias*. Malden, MA: Blackwell, 2008.
———. *Outside in the Teaching Machine*. New York: Routledge, 1993.
———. *Readings*. Calcutta: Seagull Books, 2014.
———. "Remembering Derrida." *Radical Philosophy* 129 (2005): 15–21.
Subrahmanyam, Sanjay. "Sanjay Subrahmanyam: Another Booker Flop" (diary). *London*

Review of Books, November 6, 2008. www.lrb.co.uk/the-paper/v30/n21/sanjay-subrahmanyam/diary.

Sugg, Katherine. "'I Would Rather Be Dead': Nostalgia and Narrative in Jamaica Kincaid's *Lucy*." *Narrative* 10, no. 2 (May 2002): 156–73.

Tally, Robert T., Jr. "On Always Historicizing: The Dialectic of Utopia and Ideology Today." *PMLA* 137, no. 3 (2022): 542–47.

Tambling, Jeremy. *Allegory*. New York: Routledge, 2010.

Taylor, Charles. "Modern Social Imaginaries." *Public Culture* 14, no. 1 (2002): 91–124.

Taylor, Orley R., Jr., James P. Lovett, David L. Gibo, Emily L. Weiser, Wayne E. Thogmartin, Darius J. Semmens, James E. Diffendorfer, John M. Pleasants, Samuel D. Pecoraro, and Ralph Grundel. "Is the Timing, Pace, and Success of the Monarch Migration Associated with Sun Angle?" *Frontiers in Ecology and Evolution* 7 (2019). https://doi.org/10.3389/fevo.2019.00442.

Tsing, Anna Lowenhaupt. *Friction: An Ethnography of Global Connection*: Princeton, NJ: Princeton University Press, 2005.

Vallette, Jim. "Larry Summers's War against the Earth." *Counterpunch*, June 15, 1999. www.counterpunch.org/1999/06/15/larry-summers-war-against-the-earth/.

Vance, J. D. *Hillbilly Elegy: A Memoir of a Family and Culture in Crisis*. New York: Harper Collins, 2016.

Vermeulen, Pieter. "Flights of Memory: Teju Cole's Open City and the Limits of Aesthetic Cosmopolitanism." *Journal of Modern Literature* 37, no. 1 (2013): 40–57. https://doi.org/10.2979/jmodelite.37.1.40.

Vogl, Joseph. *The Specter of Capital*. Translated by Joachim Redner and Robert Savage. Stanford, CA: Stanford University Press, 2015.

Wang, Orrin. "Disfiguring Monuments: History in Paul De Man's 'Shelley Disfigured' and Percy Bysshe Shelley's 'The Triumph of Life.'" *English Literary History* 58, no. 3 (1991): 633–55.

Wark, McKenzie. *Virtual Geography: Living with Global Media Events*. Bloomington: Indiana University Press, 1994.

Watt, Ian. *Conrad in the Nineteenth Century*. Berkeley: University of California Press, 1979.

Webster, Richard A. "For Homeless in New Orleans, Hotel Living Brings Benefits and Risks amid Coronavirus Outbreak." *Washington Post*, April 11, 2020. www.washingtonpost.com/national/for-homeless-in-new-orleans-hotel-living-brings-benefits-and-risks-amid-coronavirus-outbreak/2020/04/11/66f1ef92-7ae1-11ea-b6ff-597f170df8f8_story.html

Weheliye, Alexander G. *Habeas Viscus: Racializing Assemblages, Biopolitics and Black Feminist Theories of the Human*. Durham, NC: Duke University Press, 2014.

Williams, Raymond. *Marxism and Literature*. Oxford: Oxford University Press, 1977.

Woods, Derek. "Scale Critique for the Anthropocene." *Minnesota Review* 83 (2014): 133–42.

Wordsworth, William. "I Wandered Lonely as a Cloud." In *The Norton Anthology of Poetry*, 5th ed., edited by Margaret Ferguson, Mary Jo Salter, and Jon Stallworthy. New York: W. W. Norton, 2005.

Yusoff, Kathryn. *A Billion Black Anthropocenes or None*. Minneapolis: University of Minnesota Press, 2019.

Zhou, Yanqiu Rachel, and William D. Coleman. "Accelerated Contagion and Response: Understanding the Relationships among Globalization, Time, and Disease." *Globalizations* 13, no. 3 (May 3, 2016): 285–99. https://doi.org/10.1080/14747731.2015.1056498.

Žižek, Slavoj. *For They Know Not What They Do*. London: Verso, 2008.

INDEX

Page numbers in italics refer to figures.

9/11 attacks, 4, 66, 71, 151, 153

Abraham, Nicolas, 80
Abram, David, 180
actor-network theory (ANT), 11
Adiga, Aravind. See *White Tiger* (Adiga)
Adorno, Theodor W., 39, 201
affective labor, 35–36
Agamben, Giorgio, 4, 15, 66
agency, distributed, 166–67, 177–78, 180, 190–91, 216n53
allegory: as "American" counternarrative, 152–53; ancient vs. modern, 146; "constellation" metaphor, 147–48; gender in, 84; neoliberal, 128–29, 133–41, 141–50, 151–62; as prosopopoeia, 141–42; wordplay in, 131, 135–36, 146
Allegory (Fletcher), 134
Allegory and Ideology (Jameson), 128, 135
Althusser, Louis, 46
Anderson, Benedict, 13, 100
Aneesh, A., 114
Anthropocene: collectivity and scale, 164–65; human agency and, 165–67, 177–78, 188–89; as messianic, 183; novel as Anthropogenic form, 167–68; paradox of, 163. *See also* assemblages; climate crisis
Aravamudan, Srinivas, 162, 165, 166
Arcades Project (Benjamin), 147
Arrighi, Giovanni, 120
assemblages: characterized, 176–78, 215n37; as concept metaphor, 20–21, 200–201;

distributed agency and, 166–67, 177–78, 180, 190–91, 216n53; economic structures and, 169, 178–81; narrative description and time lapse, 170–76; planetary encounters and spatial scales, 182–86; temporal scales and agency of, 186–91; uncertainty and, 191–95
attachments: city as palimpsest and, 62–70; as concept metaphor, 20–21, 200–201; mourning, melancholia and, 70–77, 209n42; nation, citizenship and, 57–62, 208n9; outsized and irruptive memory, 78–79, 85–87; as residue, 56–57; unacknowledged loss, 77–83
autobiography: as intellectual labor, 29, 46–47; metaleptic recovery and, 46; paradox of spectrality and, 27. *See also Lucy* (Kincaid); *Open City* (Cole)

Babel (2006), 97, 112
Bal, Mieke, 172
Balibar, Étienne, 20
Bananas, Beaches and Bases (Enloe), 35
Barthes, Roland, "From Work to Text," 198
belonging and diaspora, 60, 75–76
Benjamin, Walter, 131–32, 135, 147, 201
Bennett, Jane, 176, 178–79
Berlant, Lauren, 20, 62, 69, 87
Bordwell, David, 97
Braidotti, Rosa, 199
Brooke, Stephen, 8
Brown, Wendy, 58, 130–31, 138, 150

Butler, Judith: concept metaphors and, 201; on gender-identity formation, 80–81, 83; on mourning, 81–82; on vulnerability, 62, 69, 71, 74, 84

Çalişkan, Koray, 134–35
Callon, Michel, 134–35
capital: abstraction of, 109–10, 111–12, 117–21, 127, 155; assemblages vs. economic structures, 178–81; displacement of time through, 155–56; market expansion, Don DeLillo on, 151; metaleptic rhythm of, 32, 40–46, 206n38; pandemic as byproduct of, 123; technology as cause of, 106. *See also* globalization; markets; neoliberalism
Capital (Marx): materiality, theory of, 176; metaleptic substitutions, 32, 40, 43–44, 45; personification trope, 136
Castells, Manuel, 8, 106, 107–8, 115
catachronism, 166
Chakrabarty, Dipesh, 164–65
citizenship: attachments, in defining of, 58–60; binary structures within, 88–89; openness and, 55–57. See also *Open City* (Cole)
class privilege, 84
climate crisis: distributed agency and, 190–91; home-as-location, suspension of, 191; idealized nature and, 50–51; within narrative fiction, 170–71; as problem of space and land, 11; uncertainty and, 189–90, 194–95. *See also* Anthropocene; assemblages
Cole, Teju. See *Open City* (Cole)
colonialism: fantasies of origin and, 48–49, 52, 53; partial visibility of, 30; race and postcoloniality, 72–73; timeless time and, 163. See also *Lucy* (Kincaid)
concept metaphors, 20–21, 200–201. *See also* assemblages; attachments; markets; networks; spectrality
conceptual performances, 6–7, 19–22
"constellation" metaphor for history, 147–48
contemporary, concept of: abstract and concrete time, 12–19; as ahistorical, 4–5; chronopolitics of globality, 7–12; contemporary literature, defining, 3–4, 203n3;

intersections of time and, 2–3; reading as conceptual performance, 19–22. *See also* assemblages; attachments; markets; networks; spectrality
contemporary literature: defining, 3–4, 203n3; noncoincidence with the empirical, 15–17; novel as Anthropogenic form, 167–68. *See also* novel form
Coole, Diana, 178
Cosmopolis (DeLillo): introduced, 23–24, 127, 132–33; hollowing out of the present, 153–62; market as metaphor, 200–201; as neoliberal allegory, 128, 213n50; as post-9/11 novel, 151–53
cosmopolitanism, national identity and, 87–88
Cosmopolitanisms (Robbins and Horta), 87–88
COVID-19 pandemic, 94–95, 96, 123, 124, 187
Cowan, Bainard, 146
Crang, Mike, 115
creolization, 61
critical consumerism, 174
Culture and Imperialism (Said), 64–65

DeLanda, Manuel, 177, 184, 190, 191, 192
delayed decoding, 182–83
Deleuze, Gilles, 166, 174, 176, 177
DeLillo, Don, on September 11th attacks, 151. See also *Cosmopolis* (DeLillo)
de Man, Paul, "Shelly Disfigured," 15–16
Derrida, Jacques: palimpsests and, 67; responsibility beyond the present, 18–19, 202; teleiopoiesis, coining of, 63–64; trajection/waiting, 190; on uncanniness of "live" television, 26
detachment, 56, 63–64, 75, 76, 209n42
determinate absence, 46
diaspora and identity, 60, 75–76
Dillon, Sarah, 67
distributed agency, 166–67, 177–78, 180, 190–91, 216n53
Do bigha zamin (1953), 145
Down to Earth (Latour), 11

Echographies of Television (Derrida), 26
ecological crisis. *See* climate crisis

economics. *See* capital; globalization; markets; neoliberalism
"The Ego and the Id" (Freud), 70
Enloe, Cynthia, *Bananas, Beaches and Bases*, 35, 36
epidemiological modeling, networks and, 94–95, 96
ethics: beyond the living present, 18–19; spectrality and, 28–29; of suffering, 87–89

Fletcher, Angus, 134, 155
Flight Behavior (Kingsolver): introduced, 168–70; delayed decoding and spatial scales, 182–86; human-nonhuman assemblages, 179–82; marginalized perspectives within, 24; narrative description and time lapse, 168, 172–76; temporal scales and agency of assemblages, 187–91; uncertainty, 191–95. *See also* assemblages
Foucault, Michel, 68–69
Freud, Sigmund: on memory traces, 66–67; on mourning and melancholia, 70–71, 75, 79, 80; substitutability of objects, 83
Friedman, Thomas, 98–99
"From Work to Text" (Barthes), 198
Fukuyama, Francis, 2, 10, 18
Fuller, Matthew, 191–92
future: commodification of, 126, 151–62; past-present-future continuum, 6, 12, 19, 21, 78; spectrality as disjuncture and, 18–19

Gandhi, Leela, 88
gender: in allegory, 84; gendered labor, 35–36, 207n62; identity formation, 80–81, 83; sexualized violence, 85–87
Gender Trouble (Butler), 80
Ghosh, Amitav, 170
Glissant, Édouard, 61
globalization: abstraction of capital, 109–10, 111–12, 117–21; assemblages vs. economic structures, 178–81; critical globality, narrative as tool for, 197–202; defining contemporary literature and, 3–4; as form of chronopolitics, 7–12; as form of cyberspace, 98; imagining "global community," 13–14, 18; intersections of time and, 2–3;

language of, 118–19; paradoxical tensions around, 57–58; rural-urban divide and, 142–47; "serving classes," reappearance of, 36, 207n62; as socially produced amnesia, 28; timeless time and, 107–8. *See also* capital; markets; neoliberalism
"global novel," 4, 16, 199, 204n34
Godden, Richard, 159
Goriunova, Olga, 191–92
Gramsci, Antonio, 33, 46–47
grief. *See* mourning and melancholia
Guattari, Félix, 166, 176, 177, 192
Guha, Ranjit, 60

Hale, Dorothy, 201–2
Hall, Stuart, 46, 51, 200
Hamid, Mohsin. *See How to Get Filthy Rich in Rising Asia* (Hamid)
Hamilton, Alexander, 58–59, 64, 208n9
Hamlet, Prince of Denmark (Shakespeare), 28
Harvey, David, 8, 138
"hauntology" as reading, 28
Heise, Ursula, 171
history: allegory as historical analysis, 131–32, 142–50; Anthropocene origins and, 164; contemporary as ahistorical, 4–5; durability of, 2, 10, 18–19, 20; fear of forgetting, 27–28; historical consciousness, 14, 131; literature's disfiguring of, 15–16; "privatizing history," 28; privileging of the "now," 27; systemization of the past as, 47; timeless time and, 99, 107–8, 110, 115, 124, 163. *See also* spectrality
Hollander, John, 38–39
home, as assemblage, 191–92
Horkheimer, Max, 39
Horta, Paulo Lemos, *Cosmopolitanisms*, 87–88
How to Get Filthy Rich in Rising Asia (Hamid): introduced, 23–24, 127, 131; economic doctrine personified, 133–41; as neoliberal allegory, 128, 133, 139; wordplay in, 131, 135. *See also* markets
Huyssen, Andreas, 14, 28

identity: creolization and, 61; gender-identity formation, 80–81, 83; historical layering

identity (*cont.*)
    and, 60, 75–76; labor identities, 2; telei-
    opoiesis and, 64
incorporation and introjection, 71, 80, 81
The Information Age (Castells), 106
"I Wandered Lonely as a Cloud" (Words-
    worth), 40, 42

Jameson, Fredric: on abstraction of capital,
    119–20, 121; on allegory, 128–29, 133;
    globalization as form of cyberspace, 98; on
    the "living present," 12, 17; metaphorical
    potential of networks, 117; on metaphor
    vs. simile, 135
Jay, Martin, 46
Joseph, Jonathan, 107

Kincaid, Jamaica. See *Lucy* (Kincaid)
Kingsolver, Barbara. See *Flight Behavior*
    (Kingsolver)
Klein, Melanie, 77
Kornbluh, Anna, 32, 40–41, 137
Kunzru, Hari, on abstraction of economic
    life, 111–12. See also *Transmissions*
    (Kunzru)

labor: colonial legacies in migrant, 53–54;
    gendered, 35–36, 207n62; labor iden-
    tities, 2
Lal, Vinay, 145
language: as analogy for assemblages, 177,
    184; anti-futuristic, in *Cosmopolis*, 157–58;
    of globalization, 118–19; of informational
    capitalism, 109–10, 115–16
Latour, Bruno, 10–11, 141
Levine, Caroline, 95
Levitt, Theodore, 7
the "living present," 12, 17, 18–19
localism, in environmental aesthetics,
    171–76, 180, 214n24
Lombardi, Mark, *Oliver North, Lake Re-
    sources of Panama, and the Iran Contra
    Operation, ca 1984–86*, 91–94, *92*, *93*
Lucy (Kincaid): daffodils as economic form
    of appearance, 40–46, 49–50, 51, 207n55;
    doubled vision of history, 33–37; margin-
    alized perspectives within, 24; memory

in subject formation, 28–30; metalepsis
    as spectral figure, 37–40; present violence
    and invented origin, 46–54; requiring
    metaleptic reading, 31–32. See also
    spectrality

Macron, Emmanuel, 96–97
Mandelstam, Osip, "My Century," 15
markets: allegory as historical analysis,
    131–32, 142–50; commodification of the
    future, 126, 151–62; as concept metaphor,
    20–21, 200–201; economic doctrine per-
    sonified, 130–31, 133–41; economizing of
    the social, 125–27, 138–39; market time
    as "extended present," 127–28; neoliberal
    allegory, characterized, 128–29, 133. See
    also capital; globalization; neoliberalism
Martin, Randy, 126
Marx, Karl: metaleptic argumentation, 32,
    40, 43–44, 45; money as phenomenal
    form, 19; theory of materiality, 176; use
    of personification, 136, 137
Massumi, Brian, 69, 78
memory: fear of forgetting, 14, 27–28;
    memory traces, 47, 66–67; outsized and
    irruptive, 78–79, 85–87; in subject forma-
    tion, 28–30
Mentz, Steve, 163
metalepsis: metaleptic reading, 31–32;
    metaleptic rhythm of capital, 32, 40–46,
    206n38; as spectral figure, 37–40. See also
    spectrality
metaphor vs. simile, 135–36
Metropolis (1927), 152
migrancy: attachment, citizenship, and,
    57–62, 208n9; ethics of suffering, 87–89;
    identity and, 75–76; migrant labor, 35–36,
    53–54, 207n62; mourning and, 70; sonic
    fugue as metaphor, 63–64. See also *Lucy*
    (Kincaid); *Open City* (Cole)
Miller, D. A., 79
Milton, John, *Paradise Lost*, 37–38
Morton, Timothy, 172, 174
mourning and melancholia: characterized,
    70–71; collective, 71–72; unacknowl-
    edged loss, 77–83; vulnerability and,
    73–75, 84

"Mourning and Melancholia" (Freud), 67, 70–71, 75, 79, 80
Mrs. Dalloway (Woolf), 17
"My Century" (Mandelstam), 15

Nail, Thomas, 176
narrative. *See* novel form
nationality: compromised sovereignty, 57–58; contemporary literature and, 3; cosmopolitanism and, 87–88; as imagined community, 48–49; mourning and, 70, 79. *See also* citizenship
neoliberal allegory: characterized, 128–29, 139; commodification of the future, 126, 151–62; economic doctrine personified, 130–31, 133–41; rural-urban divide, 141–50. See also *Cosmopolis* (DeLillo); *How to Get Filthy Rich in Rising Asia* (Hamid); *White Tiger* (Adiga)
neoliberalism: as end of history, 2, 10, 18; "extended present" and, 127–28; individual autonomy and, 138–39. *See also* capital; globalization; markets
networks: abstraction of capital, 109–10, 111–12, 117–21; assemblages vs., 176–77; as concept metaphor, 20–21, 200–201; divisions of space, 112–14; human agency and, 121–22; internet and cyberspace as, 101–6; metaphorical potential of, 116–17; mobility and, 114–15, 117–19; multidimensionality of, 115–16; narrative as response to, 110–12; narrative elements and topology, 95–96, 103; "network narrative" genre, 97–98; society as network, 98–99, 105, 106–8, 111, 123–24; synchronous simultaneity of, 91–95, *92, 93*
The *New York Times*, 9
normative heterosexuality, 80–81, 83
"A Note upon the 'Mystic Writing Pad'" (Freud), 66–67
novel form: as Anthropogenic, 167–68; climate crisis within, 170–71; contemporary literature, defining, 3–4, 203n3; "global novels," 4, 16, 199, 204n34; place, in narrative description, 168, 171–76; as response to "network," 110–12; serious novels, decline of, 196–97; temporal representation within, 130; as tool for critical globality, 197–202. *See also* assemblages; attachments; markets; networks; spectrality
Nowotny, Helga, 127, 161, 181, 190

Oliver North, Lake Resources of Panama, and the Iran Contra Operation, ca 1984–86 (Lombardi), 91–94, *92, 93*
Open City (Cole): introduced, 23, 55–56; citizenship and identity, 60–61; city as palimpsest, 62–70; ethics of suffering, 87–89; mourning and melancholia, 70–77, 209n42; outsized and irruptive memory, 78–79, 85–87; unacknowledged loss, 77–83. *See also* attachments
Ophir, Adi, 6, 20
Orientalism (Said), 47

palimpsest, city as, 62–70. *See also* attachments
"The Pandemic Is a Portal" (Roy), 123
Paradise Lost (Milton), 37–38
parataxis: creating a timeless time, 107–8; division of space through, 112–14; electronic network as, 103–6. *See also* networks
past-present-future continuum, 6, 12, 19, 21, 78. *See also* spectrality
Perelman, Bob, 105
personification of economic doctrine, 130–31, 133–41
place, in environmental aesthetics, 171–76
Poverty of Philosophy (Marx), 19
Pratt, Mary Louise, 118
Precarious Life (Butler), 81–82
present time: hollowing out of, 153–62; market time as "extended present," 127–28; past-present-future continuum, 6, 12, 19, 21, 78; responsibility beyond, 18–19, 202
Prison Notebooks (Gramsci), 46–47
privatizing history, 28
prosopopoeia, allegory as, 141–42

Quilligan, Maureen, 128, 135

race: postcoloniality and, 72–73; as term of identity, 76

right-wing politics, 10
Rivera, Mayra, 27–28
Robbins, Bruce, *Cosmopolitanisms*, 87–88
Rosa, Hartmut, 8
Roy, Arundhati, "The Pandemic Is a Portal," 123
rural-urban divide, 141–50

Said, Edward, 47, 64–65
Sassen, Saskia, 36, 55, 58
Self, Will, 196–97, 198
self-help genre, 133, 138–39. See also *How to Get Filthy Rich in Rising Asia* (Hamid)
September 11th attacks, 4, 66, 71, 151, 153
Serres, Michel, 113–14
setting, in environmental aesthetics, 171–76
sexualized violence, 85–87
Shakespeare, William, 27, 28
"Shelly Disfigured" (de Man), 15–16
Shklovsky, Viktor, 6
simile vs. metaphor, 135–36
slavery: as assemblage, 164, 166–67; timeless time and, 163
Sloterdijk, Peter, 1, 13
social acceleration, 8
Soja, Edward, 8
"Sonnet 18" (Shakespeare), 27
sovereignty, globalization and, 57–58
space-time compression, 8
spatial fix concept, 8
"speaking otherwise," 141–42
Specters of Marx (Derrida), 18, 28
spectrality: as concept metaphor, 20, 200–201; doubled vision of history, 33–37; as form of living-on, 26–30; metalepsis as spectral figure, 37–40; metaleptic reading, 31–32; metaleptic rhythm of capital, 32, 40–46, 206n38; as response to present violence, 46–54; as temporal disjuncture, 18–19
Spivak, Gayatri: on globalization, 33; on historical consciousness, 14; on home-as-location, 191; on literary analysis, 16–17, 199; on "privatizing of history," 28; reading of *Lucy*, 52, 53; on recoding of change, 39; on teleiopoiesis, 64
Stoler, Ann, 30
Summers, Lawrence, 9–10

Tally, Robert T., 198
Taylor, Charles, 126–27
technological change: as cause of global capital, 106; chronopolitics of globality and, 8; creating "permanent Now," 198; in flattening of time, 27, 91–94, 92, 93; satirical representation in *White Tiger*, 143; and serious novels, decline of, 196–97. See also networks
teleiopoiesis, 63–64, 66, 72, 73
A Thousand Plateaus (Deleuze and Guattari), 176
time: abstract and concrete, 12–19, 30–31; agency of assemblages and, 186–91; anachronism vs. catachronism, 166; displacement of, through capital, 155–56; flattening of, 27, 91–94, 92, 93; hollowing out of the present, 153–62; intersections of globalization and, 2–3; market time as "extended present," 127–28; narrative form and, 130, 70–71, 172; past-present-future continuum, 6, 12, 19, 21, 78; September 11th attacks and, 151–52; space-time compression, 8; timeless time, 99, 107–8, 110, 115, 124, 163
Torok, Maria, 80
Transmissions (Kunzru): introduced, 23, 97, 98, 99–100; abstraction of capital, 109–10, 111–12, 117–19; divisions of space, 112–14; human agency within networks, 121–22; internet as technological network, 101–3; levels of narration, 115–16; mobility, critique of, 114–15, 117–19; narrative as response to network, 110–12; network through parataxis, 103–6. See also networks
Tsing, Anna, 14, 94

uncertainty, 189–90, 194–95
Undoing the Demos (Brown), 130–31

Vibrant Matter (Bennett), 178
Vogl, Joseph, 126
vulnerability, 62, 69, 71, 73–75, 84, 86

Wang, Orrin, 16
Wark, McKenzie, 119

The Washington Post, 94
Watt, Ian, 182
Weheliye, Alexander, 167
"What Is the Contemporary?" (Agamben), 4, 15
White Tiger (Adiga): introduced, 23–24, 127, 131–32; as historical analysis, 131, 141–50; as neoliberal allegory, 128; "speaking otherwise," 141–42. *See also* markets

Woolf, Virginia, *Mrs. Dalloway*, 17
wordplay, 131, 135–36, 146
Wordsworth, William, "I Wandered Lonely as a Cloud," 40, 42
Wynter, Sylvia, 164

Yusoff, Kathryn, 164, 166–67

Žižek, Slavoj, 48

www.ingramcontent.com/pod-product-compliance
Lightning Source LLC
Chambersburg PA
CBHW020649230426
43665CB00008B/367